Study Guide

Volume I - To 1877

to accompany

Garraty

The American Nation:
A History of the United States

Eighth Edition

Study Guide

Volume I - To 1877

to accompany

Garraty

The American Nation:
A History of the United States

Eighth Edition

Ken L. Weatherbie
Del Mar College

**HarperCollins*CollegePublishers*

Who settled Rhode Island
Roger Williams

Study Guide, Volume I - To 1877 to accompany Garraty's THE AMERICAN NATION: A HISTORY OF THE UNITED STATES, Eighth Edition

Copyright © 1995 by HarperCollins College Publishers

All rights reserved. Printed in the United States of America. No part of this book may be used or reproduced in any manner whatsoever without written permission with the following exception: testing material may be copied for classroom testing. For information, address HarperCollins College Publishers, 10 East 53rd Street, New York, NY 10022.

ISBN: 0-673-99227-6

94 95 96 97 98 9 8 7 6 5 4 3 2 1

Contents

Preface vii

Chapter 1: Europe Discovers America 1

Chapter 2: American Society in the Making 20

Chapter 3: America in the British Empire 35

Chapter 4: The American Revolution 52

Chapter 5: The Federalist Era: Nationalism Triumphant 67

Chapter 6: Jeffersonian Democracy 82

Chapter 7: National Growing Pains 94

Chapter 8: Toward a National Economy 113

Chapter 9: Jacksonian Democracy 126

Chapter 10: The Making of Middle-Class America 139

Chapter 11: A Democratic Culture 154

Chapter 12: Expansion and Slavery 166

Chapter 13: The Sections Go Their Ways 181

Chapter 14: The Coming of the Civil War 193

Chapter 15: The War to Save the Union 206

Chapter 16: Reconstruction and the South 222

Answers Section 235

PREFACE

To the Student

This *Study Guide* is intended to help you review and deepen your understanding of the material in the textbook, Garraty's THE AMERICAN NATION: A HISTORY OF THE UNITED STATES TO 1877, Volume I, Eighth Edition.

Each chapter of the *Study Guide* follows the same format. Each chapter begins with *Learning Objectives* which introduce the key themes of the chapter and suggest what you will know and be able to do after studying the chapter. These objectives are followed by an *Overview* of the chapter. This is a summary of the chapter's content. Next is an interactive section called *People, Places, and Things*. Here you will have space to write definitions of key concepts and terminology, descriptions of significant events, and identifications of important groups and personalities that are discussed in the chapter. In several chapters there are *Map Questions* requiring you to identify historically significant places both by name and geographic location. Following these exercises is a set of *Self-Test* questions, both multiple-choice and essay, that will help you check your comprehension of the chapter material and your attainment of the Learning Objectives.

Next is a section titled *Critical Thinking Exercise*. The purpose of these exercises is to help you develop selected critical thinking skills, especially those that are crucial to the study of history: classifying information, comparing and contrasting relationships, cause and effect relationships, and distinguishing between facts, inferences, and judgments. These exercises use material from the textbook, so they will also aid your comprehension and understanding of the text.

Finally, each *Study Guide* chapter ends with a one page "Cmap" of the chapter (pronounced "see map;" the C stands for "content") The Cmap is a graphic organizer, or outline of the chapter using chapter subheadings, keywords, and connecting lines that link related keywords. Directions for using Cmaps are in the Cmap section at the end of Chapter 1 of the *Study Guide* (p. 17).

You can attain maximum benefit from the *Study Guide* by using the following procedure:

- Read the Learning Objectives.
- Read the Overview.
- Read the textbook chapter carefully using the Cmap to guide your reading.
- Complete the People, Places, and Things items.
- Complete the Critical Thinking Exercise.
- Complete the Cmap.
- Rehearse for the Self-Test by rereading the Learning Objectives and Overview carefully.

- Double-check any misunderstandings, information gaps, or confusion with the appropriate section of the textbook.
- Take the Self-Test.
- Reread the Learning Objectives. You should be confident of your ability to do what they ask.

Answers to the Map Questions, Self-Tests, and Critical Thinking Exercises are in the Answers Section beginning on page 235.

Ken L. Weatherbie

Chapter 1

Europe Discovers America

Learning Objectives

After reading Chapter 1 you should be able to:

1. Describe the significant characteristics of Native American cultures and evaluate the impact of the European invasion on those cultures.
2. Summarize the accomplishments of the Spanish in opening the New World to conquest and colonization.
3. Explain why English settlers came to America.
4. Evaluate the key role of Massachusetts Bay as a hub of English settlement in New England.
5. List the requirements of successful colonization that had evolved in English America by 1700.

Overview

Columbus and the Discovery of America

The first humans in the Americas arrived from Asia tens of thousands of years ago, and the Scandinavian Leif Ericson explored Labrador around 1000, but it was the ventures of Christopher Columbus that opened the New World to European invasion and development after 1500. Columbus explored the Caribbean basin thinking he was near the Orient. He never realized he had discovered a new world.

By the eleventh century the European manorial system was breaking down, towns and cities were growing, and urban merchants were seeking profits in trade. The Crusades stimulated trade with Asia Minor, but the fourteenth and fifteenth centuries witnessed economic decline caused by the Black Death and the drain of precious metals to the Orient. By 1450, Europe was recovering and strong rulers laid the groundwork for modern nations. Merchants exploited this concentration of wealth and power, but they needed an all-water route to the Orient to cut their costs.

Portugal's Prince Henry and his school of navigators led the search for a new route to the Orient around Africa. But Columbus believed a western route across the Atlantic would reduce the travel distance and increase the profits of the Oriental trade. Spain's Queen Isabella commissioned his expedition in 1492.

Spain's American Empire

Spanish *conquistadores* eagerly explored the new world Columbus found. They discovered the Pacific Ocean, subdued the Aztec and Inca empires, and explored Florida, the Golf Coast, and the present southwestern United States. To these regions, the Spanish brought their culture and the Catholic religion. They were motivated by greed, a spirit of adventure, and a passionate desire to Christianize the Indians. They saw the New World as a land of infinite promise, and they could not resist the opportunity to exploit it.

The Indian and the European

The European settlement of the New World was an unprovoked act of aggression. To the Indians the Europeans seemed as gods and European products fascinated them. But the Spanish tricked and cheated the Indians and, through the *Requerimiento*, compelled them to recognize the sovereignty of the Spanish monarchy. Virtually all Europeans who settled the New World mistreated the Native Americans.

Native American Civilizations

Pre-Columbian Indian cultures had evolved in different ways. Many local cultures were primitive by European standards, but others, like the Aztecs and Incas, were as highly developed as any in Europe or Asia at the time.

The 1-2 million Indians who lived in what is now the United States spoke many different languages. Some native groups were hunting and fishing nomads; others were agricultural Indians who lived in villages. Their political organization ranged from small bands and family groups to complex confederacies of tribes. They had some things in common, such as cruelty in warfare, slavery, and male chauvinism; and they were all decimated by infection from European diseases.

Cultural differences led Europeans to assume that Indians were inferior beings. The non-Christian Indians were damned as contemptible heathens even though they were a deeply religious people. Unlike Europeans, Indians lived in harmony with nature and had no concept of personal property or individual wealth. The Europeans' inability to grasp the Indians' kinship relationships and the communal nature of land tenure among Indians resulted in innumerable quarrels. The English propensity to settle on the land and change it clashed with the nomadic Indians' mobility and desire to minimize their own impact on the land.

Spain's European Rivals

England and France based their claims to the New World on the explorations of John Cabot and Giovanni da Verrazano, respectively. But, unlike Spain, these two nations were slow to follow exploration with permanent settlement. Both nations were torn by internal stride in the sixteenth century, and Catholic Spain, growing wealthy on New World gold and silver, seemed too powerful to be challenged. But, by the late sixteenth century, that very New World wealth was undermining Spain's economy, the Spanish court was corrupted, and the Protestant Reformation was disrupting the Catholic church.

The Protestant Reformation

The spiritual lethargy and bureaucratic corruption of the Roman Catholic church in the early sixteenth century made it a target for reform. Martin Luther and John Calvin challenged Rome's spiritual authority, and local monarchs established their independence from the power of the Church. In the mid-sixteenth century, Henry VIII of England founded the Anglican church and England became a Protestant nation. In parts of Europe, business classes supported Protestant leaders and English, French, and Dutch trade began to flower. In England, joint-stock companies pooled investment capital and offered limited liability to investors. These companies became important tools for expanding English trade and colonization.

English Beginnings in America

English merchants sought new routes to the Orient, a northwest passage through the Americas, and gold. Queen Elizabeth I supported these efforts because she hoped to break Spain's overseas monopoly. She also commissioned English sea dogs like Francis Drake to capture Spain's treasure ships. She was also involved in the earliest colonization efforts by Englishmen Humphrey Gilbert in Newfoundland and Walter Raleigh on Roanoke Island. These early efforts failed, but England's defeat of the Spanish Armada in 1588 ended Spain's ability to block English penetration of the New World.

In his *Discourse on Western Planting*, propagandist Richard Hakluyt made a strong argument for English colonization based on military advantage and economic benefit. But it was merchant capitalists in quest of profits and not the queen and larger national interests that was the primary organizing force behind English colonization in North America.

The Settlement of Virginia

In 1607, the joint-stock London Company founded Jamestown as England's first permanent settlement in America. There were problems from the start. The colony was located on a swamp and the settlers lacked agricultural skills, so many starved. Company officers, looking only for quick profits, directed the settlers into fruitless activities. They also failed to take advantage of the economic hardships in England that were making skilled farm laborers available for migration. In Virginia, Captain John Smith provided some discipline and leadership, but the lack of a sense of common purpose among the settlers, infection and disease, and Indian attacks all ravaged the early colony. Jamestown was saved when it began to produce its own food supply and John Rolfe began to cultivate tobacco for export. To attract new settlers, the company made it easier for settlers to obtain their own land and gave them a rudimentary form of self-government in the House of Burgesses. But with these actions the company destroyed the colonists' reliance on the company, and it lost its charter in 1624 and became a royal colony.

"Purifying" the Church of England

Economic opportunity motivated most English settlers to come to America, but religious persecution motivated many. Some religious dissidents in England objected to the ritual and hierarchical governance of the Anglican church. These Puritans accused the Anglican clergy of Arminianism—preaching a doctrine of good works instead of predetermination. Puritans also preferred a more decentralized system of church government, making each congregation self-governing or governed by representative presbyteries elected by the laymen. Though they tried to purify it of its "popish" elements, most Puritans remained members of the Anglican church.

"Of Plymouth Plantation"

Radical Puritans, called Separatists, withdrew from the Anglican church and migrated to the Netherlands, then to America. These "Pilgrims" elected William Bradford as the governor of their Plymouth Plantation in New England. Their Mayflower Compact established a society of based on laws chosen by its members. The Indian Squanto helped the new settlers, but Plymouth never grew rich nor well populated.

A Puritan Commonwealth

English Puritans organized the Massachusetts Bay Company to establish a religious refuge in America. Their Great Migration began in 1630 and their carefully planned colony was blessed with good luck and a constant influx of industrious and prosperous settlers. The colony's government was a practical democracy headed by an elected legislature—the General Court—chosen by the vote of church members, and by an elected governor, John Winthrop. Church membership was obtained through a conversion experience. Most early settlers satisfied this standard and could vote.

Troublemakers

Two zealous Puritans gave Massachusetts authorities trouble. Roger Williams insisted that the company's charter was invalid because the company did not buy its land from the Indians. This, and his advocacy both of separation of church and state and of religious libertarianism, led to Williams' banishment. He founded Rhode Island with a democratic government, rigid separation of church and state, and near-universal religious toleration.

Anne Hutchinson challenged the Massachusetts clergy's admonition to church members to lead morally pure lives in order to be models for the unregenerate. She was accused of advocating the heresy of antinomianism—that the saved were exempt from the constraints of law. Her disclosure of an experience with divine revelation led to her banishment and she too went to Rhode Island. These two outspoken individualists posed a genuine threat to the Puritan community.

Other New England Colonies

Massachusetts Bay's Puritan intolerance and its growing population produced new settlements in New England. Maine, New Hampshire, and Connecticut were all spin-off colonies from Massachusetts.

French and Dutch Settlements

While the English settled Virginia and New England, the French established in Canada and the West Indies. Dutch settlers inhabited New Netherlands in an area earlier claimed by Henry Hudson. They purchased Manhattan Island from the Indians, traded for furs, and plundered Spanish treasure ships. The Dutch also tried without success to promote large-scale agriculture in the Hudson Valley.

Maryland and the Carolinas

Outside of Virginia and New England, most English colonies were not corporate ventures, but proprietary grants to individuals. The proprietors received their grants as personal property and they assumed near sovereign political power. But the realities of life in America limited their freedom of action and their profits.

Maryland was founded by the Calvert family as a haven for English Catholics. To attract settlers Lord Baltimore had to abandon his feudal plans, make his land easily available to settlers, and give them some power over local affairs. He also agreed to a Toleration Act that guaranteed religious freedom to all Christians.

Several new proprietorships were granted following the restoration of the English monarchy in 1660. Easy access to land, religious toleration, and political rights quickly became features of each of these new colonies. The proprietors of Carolina depended on the excess population from the established colonies to settle their grant. John Locke's elaborate social plan for Carolina—the Fundamental Constitutions—proved unworkable because it restricted access to land. Carolina's first settlers were from Barbados and they organized a thriving fur trade and exported foodstuffs to the West Indies. North and South Carolina were separated in 1712.

The Middle Colonies

The Duke of York was given a proprietary grant to the Dutch settlement north of Maryland. In 1664, English forces captured New Amsterdam without a fight and renamed it New York. Quakers established settlements in New Jersey and Pennsylvania. Quakers believed in an individualistic mystical experience with God, pacifism, religious toleration, and freedom of conscience. William Penn founded the Quaker's Holy Experiment in Pennsylvania. He was unusual for his fair treatment of local Indians and his colonists were guaranteed freedom of worship and individual civil rights. Through the Frame of Government, Penn established a paternalistic approach to governing the colony, but he sold land on easy terms and Pennsylvania was one of the most prosperous colonies.

Indians and Europeans as "Americanizers"

Interaction between Indians and Europeans caused a "Columbian Exchange"—each learned from the other. The Indians' domestication of corn was an especially important contribution to the success of English colonization, while Indians eagerly adopted European technology. The fur trade best illustrates the consequences of Indian-European interaction. European demand for furs made Indians more efficient hunters and trappers and caused Indians to absorb European ideas about private property and material wealth. The trade also altered tribal organization; tribes formed confederacies to control more territory for trapping, and farming tribes relocated to be along trade routes.

Colonists learned much from the Indians, but they had no desire to be like the Indians whom they considered savage barbarians. In fact, conflicts with the Indians caused whites to draw closer together and, over time, they developed a sense of having shared a common history. This process Americanized the transplanted Europeans.

People, Places, and Things

Define the following:

conquistadores _Spanish soldiers_

Requerimiento _a speech given to Indians requiring them to reconize the sovereinty of the reining Spanish Monarch_

joint-stock company _Pooled investment capital + offered limited liability to investors_

predestination _Puritans believed in original sin + what one did on earth had no effect on a person's fate after death_

Arminianism _Preaching a doctrine of good works instead of Predeteremism_

antinomianism _the saved were exempt from the constraints of the Law_

proprietor _large tract of land given by the King as a gift_

Describe the following:

Crusades — Holy wars fought against Moslems

Black Death — mass sickness in Europe 1300's 1400's killed thousands of people

*Treaty of Tordesillas — Divided the Non Cristian world between Spain Portugal - Portugal has Africa, Spain - New World

Protestant Reformation — The change in religion from being all Cathlic to protesant / Religous upheavel

*House of Burgesses — a rudimentary form of self-goverment consisting of delegates chosen in each district.

Church of England (Anglican Church) — King Henry VIII of England founded this church

Mayflower Compact — established a societey based on laws chosen by it's members.

Great Migration — Puritans leaving Europe for New World

Toleration Act — guaranteed relegious freedom to all christians

Frame of Government — A paternalistic approach to governing

Identify the following:

Leif Ericson — First discover - Scardinavian 1000

William Laud - Anglican cleric - with King Charles help tried to bring Puritans to Heel - Embellish rituals in Anglican church, tighten control, removed ministers who were Puritan.

Christopher Columbus discovered New World 1492

Prince Henry made compass

John Cabot Explorer for England

Martin Luther religious reformist

John Calvin religious reformist

Henry VIII Founded Anglican church - England became Protestant - he also married 5 times

Sir Humphrey Gilbert Colonized New Foundland

Sir Walter Raleigh Colonized Roanoke Island

Richard Hakluyt Proponate of Colonizing the new world

Queen Elizabeth I Supported exporation of New World - wanted to find Passage to orient + to overcome Spain

London Company a joint stock Co. Founded Jamestown as Englands first permenant settlement

John Smith One of first colonist - tried to bring order

8

Puritans _Wanted to purify Anglican religion_

Separatists _Radical Puritans_

Pilgrims _Rad. Puritans - From Scrooby, Nottinghamshire_

William Bradford _Puritan - governer of Plymouth Plantation_

Squanto _Indian who helped the new settlers in New England - Plymouth_

John Winthrop _Puritan - First Elected governer of Mass_

Roger Williams _Religious disenter - Founder Rhode Island + Providence_

Anne Hutchinson _Religious disenter - Followed Roger Williams to Rhode Island, after banishment from Mass._

Lord Baltimore _____

Duke of York _____

Quakers _religious group_

William Penn _____

9

Locate the following places: Write in both the place name and its map location number.

1. That portion of North America reached by Leif Ericson about 1000.
   _____   _____

2. That portion of the New World explored by Christopher Columbus in the 1490s.
   _____   _____

3. Where Sir Humphrey Gilbert attempted to establish an early English colony in the New World.
   _____   _____

4. Location of the first permanent English settlement in the New World.
   _____   _____

5. Island purchased by the Dutch from local Indians in 1624.
   _____   _____

6. Island from which came the early English settlers to the Carolinas.
   _____   _____

7. River scouted by the explorer Cartier to help establish French claims to the New World.
   _____   _____

8. The 12 English mainland colonies founded in America in the seventeenth century.
   _____   _____
   _____   _____
   _____   _____
   _____   _____
   _____   _____
   _____   _____

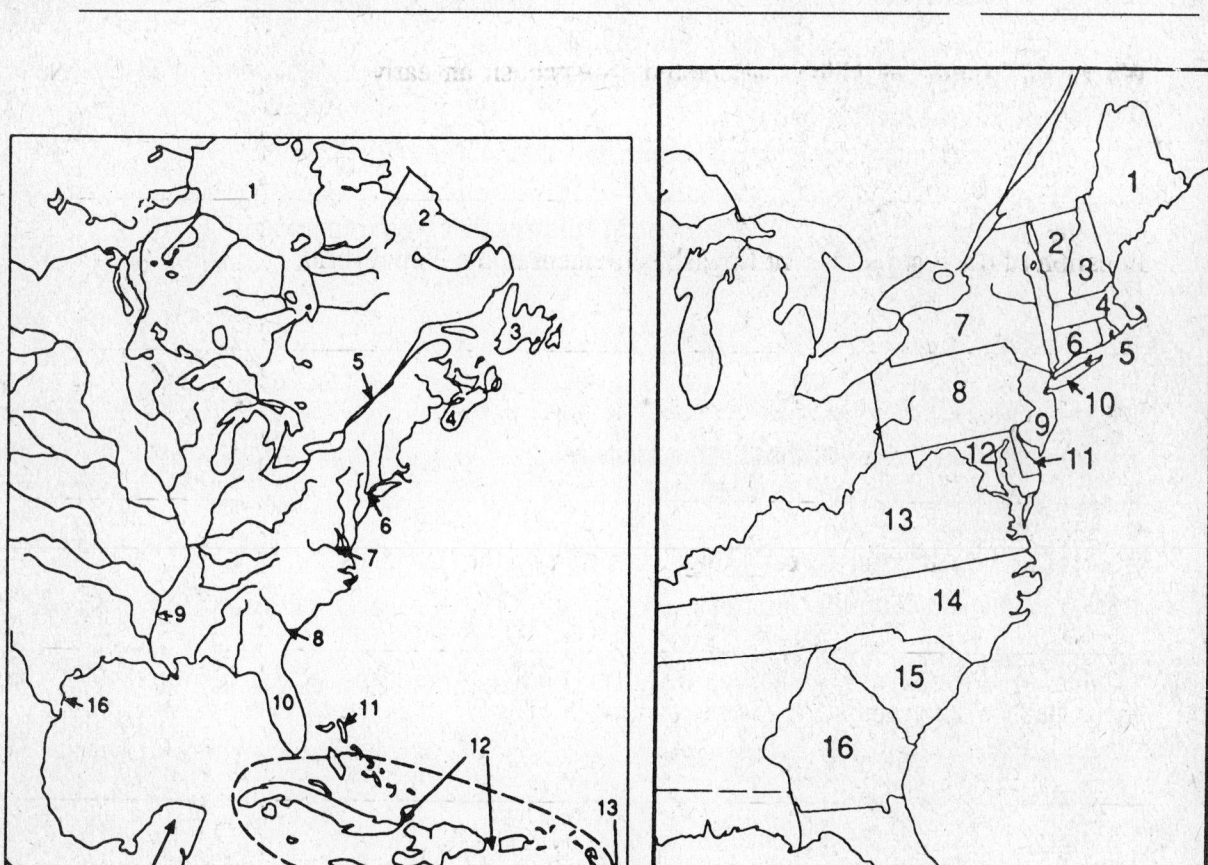

Self-Test

Multiple-Choice Questions

1. When he sailed from Spain in 1492, Columbus intended to find
    A. the fabled northwest passage
    B. a new world
    C. a new route to the Orient
    D. the lost continent of Atlantis

11

2. All of the following Spanish conquistadors explored regions of what is now the United States EXCEPT
   A. Nuñez de Balboa
   B. Pánfilo de Narvaez
   C. Hernando de Soto
   D. Alvar Nuñez Cabeza de Vaca

3. Wherever Europeans went as explorers and settlers in the fifteenth and sixteenth centuries, they
   A. established more democratic political institutions
   B. mistreated the native people they encountered
   C. enriched the local economy
   D. quickly assimilated the native people into their culture

4. Invading Europeans found Native American cultures that were remarkably
   A. underdeveloped
   B. weak
   C. savage
   D. varied

5. Europeans usually viewed Native Americans as
   A. overly possessive and materialistic
   B. politically weak and disorganized
   C. incapable of Christian education
   D. racially and culturally inferior

6. From the perspective of European invaders, Native Americans lacked respect for all the following EXCEPT
   A. private property
   B. nature
   C. God
   D. political authority

7. England was slow to colonize in the New World in the sixteenth century because
   A. it was torn by domestic political and religious differences
   B. it had no early territorial claim to the New World
   C. Queen Elizabeth I had no interest in colonization
   D. it was a Protestant nation

8. During the Protestant Reformation, which of the following challenged the authority of the Roman Catholic church?
   A. Martin Luther
   B. Henry VIII
   C. John Calvin
   D. all of the above

9. The joint-stock company was an effective tool for colonization because it
   A. created large pools of investment capital
   B. prohibited foolish investments in risky ventures
   C. held each investor personally responsible for all company debts
   D. restricted investments to short-term payoffs

10. Richard Hakluyt's *Discourse on Western Planting* was
    A. a pamphlet used to recruit English colonists
    B. a manual summarizing Indian agricultural techniques
    C. a settler's guide to the American colonies
    D. an essay promoting and justifying English colonization

11. Early Jamestown nearly failed as a colony because of all of the following EXCEPT
    A. no farming skills among early settlers
    B. poor leadership from Captain John Smith
    C. lack of a common sense of purpose among early settlers
    D. unrealistic direction from company officials

12. Eventually, the London Company encouraged immigrants to come to Jamestown by offering them an opportunity to
    A. own their own land
    B. become titled nobility
    C. gain religious freedom
    D. search for gold

13. Puritan reformers of the Anglican church hoped to focus the act of worship on
    A. traditional rituals using candles, incense, and music
    B. reading the Bible and analyzing the Scriptures
    C. sermons emphasizing the doing of good works
    D. the forgiveness of sins by the granting of indulgences

14. To establish a civil government for themselves, the Separatist Pilgrims at Plymouth Plantation signed the
    A. Frame of Government
    B. Fundamental Constitutions
    C. Toleration Act
    D. Mayflower Compact

15. Of the following, the concept most highly valued by the Puritans was
    A. religious toleration
    B. separation of church and state
    C. fair treatment of the Indians
    D. community harmony

16. Roger Williams was banished from Massachusetts Bay because he advocated
    A. separation of church and state
    B. a war of annihilation against the Indians

C. the doctrine of predestination
D. Calvinist theology

17. Anne Hutchinson's heresy of antinomianism called into question
    A. the right of Puritans to possess Indian land
    B. the application of the colony's laws to those who were in possession of saving grace
    C. the truth of predestination
    D. the possibility of divine revelation

18. The proprietary form of colonization became the usual form of planting English colonies immediately following the
    A. restoration of the monarchy
    B. Glorious Revolution
    C. chartering of the London Company
    D. founding of Jamestown

19. Quakers were NOT committed to
    A. freedom of conscience
    B. pacifism
    C. toleration of other religions
    D. placing the sermon at the center of worship

20. Arrange the following in correct time order: (A) the restoration of the English monarchy, (B) the Puritans' Great Migration, (C) the founding of Jamestown, (D) the Protestant Reformation.
    A. B, C, A, D
    B. A, D, C, B
    C. D, C, B, A
    D. D, B, C, A

Essay Questions

1. Describe the ways Native American and European cultures were similar to and different from each other when Europeans invaded America in the 1500s.
2. Explain why Spain was the first European nation to establish a New World empire and why England ultimately became so successful as a New World colonizer.
3. Compare and contrast the roles of economic and religious motives in the beginnings of English settlement in the New World.
4. Describe the religious views and social values of Massachusetts Bay Puritans and explain why Roger Williams and Anne Hutchinson posed a real threat to that colony.
5. State the motives for founding of the restoration colonies in English America and explain how they benefited from earlier colonizing experiences.

Critical Thinking Exercise

Classification

Classification is one of the historian's most important tools. Historical information usually comes in complex and confusing disarray, and it is the historian's skill at classifying this information—organizing it into patterns that make sense—that makes narrative history comprehensible.

Historians often place information into geographical, sequential (chronological), topical or other categories. For example, this chapter classifies information geographically when it separates the discussion of voyages of exploration and discovery into three categories: the Caribbean, South and Central America, and North America. Secondly, the information in the chapter has been classified sequentially: first, the European background; second, voyages of exploration; third, Spanish colonization; and last, early English settlement. Finally, some of the information in the chapter is classified topically, for example, there are discussions of Native Americans, the Protestant Reformation, and New England religious dissenters. It is with classification schemes such as these that historians make sense of the wealth of data in history that once led an observer to define history as just "One damn thing after another!"

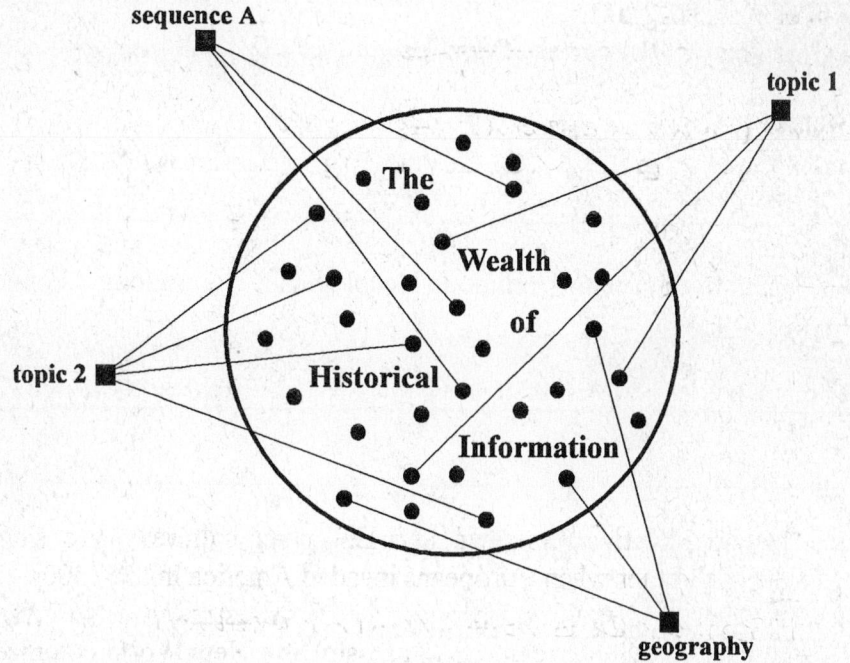

Classification is a basic critical thinking skill. It is vital to gaining control of a large amount of information and arranging it in a comprehensible order. The skill of classification requires the classifier to systematically group many seemingly isolated facts into a few categories. Placement of a fact into a category is based on the classifier's perception that some facts are related to each other in a given way, but not to other facts in the same way. It is an *inductive* process, that is, the classifier assembles several facts, then places particular facts into separate categories. These categories, called generalizations or concepts, describe the relationship among all the selected facts for that category. It is a skill that requires some familiarity with the information being classified. Greater familiarity means sharper perception of relationships and a more accurate placement of facts into proper categories.

The following exercise tests your familiarity with the information presented in Chapter 1. Of the four items in each of the ten groupings below, three of the items are related or associated with one another—that is, they can be classified together. The fourth item is not related to the other three in the same way they relate to one another. Your task is to:

1. Identify the three related items.
2. Cross out the unrelated item.
3. State the relationship of the three selected items in a single sentence.

Example: Group X

X. Queen Isabella, ~~Crusades~~, Columbus, New World

Relationship: Queen Isabella commissioned Christopher Columbus's voyage, which led to the "discovery" of the New World when he landed at San Salvador in 1492.

1. Ponce de Leon, Hernando de Soto, Francisco Pizarro, Francisco Coronado

   Relationship: *o Conquestedors*

2. geographically immobile, deeply religious, ecologically conscious, communal land ownership

   Relationship: *Native Am. were deeply religious, believed in not misuseing the land and believed the land belonged to everyone.*

3. ~~Walter Raleigh~~, John Calvin, Humphrey Gilbert, Richard Hakluyt

   Relationship: *Proponets of colonization in Americas*

4. Newfoundland, Roanoke Island, Chesapeake Bay, Florida

   Relationship: *the First colonies founded by Britan*

5. Puritans, Anglicans, Separatists, Quakers

   Relationship: _All disenting sects of the Anglican church_

6. William Bradford, John Smith, John Winthrop, John Cabot

   Relationship: _Bradford- Plymouth Col., Winthrop- Mass. Bay Cabot- Jamestown- All early Gov._

7. revelation, Arminianism, antinomianism, ~~predestination~~

   Relationship: _Puritans considered all of these heresey_

8. Maine, Connecticut, New Netherlands, New Hampshire

   Relationship: _all spin offs of colonies from Mass._

9. ~~social~~ experimentation, access to land, political rights, religious toleration

   Relationship: _Colonal Proprietors + land Co's offered these to colonist to settle on their land_

10. New York, Carolinas, Pennsylvania, Massachusetts,

    Relationship: _Proprietary colonies founded after restoration of Monarchy in 1660_

Cmap

Each chapter of this *Study Guide* includes a Cmap. The Cmap is a graphic representation of the key material in the chapter. Cmaps are designed to help you see the structure of the information in your text all at once on a single page. It is a kind of outline of the chapter. The Cmap, read left to right, follows the sequence of the material as it is presented in the chapter. Read top to bottom, the Cmap reveals the hierarchy of information in the chapter: chapter and subtopic titles are at the top; important points are below them; and examples and "details" are near the bottom. The following partial Cmap illustrates the "outline" characteristic of the Cmap.

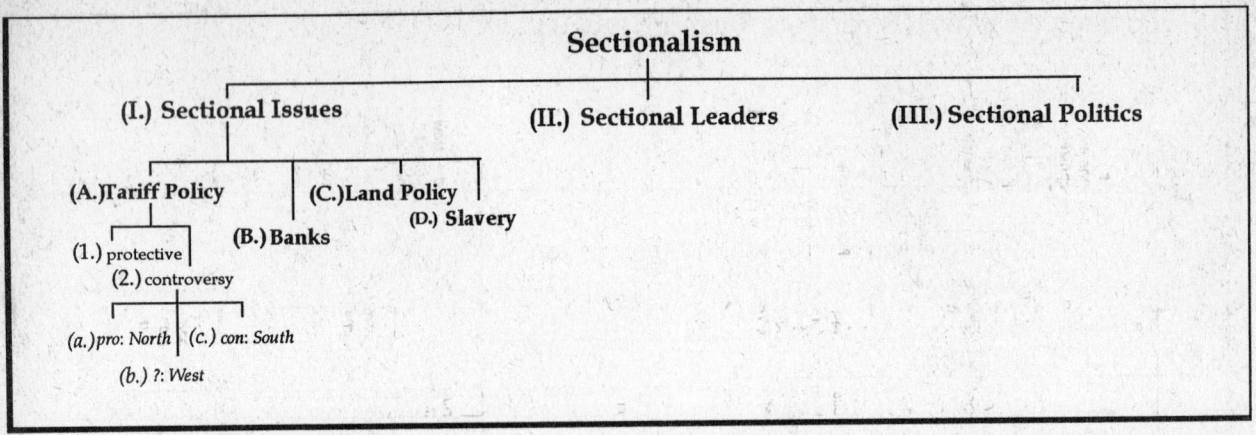

As you can see from the example, the Cmap is a way of representing the sequential and hierarchical structure of information in a text. Unlike the usual outline of material, however, by using keywords and linking lines, the Cmap represents a large amount of information in a single viewing.

Cmaps are most helpful when you construct them yourself. As a way to help you develop this useful skill, in this *Study Guide* each Cmap contains some question marks (**?**) in place of keywords that should be placed there. From your reading of the chapter, you should be able to place an appropriate keyword where each **?** appears. As you move through each chapter of the *Study Guide* and become increasingly skilled at discerning the structure of the information presented in the text (a skill that is critical to your successful comprehension and retention of what you read), each Cmap challenges you with an increasing number of **?**s. On some Cmaps there are opportunities for you to list information in boxes or to compare and contrast (c/c) information within the chapter.

The Cmap for Chapter 1 is nearly completed. You are to complete the Cmap by noting in the c/c box how Indian and European views compared and contrasted in such areas as religious beliefs, property ownership, material interests, etc. The information you need to do this is near the end of the subtopic section titled "Native American Civilizations." In that section, the author emphasizes the *diversity* of Native American cultures and the *European impact* on Native Americans (Their bringing of *diseases* and *assumption* that Indians were *inferior* to them had important consequences.); and the author compares and contrasts (*c/c*) important cultural characteristics and world views of *Indians and Europeans*.

Where the three **?**s appear under "The Settlement of Virginia" subtopic title, you are to write in three keywords that represent three problems experienced in early Jamestown. The information you need to do this is in the subtopic section titled "The Settlement of Virginia." In that section, the author tells of the *London Company's* founding of the *Jamestown* settlement, the *problems* it faced in its early years, the leadership provided by *Captain John Smith*, and the early settlers' relations with the local *Powhatan Indians*.

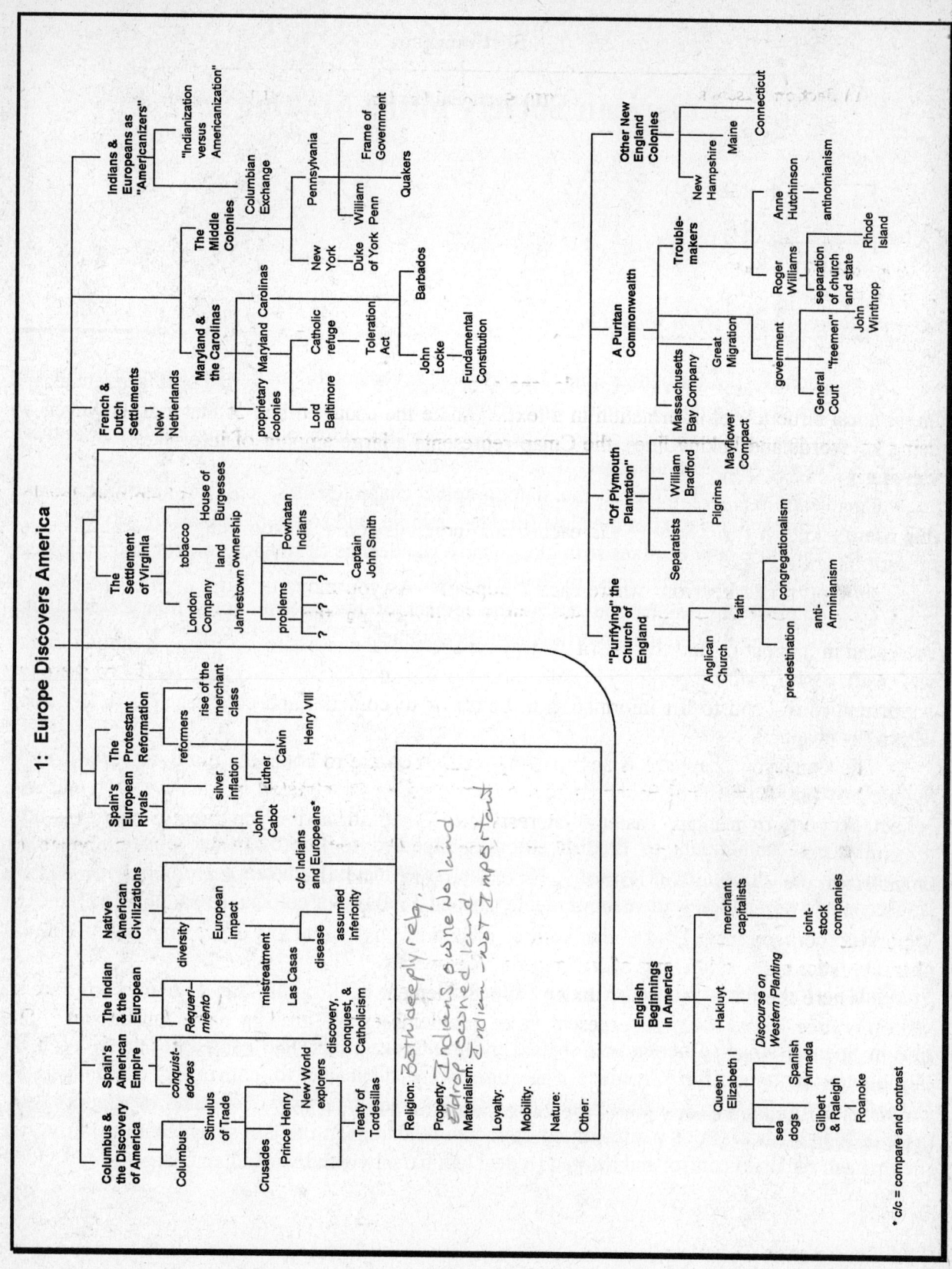

Chapter 2

American Society in the Making

Learning Objectives

After reading Chapter 2 you should be able to:

1. Identify the influences that transformed seventeenth- and early eighteenth-century European immigrants into "Americans."
2. Explain why slavery came to be the dominant labor system in England's southern North American colonies.
3. Compare and contrast the demographic characteristics, political institutions, and economic pursuits of the New England, middle, and southern colonies.
4. Describe how Puritans struggled against the decline of religious fervor and the rise of economic acquisitiveness in New England.
5. Explain the origins and assess the impact of the several domestic rebellions that occurred in England's North American colonies.

Overview

What Is an American?

The first immigrants to English colonies expected to improve their position within a recognizably European social system. Nevertheless, America's distance from Europe and its landscape and population settlement gradually shaped a mosaic of colonial social patterns.

Spanish Settlements in New Mexico and Florida

Life in Spanish North America was shaped by Franciscan friars who established missions from Florida to the upper Rio Grande. The friars were dedicated to converting the Indians to Catholicism, but in so doing undermined the Indians' traditional way of life and exacted a heavy price in Indian labor. Poor treatment led to Indian rebellions in the late seventeenth century, but the Spanish regained control and learned to deal less harshly with their Indian charges.

The Chesapeake Colonies

The seventeenth-century colonial South included the tidewater around Chesapeake Bay, the low country of the Carolinas, and the back country west of the fall line. Gradually a common South emerged characterized by cash crop agriculture, slavery, and a rural society.

In the disease-ridden Chesapeake colonies life expectancy was short and women were scarce. Life was precarious, frustrating, and often violent, but those who maintained their health could amass a fortune in land.

The Lure of Land

All southern colonies adopted the headright and indentured servant systems to trade their plentiful land for needed labor. Indentured servants who came to America under the terms of these systems were often abused, but binding contracts limited their time of service to a few years. Over half of the white settlers in the southern colonies came as indentured servants. Most eventually became small landowners, but poor land, low prices, and high taxes kept them impoverished. As their number increased and many squatted on unclaimed land, the resulting conflicts caused the large landowners to seek an alternative source of labor.

The Resort to Slavery

Blacks first came to America in 1619, but slavery was not codified into law until the 1660s. The English were already racially prejudiced against blacks, and they followed the Portuguese and Spanish example of enslaving Africans. These factors, and the demand for a reliable labor force, eventually spread slavery throughout the colonies. Still, until late in the seventeenth century, white indentured servitude remained the primary source of labor because Africans were so utterly alien, and slaves were expensive. But when England's economic conditions improved in the 1670s, few indentured servants left for the colonies. Africans now became a more attractive labor force because they were more readily available, and, as life-long slaves, they could never compete with whites for land and political power.

"Their Darling Tobacco"

Tidewater tobacco was exported when English merchants recognized its marketability. It was easy to plant and grow, but it required lots of human labor. In fact, overproduction of tobacco caused prices to fall in the late seventeenth century, drove many small farmers out of business, and improved the position of large landowners who could absorb the losses. Unfortunate losers in this competition moved to the frontier where they became involved in conflicts with the Indians.

Bacon's Rebellion

In 1676, Virginia's western settlers rebelled against the colony's governor, William Berkeley, because he was insensitive to their problems with the Indians. In defiance of Berkeley's authority, frontiersmen rallied behind Nathaniel Bacon. They attacked the troublesome Indians, then raided Jamestown and briefly unseated the governor, but Bacon died and the rebellion collapsed. Nevertheless, Bacon's Rebellion helped fix slavery and the plantation system on the colony, and it produced a harmony among whites that was based on assumptions of white supremacy and black exclusion.

The Carolinas: "More Like a Negro Country"

Like the Chesapeake, North Carolina grew tobacco, but South Carolina's cash crop was rice. Together with furs, indigo and timber products, it was traded to English factors for manufactured goods. But the factor system made southerners dependent on European middlemen, inhibited the development of a diversified economy, and retarded the growth of cities. Slavery was used in South Carolina from the beginning, and by 1730 blacks were a majority of the colony's population. There, as throughout the South, as slaves grew in numbers, regulations governing their behavior became more restrictive and severe.

Slaves resented their condition, but their response to it depended on their place in slave society. Acculturation to white society made a slave more valuable to the owner, but it also increased the slave's independence and mobility; most runaways were slave artisans, not field hands. Organized slave rebellions were rare, although whites were always on guard. Whites saw their "peculiar institution" of slavery as a fact of life and, except for a few Quakers, talk of abolishing slavery was almost nonexistent.

Home and Family in the Colonial South

Life for most people in the colonial South was isolated, crude, and uncomfortable. Houses were small and furniture was crudely built, but there was plenty of food. White women rarely worked in the fields; they maintained the household and, in rare instances, managed the farm or plantation. Children were not as strictly disciplined as in New England, there were few schools, and most people were illiterate. Large planters led more comfortable lives. They controlled the region's politics, but were usually responsible leaders and hardworking plantation managers, not idle grandees.

Georgia and the Back Country

The South's back country included land that lay west of the fall line—the Virginia Piedmont and Georgia. Georgia was founded as a buffer between Spanish Florida and South Carolina, and to provide a new life for debtors in English prisons. Hoping to build a colony of sober and industrious yeomen, James Oglethorpe and Georgia's trustees limited the size of land grants, banned liquor, and prohibited slavery. But settlers rejected these restrictions and Georgia gradually developed along the lines of the Carolinas.

Movement to the back country was delayed as long as Indians were a threat and land remained available in the tidewater and low country. But a rush to the frontier began in the 1750s, headed by Scotch-Irish and German immigrants. The result was often conflict between politically underrepresented western settlers and the governing elite in the eastern counties.

Colonial New England: A Covenanted People

New England, with its dependable water supply, was a healthier place than the tidewater or low country. With early death less a threat, New England settlers found it easier to attend to their spiritual, economic, and social well-being.

The Stamp of Puritanism: Family Bonds

Central to the Puritans' plan for the proper order of society was a covenant—an agreement to insure the good behavior of each and everyone in the community. The primary vehicle for achieving this was the Puritan family. Each New England household was nuclear–containing one family, and each family was patriarchal—the father was boss. The woman's role was subordinate—she was to be a good wife and mother.

Women and Children

Infant mortality rates in New England were lower than in the Chesapeake or in Europe; consequently, new England families were often quite large. As in the Chesapeake, New England children were expected to be obedient, and corporeal punishment, chore assignments, and apprenticeships were used to train and discipline them.

The Puritans' Great Migration ended in the early 1640s, and population growth in New England thereafter resulted from a high birth rate and low mortality rate. Unlike in the South, the male/female ratio was nearly equal.

Visible Saints and Others

The first arrivals in New England had to meet strict standards to become members of the Puritan church and qualify their children for baptism. Second-generation settlers were less often members of the church, and the ministers adopted a Half-Way Covenant so that they and their children could be baptized. This new covenant signaled a loss of some religious intensity in New England, but church membership rose.

Democracies Without Democrats

New England governments used their relative independence from British supervision to protect the prerogatives of the Puritan church and enforce its system of laws and values. The primary responsibility for monitoring the peace and good order of society fell to local town governments.

Dedham: A "Typical" Town

The primary governing institution in New England was the town meeting where most male adults could vote, but often did not. As in the South, the officeholders consistently came from the wealthier classes.

The Dominion of New England

In the 1680s, the Crown tried to bring its American colonies under firmer control. Massachusetts' charter was annulled and the New England colonies were placed in the Dominion of New England governed by Edmund Andros. Andros made himself unpopular by abolishing popular assemblies, enforcing religious toleration, and altering the land grant system. But the Glorious Revolution in England in 1688 toppled Andros from power, and Massachusetts became a royal colony.

Crisis in Salem Village

In Salem Village, social discord resulted in a series of witchcraft trials that led to 20 executions. The mass hysteria associated with this event eventually marred the reputation of the Puritan ministers.

"To Advance Learning"

New England Puritans established schools to train ministers. Both Harvard College and new laws requiring local towns to provide grammar schools appeared in the mid-seventeenth century. With the help of the family and church, these schools produced a highly literate population in New England. Generally, schooling promoted secularism in Puritan New England. Puritan minister Cotton Mather invoked modern science when he advocated inoculation against smallpox, and Boston's Ben Franklin satirized the pretentious intellectualism of colonial leaders.

"The Serpent Prosperity"

Most New Englanders were farmers who produced their own food. They also fished the Atlantic and generally had plenty to eat and a nutritious diet. Unlike in the South, however, New Englanders did not produce surplus cash crops for export. This was not a problem for the earliest Puritan settlers since theirs was a spiritual mission, not a commercial enterprise, and they held the accumulation of wealth in low regard.

A Merchant's World

The first generation of New Englanders tried to establish direct trade links to Europe, then turned to indirect trading schemes. Their "triangular trade" became immensely profitable and it brought New England merchants both wealth and status. Boston was the commercial hub of the region, and it became the home of wealthy merchants, middle-class artisans and shopkeepers, and propertyless sailors, workers, and transients. This had not been the social vision of the early Puritans.

The Middle Colonies: A Rising People

The Middle Colonies were similar to New England in that most people were farmers who grew their own food for consumption, or worked in seacoast cities and interior towns. They were similar to the southern colonies in that they had slavery, grew a cash crop for export, and developed a rural society.

"This Promiscuous Breed"

The Middle Colonies were distinctive for their ethnic and religious diversity. This mix of ethic groups gave rise to prejudice and discrimination. Generally, however, the different groups got along, probably because in the unusually prosperous Middle Colonies, there was enough for everyone.

"The Best Poor Man's Country"

Ethnic differences seldom produced conflict because they seldom limited opportunity. Non-English settlers came to America for the promise of prosperity, and, especially in Pennsylvania, they found it. Most became farmers, but others became artisans. Countless opportunities existed in cities like New York and Philadelphia, cities that benefited from navigable rivers that penetrated deep into the back country.

The Politics of Diversity

Politics in the Middle Colonies was as contentious as it was sophisticated. Like the colonies in New England and the South, the Middle Colonies all had popularly elected representative assemblies and adult white male suffrage. As in the Chesapeake, representatives were elected from counties, but in the Middle Colonies, voters did not defer to the leadership of the landed gentry.

In New York, politics first became polarized after Jacob Leisler's Rebellion in 1689, then polarized again between large landowners and wealthy merchants. Their squabbles produced John Peter Zenger's trial for seditious libel—a celebrated test of freedom of the press in America.

Two interest groups also contested for power in Pennsylvania: William Penn, the proprietor, battled a coalition of Philadelphia Quakers and Pennsylvania Dutch who controlled the assembly. In their stand-off, popular opinion became important. The colony's leadership was tested by the Paxton Boys' uprising in 1763—a revolt triggered by eastern indifference to the western settlers' Indian problems.

People, Places, and Things

Define the following:

headright system _____
_____

quitrent _____
_____

indentured servitude _____
_____

squatters' rights _____
_____

slavery _____
_____

peculiar institution _____
_____

covenant _____
_____

nuclear family _____
_____

town meeting _____
_____

triangular trade _____
_____

Describe the following:

    Royal African Company _____

    Bacon's Rebellion _____

    Half-Way Covenant _____

    Dominion of New England _____

    Glorious Revolution _____

    Leisler's Rebellion _____

    Paxton Boys uprising _____

Identify the following:

    William Berkeley <ins>Gov. of Va. during Bacon rebellion – 1676</ins>

    Eliza Lucas _____

    factors _____

James Oglethorpe _____

_____

Edmund Andros _____

_____

Cotton Mather _____

_____

Scotch-Irish _____

_____

Ben Franklin _____

_____

John Peter Zenger _____

_____

Pennsylvania Dutch _____

_____

Self-Test

Multiple-Choice Questions

1. Franciscan friars who staffed Spanish missions in the regions that are now part of the United States were committed to all the following EXCEPT
    A. instructing Indians in the rudiments of the Catholic faith
    B. using Indian labor to serve the needs of the friars and other Spanish colonists
    C. protecting the lives of individual Indians
    D. preserving the Indians' traditional way of life

2. Most immigrants to England's seventeenth-century mainland American colonies
    A. intended to develop a new civilization
    B. were not from England
    C. wanted to improve the condition of their own lives
    D. settled in the back country

3. In which of the following pairs is the geographical subdivision NOT correctly matched with one of colonies in it?
   A. tidewater—Virginia
   B. Chesapeake—Pennsylvania
   C. low country—South Carolina
   D. back country—Georgia

4. In contrast to the New England colonies, the Chesapeake colonies had a
   A. low mortality rate
   B. scarcity of women
   C. high birth rate
   D. healthy environment

5. Indentured servants
   A. were bound by temporary labor contracts
   B. were given headrights when they agreed to migrate to the American colonies
   C. had no legal rights
   D. constituted a small part of the southern colonies' population

6. Slavery in England's North American colonies was first used on a large scale
   A. in 1619 when the first blacks arrived
   B. late in the seventeenth century when the demand for labor increased
   C. in the Carolinas and Georgia
   D. in the mid-eighteenth century when England began losing control over the colonies

7. In 1676, frontier settlers rebelled against the royal governor of Virginia. This was
   A. Bacon's Rebellion
   B. the Paxton Boy's uprising
   C. the Regulator movement
   D. Leisler's Rebellion

8. The enactment and severity of slave codes in each colony was closely related to the
   A. kind of crops grown there
   B. structure of that colony's government
   C. ethnic origins of the white settlers
   D. size of the black population

9. Skilled slaves were generally LESS _____ than field hands.
   A. valuable
   B. independent
   C. mobile
   D. satisfied

10. In the colonial South,
    A. white women often worked in the fields
    B. food was scarce

29

C. most people were illiterate
D. children were more strictly disciplined than in New England

11. Georgia's original trustees did NOT restrict their settlers'
    A. ownership of slaves
    B. access to land
    C. religious freedom
    D. use of liquor

12. In New England families it was usual that
    A. the father and mother equally shared authority
    B. more than one family inhabited a household
    C. children were held to strict obedience
    D. wives had servants to do their housework

13. As compared to the Chesapeake colonies, New England had
    A. a high infant mortality rate
    B. smaller families
    C. a low birth rate
    D. a balanced gender ratio

14. The Half-Way Covenant was intended to allow the baptism of
    A. the children of those who were not full church members
    B. adult church members only
    C. the children of church members only
    D. the grandchildren of adult nonchurch members

15. The primary governing institution of the New England colonies was the
    A. governor's council
    B. county court
    C. Congregational church
    D. town meeting

16. In the 1680s, the English monarchy tried to gain greater control over the New England colonies by appointing Edmund Andros to govern the
    A. New England Confederation
    B. House of Burgesses
    C. Dominion of New England
    D. Puritan church

17. The driving force of New England's economy in the early eighteenth century was
    A. local agriculture
    B. fishing
    C. production of cash crops for export
    D. the "triangle trade"

18. The Middle Colonies were similar to South Carolina in all the following ways EXCEPT
    A. slavery was legal
    B. they grew a cash crop for export
    C. most people were farmers
    D. the majority of the population was black

19. The most distinctive feature of the Middle Colonies was
    A. the ethnic and religious diversity in their populations
    B. the absence of ethnic and religious prejudice among their inhabitants
    C. the limited economic opportunity there
    D. their lack of cities

20. John Peter Zenger was charged with
    A. organizing an armed rebellion
    B. religious heresy
    C. seditious libel
    D. advocating the abolition of slavery

Essay Questions

1. Explain how Europeans who settled in England's North American colonies were "Americanized" by that experience. Write a statement that defines a colonial "American."
2. Explain the origins of slavery in England's North American colonies.
3. Compare and contrast the economic, political, and social features of life in the New England, middle, and southern colonies.
4. Explain why the religious fervor of New England Puritans declined after 1660. Show how the Salem witchcraft trials were related to this decline.
5. Account for the several little rebellions that broke out periodically in England's North American colonies; notably, Bacon's Rebellion, Leisler's Rebellion, and the Paxton Boys uprising.

Critical Thinking Exercise

Comparing and Contrasting

Comparing and contrasting is a fundamental critical thinking skill. It involves classifying information into two categories: similarities (comparisons) and differences (contrasts). Comparative and contrasting relationships help historians relate facts and generalizations in a way that promotes greater understanding of both items being compared.

There are at least three specific ways that this form of classification is useful to historians. First, it helps define or clarify key terminology. For example, "slavery" and "indentured servitude" can both be clarified by comparing and contrasting the characteristics of each of the two labor systems. Second, comparing and contrasting helps generate useful generalizations. For example, contrasting the number of blacks as a percentage of the population in each colony helps produce the generalization, "Black codes were more strict where the percentage of blacks in the population was highest." Third, comparing and contrasting helps establish a frame of reference; it always poses the question, "Compared to what?" For example, any information or generalization about slavery in England's southern colonies in the seventeenth century can be better understood by comparing and contrasting it to slavery in the middle colonies and New England, or to southern slavery in the eighteenth century, or to slavery in the British West Indies, or to Spanish and Portuguese slavery in the Americas, or to slavery in antiquity, and so on.

Thus, comparing and contrasting helps clarify the characteristics of a topic of study, and like classification, of which it is a special kind, comparing and contrasting helps the historian order otherwise seemingly unrelated facts.

Contrast
Ways the New England colonies were different from the southern colonies

Comparison
Ways the the New England and southern colonies were similar

Contrast
Ways the southern colonies were different from the New England colonies

A *matrix* is a useful way to represent information for comparing and contrasting. It helps organize the similarities and differences of two or more topics being compared. Chapter 2 considers two topics we can compare: the development of life in colonial New England, and the southern colonies in the seventeenth century. Along the way, the authors discuss each regions' economy, society, demography (characteristics of the population), and politics. A matrix will help us quickly determine the similarities and differences between 17th century New England and the southern colonies.

Your task is to draw information from throughout Chapter 2 that helps you complete the boxes in the matrix on page 33. Some boxes have been filled in to cue you to specific areas of comparison and contrast.

A COMPARISON OF NEW ENGLAND AND SOUTHERN COLONIES

	SOUTH	NEW ENGLAND
Economy	cash crop agriculture	fishing, trade, agriculture
	undiversified	
		self-sufficient farms
	slavery vital to the economy	
Society	rural, no cities	
		strict child discipline
	female subordination	
	Protestant English settlers	
		high literacy
Demography	unhealthy environment	
	low life expectancy	
		low infant mortality
	unstable families	
	scarcity of women	
		immigration in family units
Politics	deference to wealthy planters	
	east-west conflict	
		popularly elected assemblies
	appointed governors and councils	
		township governments
		white male adult suffrage

2: American Society in the Making

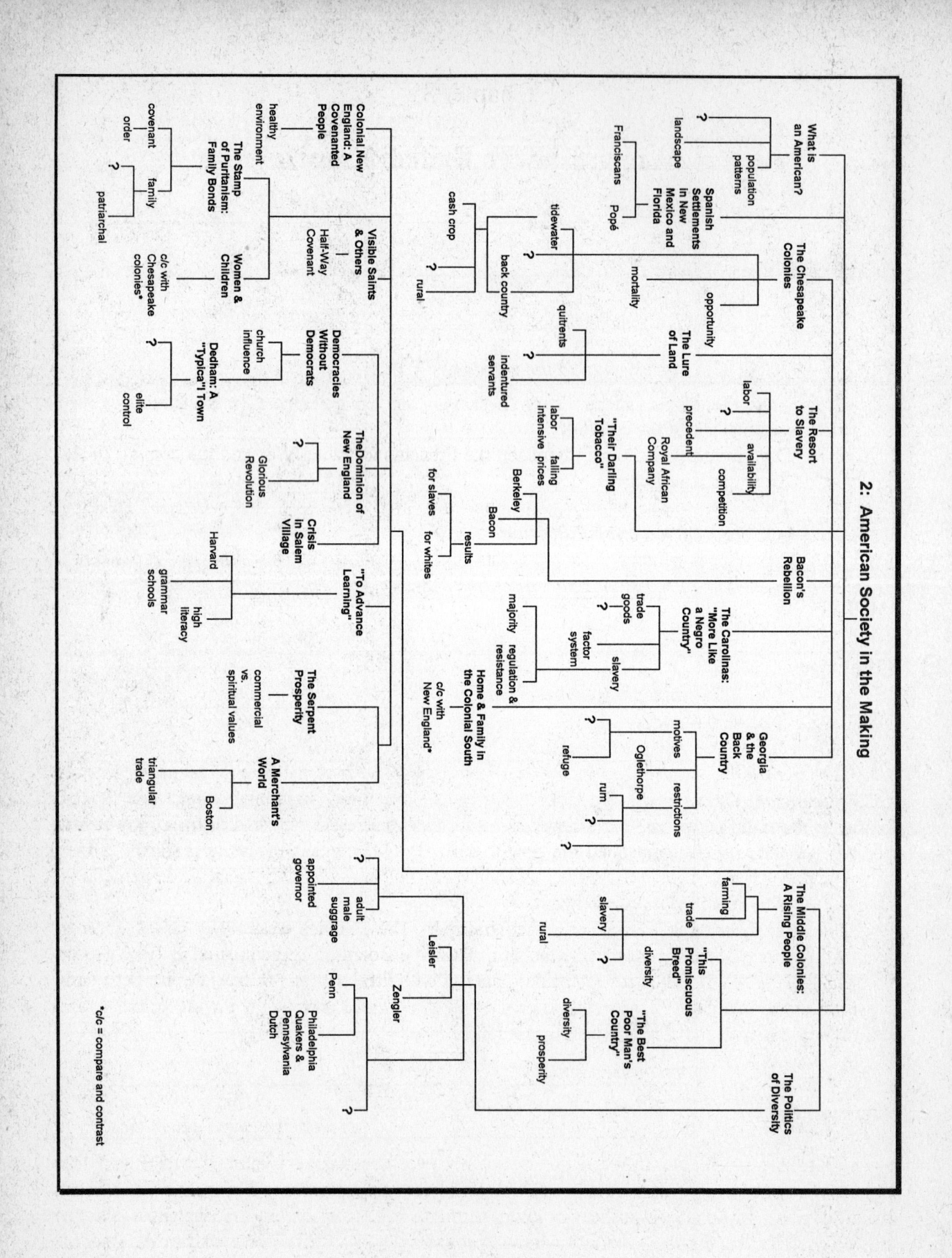

A hierarchical outline/bracket diagram with the following structure:

- **What is an American?**
  - ? — population patterns
  - landscape

- **Spanish Settlements in New Mexico and Florida**
  - Franciscans
  - Popé

- **The Chesapeake Colonies**
  - cash crop
  - tidewater — ? — back country / rural
  - mortality

- **The Lure of Land**
  - opportunity
  - quitrents — ?
  - indentured servants

- **The Resort to Slavery**
  - labor — ? — precedent / availability / competition
  - Royal African Company

- **"Their Darling Tobacco"**
  - labor intensive
  - falling prices
  - Berkeley
  - Bacon

- **Bacon's Rebellion**
  - results — for slaves / for whites

- **The Carolinas: "More Like a Negro Country"**
  - trade goods — ?
  - factor system
  - slavery

- **Georgia & the Back Country**
  - motives — ? — refuge / restrictions
  - Oglethorpe
  - rum — ?

- **Home & Family in the Colonial South**
  - majority
  - regulation & resistance
  - c/c with New England*

- **The Middle Colonies: A Rising People**
  - farming
  - trade — ? — rural / slavery
  - diversity

- **"This Promiscuous Breed"**
  - diversity

- **"The Best Poor Man's Country"**
  - diversity
  - prosperity

- **The Politics of Diversity**
  - Leisler
  - Penn — Philadelphia / Quakers & Pennsylvania Dutch
  - Zenger
  - adult male suffrage
  - appointed governor — ?

- **Colonial New England: A Covenanted People**
  - healthy environment

- **The Stamp of Puritanism: Family Bonds**
  - covenant — ? — order
  - family — ? — patriarchal
  - c/c with Chesapeake colonies*

- **Visible Saints & Others**
  - Half-Way Covenant
  - Women & Children

- **Democracies Without Democrats**
  - church influence
  - Dedham: A "Typical" Town — ? — elite control

- **The Dominion of New England**
  - Glorious Revolution — ?
  - Crisis in Salem Village

- **"To Advance Learning"**
  - Harvard
  - grammar schools
  - high literacy

- **The Serpent Prosperity**
  - commercial vs. spiritual values

- **A Merchant's World**
  - Boston
  - triangular trade

*c/c = compare and contrast

Chapter 3

America in the British Empire

Learning Objectives

After reading Chapter 3 you should be able to:

1. Define the basic assumptions of the British colonial system and describe its operation
2. Assess the impact of the Great Awakening and Enlightenment on the intellectual and spiritual life of the colonies.
3. Describe the relationship between the French and Indian War and the coming of the American Revolution.
4. Trace the course of key events between 1763 and 1775 that worsened relations between England and the colonies.
5. Identify the principles the colonists used to justify their resistance to Parliament's legislation between 1763 and 1775.

Overview

The British Colonial System

Their distance from England combined with British political inefficiency to give colonists considerable political freedom. Most colonies had an appointed governor, council and judges, and all had elected representative assemblies. Assemblies, because they had financial power and popular support, usually controlled the government. While colonial legislators gradually gained power and experience, royal officials were handicapped by lack of tenure, impractical instructions, and few ways to influence the assemblies.

The British colonial system was decentralized. The colonies were never called upon to conform to a single set of governing principles. Even the Board of Trade created in 1696 was an inconsistently efficient policy recommending agency with little power. In fact, Parliament nearly always accepted the board's recommendations, rarely legislated specifically for the colonies, and only infrequently vetoed acts of colonial assemblies.

Mercantilism

English mercantilists believed that national power depended on national wealth and that colonies could contribute to national wealth by supplying raw materials and by consuming English manufactures. National self-sufficiency and a favorable balance of trade were England's ticket to power, merchants were the agents of national prosperity, and colonies were vital to the imperial system.

The Navigation Acts

The Navigation Acts were designed to implement mercantilist principles. They barred foreign ships from colonial ports, prohibited the colonists from marketing "enumerated articles" outside the empire, and required that all colonial imports be transshipped from England. The British gave southern tobacco planters a monopoly within the empire, paid bounties to producers of indigo and naval stores, and regulated colonial manufactures.

The Effects of Mercantilism

England was the colonies' main trading partner, but much colonial trade and manufacturing was left untouched by the Navigation Laws. The Navigation system stimulated colonial shipbuilding, but it also caused colonists to pay higher prices for certain imports. The system had the potential for hampering colonial economic development, but serious problems were alleviated by the inefficiency of British enforcement; smuggling and bribery were common. The fact is, the colonial economy was almost continuously prosperous and practical British leaders followed a policy of "salutary neglect"—ignoring American violations of the Navigation Acts.

The Great Awakening

The Great Awakening was one of the colonists' first nationalizing experiences. Its outbreak in the 1730s ended a period of slackening religious fervor. George Whitefield's uncomplicated theology released an epidemic of religions enthusiasm for a God that responded to good intentions and was willing to give salvation to all. The Awakening often split established churches, and it led many people to question authority.

The Rise and Fall of Jonathan Edwards

By 1750, a traditionalist backlash had set in against Jonathan Edwards' and other Awakening preachers' emotion-charged style. While it caused divisions and controversy, the Great Awakening also fostered religious toleration and it marks the time when the previously distinct histories of the colonies began to intersect.

The Enlightenment in America

The Enlightenment had a great impact on American intellectuals. Enlightenment thinkers believed that universal natural laws governed all behavior. They saw God as the Creator, but not as an intrusive force in ordinary life. Human reason, they thought, not God's revelations was the key to knowledge. This view implied mankind's ability to control its own destiny.
Enlightenment thinkers challenged orthodox religious beliefs and many embraced Deism, a faith that revered God for the wonder of his creation, not for his omnipotence. American intellectuals avidly read and discussed the publications of Europe's political theorists and philosophers. As a result, ministers lost their monopoly of the intellectual life of America.

Colonial Scientific Achievements

Ben Franklin was the representative Enlightened man in America. He personified the colonies' mid-eighteenth century intellectual climate that was characterized by curiosity, practicality, flexibility, and confidence.

Other People's Wars

Seventeenth- and eighteenth-century mercantilistic competition for markets and raw materials generated conflict among European powers, their colonists, and the Indians. Colonists played only a minor role in England's colonial wars with France between 1689 and 1748. Frontier settlers were sometimes killed, some colonies suffered inflation and higher taxes, and some colonists were killed in militia campaigns against enemy strongholds like Louisbourgh.

The Great War for the Empire

By the mid-eighteenth century, English colonists' land interest in the Ohio Valley were challenging France's dominance in the area. The resulting showdown, called the French and Indian War, at first went poorly for the British. The English outnumbered French colonists, but British campaigns were mismanaged and most Indians sided with the French. In 1756, William Pitt took charge of England's war effort. He recognized the potential value of North America, so he poured the full resources of the empire into the campaign to drive the French from the continent. By 1760, both Quebec and Montreal had fallen and France abandoned Canada.

The Peace of Paris

The 1763 Treaty of Paris ended the Great War for the Empire. France lost almost all her American claims, while Britain took control of Canada and the eastern half of the Mississippi Valley. Britain also got East and West Florida from Spain, and (in a separate treaty) Spain received New Orleans and former French claims lying west of the Mississippi River. British regular troops and the royal treasury had cleared North America of the French threat to the colonial frontier. Colonial troops and assemblies contributed little to the fighting or costs of the war except in defense of their own homes.

Putting the Empire Right

England now had a larger, more complex, and more costly empire. Colonists were eager to expand into the newly conquered territories, so British authorities now faced problems with conflicting land claimants, rival land companies, unpacified Indians, and fur traders hoping to hold back the wave of new settlement. Unfortunately, British officials failed to provide effective leadership. King George III proved to be inept, and even the best English statesmen were wholly ignorant of American conditions. They generally held the colonists in low regard, and many English people resented the colonists' relative wealth and potential power.

Tightening Imperial Controls

The American Revolution resulted from the inefficient British government's failure to deal effectively with postwar problems following the Great War for the Empire. Colonists, having grown used to managing their own affairs, resisted England's attempts to both restrict their freedom of action and to intervene in their affairs. As early as 1759 colonists questioned British officials' authority to issue writs of assistance to control colonial smuggling. Pontiac's Rebellion provoked the English to station British regular troops on the colonial frontier and proclaim a new western policy. The Proclamation of 1763 frustrated many colonial land development schemes by prohibiting settlement in the Ohio Valley. The British saw the Proclamation as a way to save money, prevent trouble with the Indians, and keep the colonists closely tied and subordinate to England.

The Sugar Act

Even more alarming to colonists was Prime Minister George Grenville's plan to use the new Sugar Tax—a revenue tax on colonial imports—to compel the colonists to help pay the costs of colonial administration. Grenville planned to end salutary neglect, smuggling, and the corruption and inefficiency of the customs service. Colonists were further alarmed when Grenville restricted the printing of paper money—a threat to the power of the colonial assemblies and to the health of the depressed colonial economy. More fundamentally, however, the colonists saw the Sugar Act as a threat to their rights as English subjects not to be taxed without their consent or that of their representatives.

"Essential Rights and Liberties"

The British and Americans disagreed over the meaning of representation. By "virtual" representation the English asserted that colonial interests were represented by each member of Parliament. American colonists insisted on "actual" representation that was geographically based, as with the colonial assemblies. Colonists were provincials who defined their obligations to the empire very narrowly. They had prospered without a Parliamentary tax burden before 1763, and they saw no reason to change. Still, calls for coordinated protest against the Sugar Act were met with widespread indifference.

The Stamp Act: The Pot Set to Boiling

The 1765 Stamp Act was a direct tax on all kinds of printed matter that Grenville hoped would defray the costs of empire by raising revenue in the colonies. Colonial resistance was swift and widespread. Patrick Henry denied Parliament's authority to tax the colonies, and the Stamp Act Congress claimed the colonists' right to no taxation without representation. The Sons of Liberty initiated extralegal organized resistance against British tax policies, often resorting to violence.

Rioters or Rebels?

The resort to violence worried the colonial elite who feared a social revolution within the colonies. But most colonists were property owners and could vote, so they were not social revolutionaries seeking to overthrow the established order. Protests against the Stamp Act were so strong because it was imposed while the colonies were still in a postwar depression and it struck directly at the interests of the most articulate and influential groups in America. More basically, it was a clear British rejection of the principle of no taxation without representation, thus, it was a threat to colonial self-government and the colonists' constitutional rights as English subjects. The Quartering Act further heightened colonists' fears that British authorities were conspiring to subvert English liberties.

Taxation or Tyranny?

Colonists saw the English system of balanced government that was designed to protect their liberties being corrupted by greedy and ambitious politicians. British leaders were not conspiratorial tyrants, but they were committed to centralizing imperial authority at the expense of colonial autonomy. They wanted a British army in America to control both the Indians and troublesome colonists. British leaders saw the colonists as dependent "children" and refused to deal with them as equals. But by resolution, mob violence, and especially economic boycott, colonists eventually forced Parliament to repeal of the Stamp Act in 1766.

The Declaratory Act

When it repealed the Stamp Act, Parliament passed the Declaratory Act as a bold statement of Parliament's authority and colonial subordination. The British and Americans now disagreed about the meaning of representation, constitution, and sovereignty. To the British, a constitution was the totality of laws, customs and institutions that governed the realm. Americans defined a constitution as a written document that limited the powers of government. The British saw Parliament's sovereignty as absolute and necessary for the preservation of social order. Americans were beginning to conceive of the possibility that "unconstitutional" Parliamentary laws had no force in America.

The Townshend Duties

Charles Townshend, new head of the British government in 1767, mistakenly believed that colonists would accept an indirect tax on trade. The Townshend duties imposed taxes on several colonial imports, and colonists responded with a boycott of British goods. Townshend also insisted on strict enforcement of the trade laws and extraordinary penalties for smugglers. In response, Massachusetts circulated a Circular Letter asserting the unconstitutionality of the Townshend Duties; conservative John Dickinson stated plainly that Parliament had no right to tax the colonies; and radical Samuel Adams believed Parliament had no right to legislate for the colonies at all. The British dismissed these protests and sent troops to Boston.

The Boston Massacre

The presence of British troops in Boston created tensions that finally broke in the Boston Massacre in 1770. British troops, taunted by local citizens, fired upon a crowd and killed five colonists. The Townshend duties were repealed except for the tax on tea, and a postmassacre truce settled over the empire for the next two years.

The Pot Spills Over

Colonists broke the truce by burning a British customs ship in 1772. The British now viewed the colonists as utterly lawless. When news arrived that henceforth governors would be paid by the Crown and not by local assemblies, colonists knew they had lost their control of royal officials. They formed committees of correspondence to coordinate intercolonial resistance.

The Tea Act Crisis

In 1773, Lord North decided to assist the financially strapped British East India Company by allowing it to sell its tea directly to the colonies at bargain prices. Colonists viewed this as a diabolical attempt to entice them to violate their principles and buy the tea—on which they would have to pay the Townshend duty. But colonists would have to pay the Townshend tea tax to buy the tea, and Parliament's favoritism threatened colonial merchants. So, in Boston, colonists threw the tea into the harbor. In Britain, leaders now agreed that colonists must be taught a lesson in obedience.

From Resistance to Revolution

In 1774, Parliament passed the Coercive Acts which threatened the economic health and political freedom of Massachusetts. These acts signaled a shift in British policy from persuasion and conciliation to coercion and punishment. Further, and ominously, the unrelated Quebec Act created a new American colony with a centralized and authoritarian government.

Colonists had been driven by British policies and a growing awareness of their common interests to take political action into their own hands and act in concert. When the First Continental Congress met in Philadelphia in 1775, Joseph Galloway called for a restructuring of the empire, but the majority of delegates denied Parliament had any authority to govern the colonies. The Congress drafted a list of grievances and proposed that people take up arms to defend their rights. It also organized the Continental Association to enforce a total boycott against British goods. In the minds of the people, the Revolution had already begun.

People, Places, and Things

Define the following:

mercantilism _____
_____

favorable balance of trade _____
_____

enumerated articles _____
_____

salutary neglect _____
_____

Deism _____
_____

writs of assistance _____
_____

no taxation without representation _____
_____

virtual and actual representation _____
_____

provincials _____
_____

direct and indirect taxation _____
_____

boycott _____
_____

Describe the following:

Navigation Acts _____

_____

Hat, Iron, Wool Acts _____

_____

Great Awakening _____

_____

Enlightenment _____

_____

Colonial Wars _____

_____

Great War for the Empire _____

_____

Treaty of Paris (1763) _____

_____

Pontiac's Rebellion _____

_____

Proclamation of 1763 _____

_____

Sugar Act _____

_____

Stamp Act _____

_____

Declaratory Acts _____
_____

Circular Letter _____
_____

Boston Massacre _____
_____

Boston Tea Party _____
_____

Coercive/Intolerable Acts _____
_____

Quebec Act _____
_____

Continental Association _____
_____

Identify the following:

Board of Trade _____
_____

George Whitefield _____
_____

Old and New Lights _____
_____

Jonathan Edwards _____
_____

Benjamin Franklin _____

_____

Five Nations _____

_____

William Pitt _____

_____

James Otis _____

_____

George Grenville _____

_____

Patrick Henry _____

_____

Sons of Liberty _____

_____

Charles Townshend _____

_____

John Dickinson _____

_____

committees of correspondence _____

_____

First Continental Congress _____

_____

Joseph Galloway _____

_____

Self-Test

Multiple-Choice Questions

1. The most effective governmental institution in the colonies was the
   A. appointed governor
   B. elected assembly
   C. appointed council
   D. customs office

2. English mercantilists believed that England's power depended on
   A. finding gold and silver in America
   B. a ruthless exploitation of the colonists
   C. subsidizing colonial manufactures
   D. a favorable balance of trade with other nations

3. England's Navigation Acts
   A. banned Dutch ships from colonial ports
   B. allowed the colonists to sell certain enumerated articles to foreign markets
   C. failed to implement mercantilistic assumptions
   D. were strictly but fairly enforced

4. Mercantilism and the Navigation Acts stimulated the _____ industry in the colonies.
   A. hat
   B. shipbuilding
   C. iron
   D. woolen

5. One effect of the Great Awakening was that it
   A. weakened religious fervor in the colonies
   B. promoted religious toleration in the colonies
   C. unified colonial congregations
   D. renewed colonists' respect for authority

6. Enlightenment thinkers believed that mankind's future was tied to the
   A. arbitrary actions of an omnipotent God
   B. instance of divine revelation
   C. exercise of human reason
   D. unpredictability of uncontrollable fate

7. Which of the following statements is TRUE?
   A. Mercantilistic principles reduced the level of international conflict.
   B. Left alone by their imperial governments, French and English colonists in America had little reason for conflict.
   C. Before 1750, colonists played a minor role in the imperial wars between Britain and France.
   D. The early colonial wars created serious strains between England and the colonies.

8. William Pitt made the _____ the primary British objective in the French and Indian War.
   A. acquisition of the Caribbean sugar islands
   B. domination of North America
   C. banning of Dutch trade from America
   D. elimination of Indian resistance on the colonial frontier

9. In the 1763 Treaty of Paris,
   A. France lost all her American possessions
   B. England got New Orleans and former French territory west of the Mississippi River
   C. Spain got East and West Florida
   D. England got Canada

10. Which of the following statements about the British in 1763 is NOT true?
    A. Most British officials new little about America.
    B. British leaders held colonists in contempt
    C. British officials finally began to exercise effective leadership of the empire
    D. the expanded empire in America presented several new problems for British administration

11. The Proclamation of 1763
    A. held that writs of assistance were unconstitutional
    B. declared war on Chief Pontiac and his followers
    C. invalidated all colonial land claims
    D. prohibited colonial settlement in the Ohio Valley

12. The Grenville administration did NOT enact
    A. new duties on glass, paint, and tea
    B. direct taxes on all legal papers
    C. lower taxes on West Indian sugar
    D. strict enforcement of the trade laws

13. Colonial resistance to the Sugar Act generated a debate between Parliament and the colonists about the definition of
    A. representation
    B. imperialism
    C. federalism
    D. mercantilism

14. Protest against the Stamp Act was very strong and widespread for all of the following reasons EXCEPT it
    A. was imposed at a time when the colonial economy was depressed
    B. provoked the most vocal interest groups in the colonies
    C. was an indirect tax designed to regulate colonial trade
    D. was an open threat to colonial self-government

15. The Declaratory Act was
    A. an invitation to colonists to work out a system for sharing governing power between Parliament and the colonial assemblies
    B. a statement of the colonists' claim that they could not be taxed without their consent
    C. a bold assertion of Parliament's sovereign power over the empire
    D. a strongly worded colonial protest against the Stamp Act

16. Charles Townshend, author of the Townshend Acts in 1767, believed that colonists
    A. made no distinction between direct and indirect taxes
    B. objected to both direct and indirect taxes
    C. objected only to indirect taxes
    D. objected only to direct taxes

17. The Boston Massacre was directly followed by the
    A. repeal of the Stamp Act
    B. enactment of the Declaratory Act
    C. repeal of the Townshend Acts
    D. enactment of the Quartering Act

18. After the *Gaspee* was burned in 1772, colonists created _____ to coordinate intercolonial resistance to British "tyranny."
    A. the Continental Association
    B. the Sons of Liberty
    C. committees of correspondence
    D. the First Continental Congress

19. Parliament intended the Tea Act to
    A. compel the colonists to pay import taxes
    B. aid the financially troubled British East India Company
    C. punish Massachusetts for the Boston Tea Party
    D. provoke the colonies to armed rebellion

20. Most delegates to the First Continental Congress
    A. accepted the concept of virtual representation
    B. denied that Parliament had any authority to legislate for the colonies
    C. called for a restructuring of the British colonial system
    D. demanded independence for the colonies

Essay Questions

1. Describe the relationship between mercantilistic assumptions and the operation of the Navigation Acts as central elements in the British colonial system.
2. Identify the basic beliefs and assumptions of the Enlightenment and the Great Awakening. Evaluate their importance to colonial development.
3. Explain how the Great War for the Empire can be seen as a major cause of the American Revolution.

4. Explain how the Sugar Act, Stamp Act, Townshend Acts, Tea Act, and Coercive Acts led to an open breach between England and her North American colonies.
5. Make an argument that the American colonists' resistance to British authority between 1763 and 1775 was based on either principle or self-interest (pick one).

Critical Thinking Exercise

Cause and Effect

Discerning cause-and-effect (or *causal*) relationships is perhaps the most important critical thinking skill for the study of history. Historians are always asking the cause-and-effect questions, how and why did something happen? It involves identifying a cause (whatever brings about something else) and an effect (the result of the cause). Cause-and-effect is the most basic organizing and structuring scheme for historical information.

Like classifying and comparing and contrasting, historians use cause-and-effect relationships to organize otherwise seemingly isolated facts into comprehensible patterns. These patterns take at least two forms. First, a *causal chain* is a sequence of events each of which was the effect of the preceding event that then becomes the cause of the next event until a whole series of causes produces a climactic event at the end of the chain. For example, the outcome of the Great War for Empire caused the British to reorganize their North American empire, which resulted in the enactment of new tax laws that provoked colonial resistance, culminating in the American Revolution.

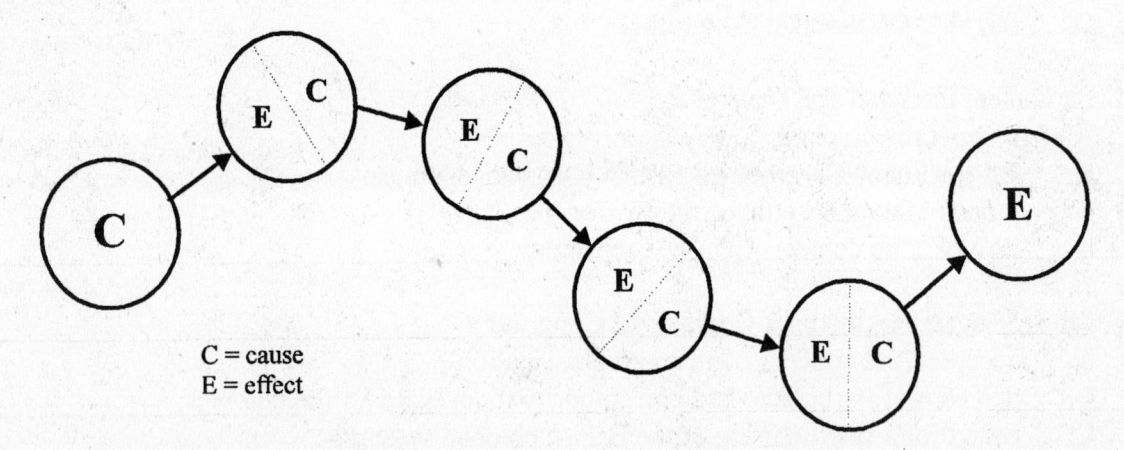

C = cause
E = effect

A second cause-and-effect pattern involves *contributory causes*—a set of causes that act simultaneously to bring about an effect. Each cause contributes to producing the effect, and each cause reinforces the other causes. Thus, the effect is the result of several different factors working together. For example, it might be said that the simultaneous interaction of the colonist's assimilation of ideas from the Enlightenment, the consequences of the Great War for the Empire, and the ineffective handling of colonial issues by the British government contributed to the coming of the American Revolution.

Your task in the following cause-and-effect exercise is to rearrange the items in each group into a causal chain. Correctly arranged, the items will show a series of events each of which will be the effect of the preceding event that then became the cause of the next event. Therefore, the chain must be sequential. The first event on your list (give it number 1) should be the event that initiated the chain, the last event (give it the highest number) on your list will be the last effect in the preceding chain. Number the intermediate events in their proper cause-and-effect sequence. Finally, link all the items in the group in a short explanatory paragraph that clearly expresses the cause-and-effect relationship among the items in the group. Group One is an example.

Group One

____3____ British need to maintain peace on the frontier

____2____ Pontiac's Rebellion

____4____ Proclamation of 1763

____1____ End of the Great War for the Empire

    The end of the Great War for the Empire resulted in Pontiac's Rebellion, a defensive war against the westward migration of colonists into former French territory. As a way to minimize Indian-white conflict and maintain peace on the frontier, the British government adopted the Proclamation of 1763 which delayed the westward migration of colonists.

Group Two

_____ Sugar Act passed

_____ British argue for virtual representation

_____ British face new expenses in their expanded empire

_____ Americans protest being taxed without their consent

_____

_____

_____

Group 3

_____ Declaratory Act passed

_____ Sugar Act fails to produce needed revenue

_____ Stamp Act Congress claims "no taxation without representation"

_____ Stamp Act passed

_____ Stamp Act repealed

Group 4

_____ Circular Letter issued

_____ Townshend duties adopted

_____ Boston Massacre occurs

_____ British send troops to Boston

_____ Townshend duties repealed

Group 5

_____ Coercive Acts passed

_____ Tea Act passed

_____ First Continental Congress meets

_____ Boston Tea Party occurs

_____ British East India Company needs to dump surpluses

3: America in the British Empire

A hierarchical concept map covering the following topics and subtopics:

- **The British Colonial System**
  - inefficient
    - distant
    - decentralized
    - assemblies

- **Mercantilism**
  - wealth/power
  - national self-sufficiency
  - favorable balance of trade
  - **The Navigation Acts**
    - Dutch
    - bounties
    - manufactures
    - ?
  - **The Effects of Mercantilism**
    - colonial debt
    - high prices
    - poorly enforced
    - ?

- **The Great Awakening**
  - George Whitefield
    - split churches
    - emotional enthusiasm
    - stimulated toleration
    - undermined authority
  - Old/New Lights
  - **The Rise & Fall of Jonathan Edwards**

- **The Enlightenment in America**
  - natural law
  - human reason
  - Deism
  - **Colonial Scientific Achievements**
    - ?

- **Other People's Wars**
  - three Colonial Wars
  - ?
  - **The Great War for the Empire**
    - Louisbourg
    - Ohio Valley
    - William Pitt
    - Ft. Duquesne
  - **The Peace of Paris**
    - territorial settlements
      - England:
      - France:
      - Spain:

- **Tightening Imperial Controls**
  - **Putting the Empire Right**
    - new empire — George III
    - war debt
    - defense
    - administration costs
    - British views of Americans

- **The Sugar Act**
  - writs of assistance
  - Otis
  - Pontiac's Rebellion
  - ?
  - Grenville
  - Currency Act
  - **"Essential Rights and Liberties"**
    - "no taxation without representation"
    - virtual/actual representation

- **The Stamp Act: The Pot Set to Boiling**
  - direct tax
  - Patrick Henry
  - Stamp Act Congress resolutions
  - **Rioters or Rebels?**
    - ?
    - boycott
    - riot
    - depressed economy
  - **Taxation or Tyranny?**
    - balanced government
    - constitutional rights of Englishmen
    - conspiracy?
    - "no taxation without representation"
    - dependence
    - authority v. autonomy
    - representation
  - **The Declaratory Act**
    - constitution
    - ?

- **The Townshend Duties**
  - indirect tax
  - John Dickinson
  - circular letter
  - Sam Adams
  - **The Boston Massacre**
    - repeal of the Townshend duties

- **The Pot Spills Over**
  - committees of correspondence
  - *Gaspee*
  - **The Tea Act Crisis**
    - British East India Company
    - a "plot"
    - ?

- **From Resistance to Revolution**
  - **Coercive Acts**
    - Quartering Act
  - **Intolerable Acts**
    - ?
  - **First Continental Congress**
    - Galloway Plan
    - continental association

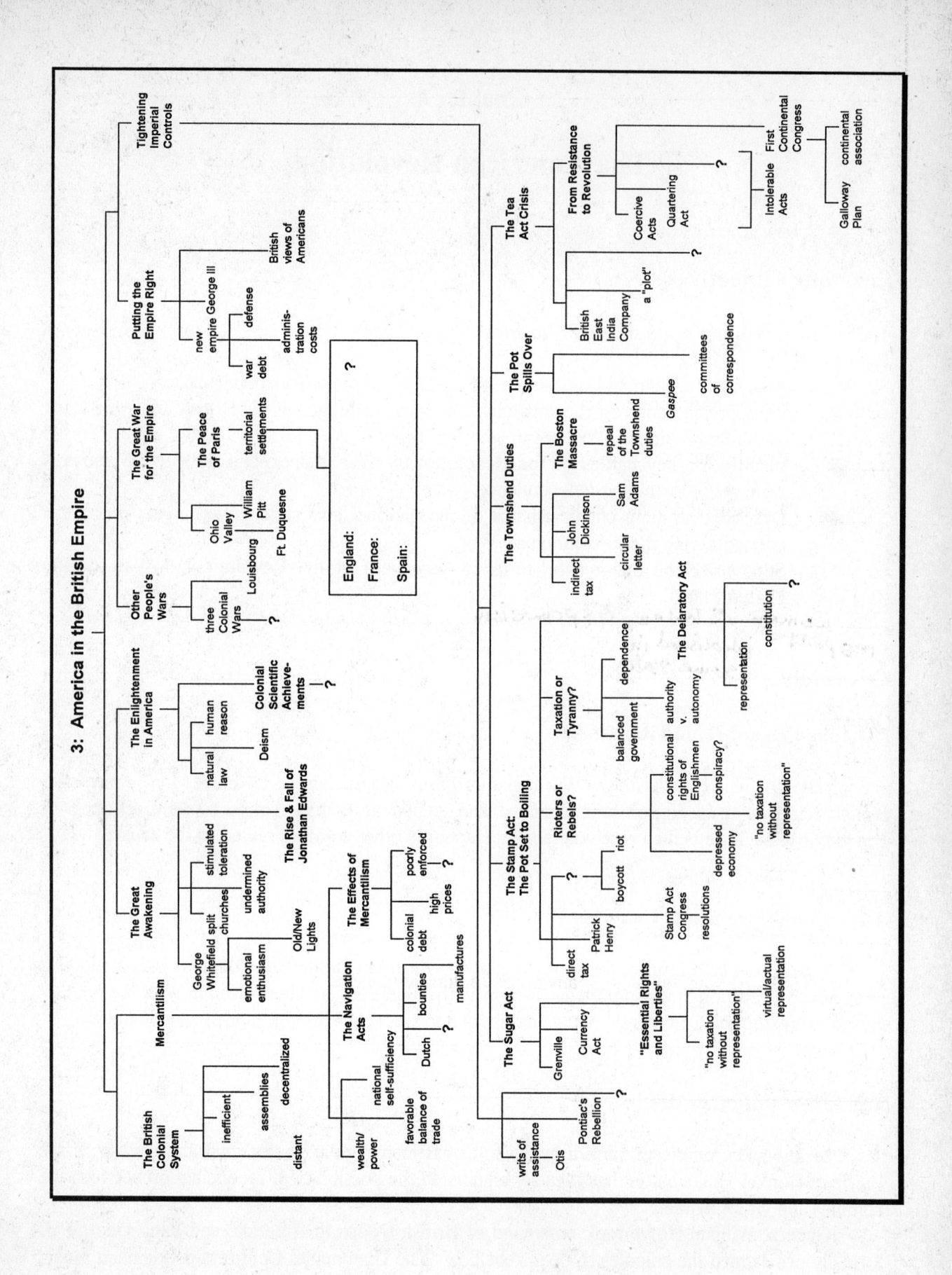

51

Chapter 4

The American Revolution

Learning Objectives

After reading Chapter 4 you should be able to:

1. Analyze the intent and the content of the Declaration of Independence.
2. Compare and contrast the advantages and disadvantages of the British and Americans as the Revolutionary War began.
3. Identify the key battles of the Revolutionary War and explain how the Americans were able to win their independence.
4. Describe the main characteristics of the national and state governments that were created during the Revolutionary War.
5. Summarize the major short-term consequences of the Revolutionary War for the United States.

[handwritten notes: respect of Women, Slaves, Expansion — abolished in some states]

Overview

"The Shot Heard Round the World"

The American Revolutionary War began in 1775. Massachusetts "Minute Men" confronted British regulars at Lexington and Concord and sniped at British troops as they returned to Boston. Massachusetts then received reinforcements as other colonies rallied to the cause.

The Second Continental Congress

A more radical group of delegates met at the Second Continental Congress in Philadelphia in May 1775. Although it had no legal authority, the Congress set about dealing with the military crisis. It created the Continental Army and appointed George Washington as its commander.

The Battle of Bunker Hill

Meanwhile, Americans took a heavy toll of British regulars before withdrawing from the Battle of Bunker Hill, a battle that virtually eliminated the possibility of reconciliation between the colonies and Great Britain.

General William Howe took command of British troops in America, and King George III formally proclaimed the colonies to be in rebellion. The Continental Congress condemned recent British policies and refused to submit to British "tyranny." Congress then ordered an attack on Canada, commissioned a navy, and began seeking foreign aid.

The Great Declaration

Still, some hesitated at declaring independence. They disliked being called traitors, feared the possibility of social revolution and were apprehensive about self-government. But two events moved the colonies toward independence: British employment of Hessian soldiers, and Thomas Paine's publication of *Common Sense*. Paine's call for independence and republican government profoundly affected public opinion. Congress commissioned privateers, opened all ports, and called upon the states to draft constitutions and establish independent governments.

Finally, Congress appointed a committee to draft a Declaration of Independence. Thomas Jefferson's Declaration justified the right of revolution and defined republican government. It also contained a bill of indictment against George III. The Declaration was a self-conscious attempt to favorably influence world opinion toward the colonies.

1776: The Balance of Forces

Americans had the home-court advantage. The British had the task of bringing men and supplies all the way from England. Britain was also hampered by the mismanagement of its army, a reluctance to expend blood and money in another American war, and the need to protect its European flank. Nevertheless, Britain had superior resources in population, war materials, and industrial capacity, and it had a well-trained and experienced army and navy.

Americans were chronically short of money and the tools of war. George Washington commanded an inexperienced and poorly supplied army.

Loyalists

Perhaps a fifth of the colonists were Loyalists (Tories) who rejected independence for the colonies. Colonists who were most likely to be Loyalists were royal appointees, Anglican clergymen, merchants with close connections in Britain, or minority groups who counted on London for protection. Loyalists were not well organized and were often mistreated by Patriots through physical abuse, forced exile, or by having their property confiscated.

Early Defeats

British general William Howe failed to pursue his advantage promptly, or he may have ended the war with the Battle of Long Island in 1776. Washington learned rapidly, however, and he was seldom thereafter caught so vulnerable. Howe went into winter quarters in New York, but the Americans boosted their morale with victories at Trenton and Princeton.

Saratoga and the French Alliance

The British plan to isolate New England from the other colonies in 1777 ended in a fiasco. Instead of following prearranged plans, Howe left New York to captured Philadelphia, and General Burgoyne's army was forced to surrender at the key Battle of Saratoga. With the victory at Saratoga, France allied itself with the colonies. This changed the course and character of the war in the Americans' favor, but they did not yet have it won.

The War Moves South

In 1778, the British replaced Howe with General Clinton, moved their base back to New York, and changed strategy. They now focused on the southern colonies, hoping to utilize their sea power, Loyalist supporters, and southern slaves. They dealt the Americans their worst defeat of the war at Charleston. Nathanael Greene then conducted a guerrilla campaign against British general Cornwallis' army as it moved north toward Virginia.

Victory at Yorktown

Cornwallis encamped at Yorktown, Virginia, where he hoped to be resupplied by sea. But the French navy took control of Chesapeake Bay, and Washington's Continental Army, the Virginia militia, and French troops trapped Cornwallis' army. Cornwallis surrendered in October 1781.

The Peace of Paris

The British government gave up trying to suppress the rebellion after Yorktown and opened peace negotiations. American peace commissioners maneuvered the British into a generous peace. In the 1783 Treaty of Paris the British acknowledged American independence and transferred control of trans-Appalachia to the new nation. Further, the United States won fishing rights off Canada, and the British agreed to evacuate United States territory. The United States promised to recommend the restitution of Loyalist properties and not to impede the British collection of prewar debts.

Forming a National Government

In 1777, the Continental Congress submitted a national constitution—the Articles of Confederation—for ratification by the states. But the Articles were not ratified until disputes over state representation and western land claims were resolved in 1781. Under the Articles, each state retained its essential sovereignty and was equally represented in the national congress. The central government had no power to tax nor to enforce its authority.

Financing the War

The Continental Congress and the states cooperated in conducting the Revolutionary War. Congress supported the Continental Army and each state raised a militia. States spent money in support of the war and met Congress' request for military supplies. Congress borrowed money by selling war bonds and accepting foreign loans. It also issued millions in depreciating paper currency. Superintendent of finance Robert Morris inspired confidence in the new government's financial stability.

State Republican Governments

States began writing their constitutions even before the Declaration of Independence. In general, the new state governments were responsive to public opinion, had a powerful elected legislature, and limited the power of governors and judges. Americans saw their legislators as actual representatives carrying out the wishes of the voters in their home districts. Each state constitution had a bill of rights to protect individual civil liberties. These state constitutions, written frames of government based on the compact principle of government, represented one of the most important innovations of the Revolutionary era: a peaceful method for altering the political system.

Social Reform

Many states introduced important new social and political reforms. Steps were taken to reapportion representatives, reform inheritance laws, and separate church and state. Many states also moved against slavery. Enlightenment thought, Revolutionary rhetoric, and blacks' service in the Patriot army and navy posed questions about the morality of slavery. During the Revolution, all the states abolished the slave trade. Beginning in 1780, northern states gradually abolished slavery, and most southern states removed restrictions on voluntary emancipation. Still, slavery died only in the North where it was economically unimportant.

Overall, the Revolution produced little of the economic and political upheaval usually associated with revolution. People paid lip service to equality and less willingly deferred to elite leadership, but property confiscated from Loyalists was not redistributed to the poor, and high property ownership requirements for office holding remained the rule. Another major consequence of the Revolution was that the states adopted the convention system of drafting and rewriting constitutions.

Effects of the Revolution on Women

Revolutionary rhetoric and the Declaration of Independence, with their stress on liberty and equality, strengthened the legal rights of women. It became easier for women to obtain divorces. Male attitudes were not changed, but the war effort increased the influence of women. During the war they demonstrated their competence by managing farms and shops. The education of women was vitalized by recognition of their role in training the young to be well-educated citizens of the new republic.

Growth of a National Spirit

The common goal of independence united the colonies, and American nationalism developed during the conflict with Great Britain. American nationalism sprang from the experience of shared sacrifices, the wartime mobility of leaders, and the need to find common solutions to wartime problems. Disruption of the economy encouraged manufacturing and interstate trade that in turn encouraged pride in America's greater self-sufficiency.

The Great Land Ordinances

When ceded to the national government, western lands also became a source of unity. The Land Ordinance of 1785 stipulated that the national government survey and sell the public lands. The Northwest Ordinance of 1787 established governments for the west, set guidelines for transforming territories into republican states, and banned slavery from the Northwest Territory. While they were territories, western governments had appointed governors and judges, elected legislatures, and nonvoting delegates to Congress. Under these provisions, territories were nurtured toward guaranteed statehood.

National Heroes

The Revolution further fostered nationalism by providing national heroes. Above all others was George Washington who was revered for his personal sacrifice while leading his forces in adversity. Washington was admired as a man of deeds, a bold Patriot, and a respected leader of unquestionable integrity.

A National Culture

Post-Revolutionary nationalism strengthened the desire for a distinctly American culture. American churches broke their ties to Europe; Noah Webster promoted nationalizing influences in language and education; and painters and writers chose patriotic themes. Though still intensely loyal to their own states, Americans were becoming increasingly aware of their common interests and increasingly proud of their common heritage.

People, Places, and Things

Define the following:

right of revolution _____

_____

actual representation _____

_____

convention _____

_____

nationalism _____

_____

Describe the following:

    Battle of Bunker Hill _____

_____

    Declaration of Causes and Necessity for Taking up Arms _____

_____

    Common Sense _____

_____

    Declaration of Independence _____

_____

    Battle of Long Island _____

_____

    Battle of Saratoga _____

_____

    Battle of Yorktown _____

_____

    Peace of Paris, 1783 _____

_____

    Articles of Confederation _____

_____

Land Ordinance of 1785 _____

_____

Northwest Ordinance of 1787 _____

_____

Identify the following:

Second Continental Congress _____

_____

George Washington _____

_____

William Howe _____

_____

Hessians _____

_____

Thomas Paine _____

_____

Thomas Jefferson _____

_____

George III _____

_____

Loyalists/Tories _____

_____

John Burgoyne _____

_____

Horatio Gates _____

_____

Nathanael Greene _____

_____

Charles Cornwallis _____

_____

Benedict Arnold _____

_____

Noah Webster _____

_____

Locate the following places: Write in both the place name and its map location number.

1. Where the first skirmishes of the Revolutionary War occurred.

   _____ _____

2. Site of the first pitched battle of the Revolutionary War.

   _____ _____

3. Where Washington's army won two strategically insignificant, but psychologically important victories over British forces in 1776.

   _____ _____

4. Where Washington's army suffered a difficult winter encampment in 1777.

   _____ _____

5. Where Americans suffered their worst defeat of the Revolutionary War.

   _____ _____

6. Where the surrender of a British army helped forge a formal alliance between the colonies and France.

   _____   _____

7. Where the surrender of a British army effectively ended the British effort to try to suppress the rebellion in the colonies.

   _____   _____

8. The area which, in addition to the independence of the original 13 states, America acquired from Britain in the Peace of Paris of 1783.

   _____   _____

9. The area banned to slavery by the Northwest Ordinance of 1787.

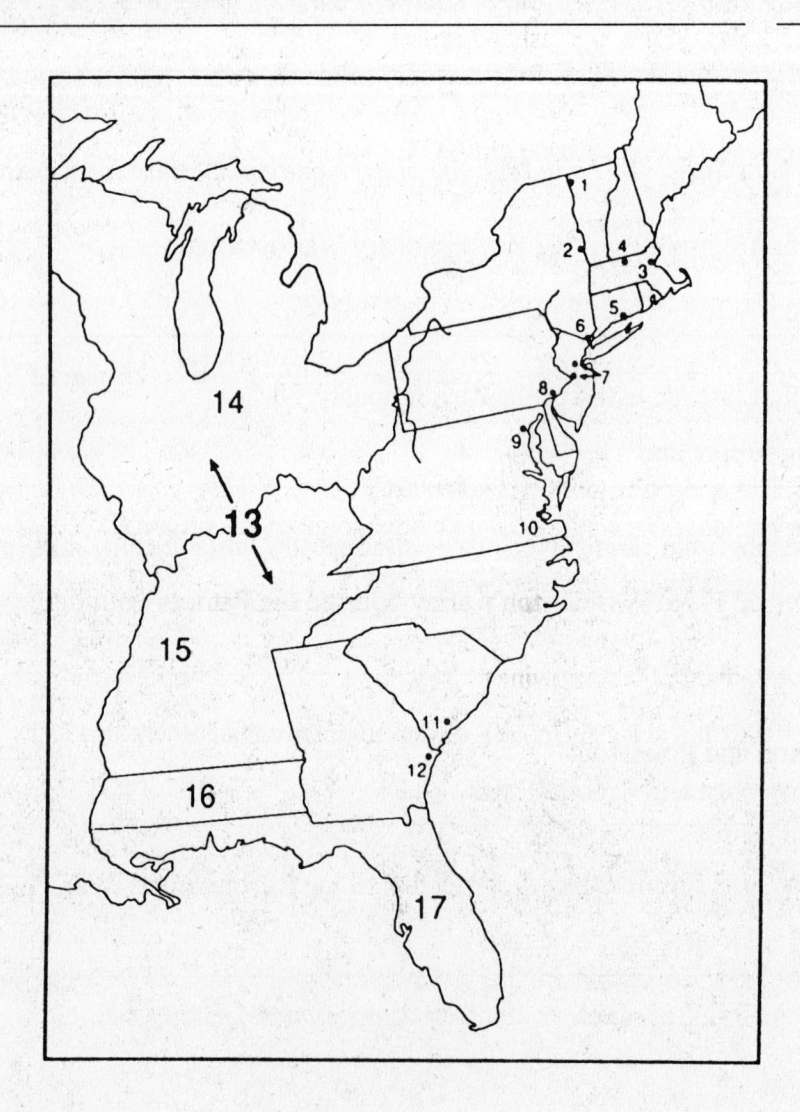

   _____   _____

Self-Test

Multiple-Choice Questions

1. What is the correct time order of (A) Battle of Bunker Hill, (B) George III proclaims the colonies in open rebellion, (C) Congress adopts the "Declaration of the Causes and Necessity of Taking Up Arms"?
   A. C, B, A
   B. B, A, C
   C. A, B, C
   D. A, C, B

2. The British view following the Boston Tea Party that other colonies would not rally to the aid of New Englanders was based on
   A. the behavior of colonial militia units during the French and Indian War.
   B. information provided by colonial agents who represented the colonies in Parliament.
   C. the hesitancy of other colonies, southern colonies in particular, to resist the Sugar and Stamp acts and the Townshend duties.
   D. intelligence reports from British spies in the colonies.

3. The Declaration of Independence did NOT
   A. call upon the states to draft constitutions
   B. justify the right of revolution
   C. describe a theory of republican government
   D. blame George III for the colonies' discontent

4. As the Revolutionary War began, Britain faced all the following problems EXCEPT
   A. a poorly disciplined army
   B. a long supply line
   C. inefficient and poor military leadership
   D. European enemies anxious to take advantage of the situation

5. In the winter of 1776, Washington's army boosted the Patriots' morale by winning victories at
   A. Philadelphia and Brandywine
   B. New York and Long Island
   C. Trenton and Princeton
   D. Ticonderoga and Crown Point

6. The British military strategy for 1777 was to
   A. occupy Boston
   B. invade the southern colonies
   C. isolate New England from the other colonies
   D. hold colonial cities and let the Americans have the countryside

7. The key significance of the Battle of Saratoga was that it
   A. forced Britain to sue for peace
   B. began a successful colonial invasion of Canada
   C. encouraged the French to ally with the colonies
   D. proved the Continental Army was superior to colonial militia

8. The worst American defeat of the Revolutionary War was at
   A. Bunker Hill
   B. Trenton
   C. Saratoga
   D. Charleston

9. The major fighting of the Revolutionary War began in _____, then moved to _____, and ended in _____.
   A. New England; the South; the Middle Colonies
   B. the South; New England; the Middle Colonies
   C. New England; the Middle Colonies; the South
   D. the Middle Colonies; New England; the South

10. In the 1783 Peace of Paris, the new boundaries of the United States did NOT included the
    A. Gulf of Mexico
    B. Great Lakes
    C. Mississippi River
    D. St. Lawrence River

11. In the 1783 Peace of Paris, Americans did NOT agree to
    A. recommend the return of Loyalists' property
    B. allow the British to collect prewar debts
    C. end the alliance with France
    D. accept British terms on Canadian fishing rights

12. Ratification of the Articles of Confederation was delayed by a dispute over
    A. the financial obligation of each state to the national government
    B. the cession of state-claimed western lands to the national government
    C. the expansion of slavery into western lands
    D. using actual or virtual representation in the national government

13. Congress did NOT use _____ to finance the Revolutionary War.
    A. bond sales
    B. foreign loans
    C. currency issues
    D. heavy taxes

14. The most powerful institution in the new state governments was the
    A. governor
    B. courts

C. legislature
D. bureaucracy

15. During or just after the Revolutionary War, all of the following were true EXCEPT
    A. northern states abolished slavery
    B. blacks served in the Patriot army and navy
    C. southern states outlawed voluntary emancipation
    D. slavery was banned from the Northwest Territory

16. A political innovation of the new states as they established their independence was
    A. constitutional conventions
    B. political parties
    C. representative assemblies
    D. bicameral legislatures

17. An important consequence of the American Revolution was that
    A. each colony separated church and state
    B. it produced major social and economic upheaval
    C. governments became more responsive to public opinion
    D. confiscated properties were redistributed to the poor

18. The American Revolution did NOT significantly improve
    A. women's ability to obtain divorce
    B. women's legal rights
    C. men's attitude toward female equality
    D. the appreciation of women's role in the education of the young

19. The Northwest Ordinance of 1787 did NOT provide for
    A. the survey and sale of public lands
    B. a territorial form of government
    C. a procedure for transforming territories into states
    D. the banning of slavery from the Northwest Territory.

20. All of the following contributed to the development of American nationalism EXCEPT
    A. George Washington
    B. George Clinton
    C. Benjamin Franklin
    D. Noah Webster

Essay Questions

1. Compare and contrast the relative strengths and weaknesses of the British and Americans as they went to war in 1775.
2. Explain why, in mid-1776, Americans were prepared to declare their independence from Britain.

3. Explain how the Americans were able to win their independence in the Revolutionary War.
4. Describe the key features of the Articles of Confederation national government, the several state governments, and the land ordinances of the 1780s. Suggest how they each reflect the democratic republicanism of the Revolutionary generation.
5. List the significant consequences of the American Revolution for blacks and women, and for the national spirit.

Critical Thinking Exercise

Facts, Inferences, and Judgments

Being able to distinguish between a statement of fact, an inference, or a judgment is an important skill to critical thinking. It involves knowing what can be proven directly, what is a legitimate implication derived from the facts, and what is fair to conclude from the historical record.

Historians typically interweave facts, inferences they derive from the facts, and their own judgments into a seamless historical narrative. Active and analytical readers—critical thinkers—must be able to distinguish between these three types of communication:

- A *fact* reports information that can be directly observed, or can be verified or checked for accuracy.
    Example: The statement, "Until the adult male population of the entire area reached 5,000, it was to be ruled by a governor and three judges . . ." can be checked for factual accuracy by consulting the Northwest Ordinance.

- An *inference* is a logical conclusion based on factual information, yet goes beyond factual information to make a more general statement about something.
    Example: The statement, "The western lands . . . became a force for unity once they had been ceded to the national government" implies that by their act of giving up their individual claims to western territories, each state placed the union of all the states above their individual interests; thus, the western lands became a force for unity.

- A *judgment* expresses an evaluation based on certain criteria which may or may not be expressed but assesses the rightness or wrongness of an act, whether it was good or bad.
    Example: The statement, "Seldom has a legislative body acted more wisely," expresses the author's judgment that the enactment of the Northwest Ordinance was a good thing; that it was the right thing to do to advance the interests of the nation.

Generally, facts are constants in historical study. But a compendium of facts is inevitably incomplete and dull reading. Historians narrow the gaps in their knowledge about the past, increase our understanding, and enliven historical narrative by drawing logical inferences from facts they have assembled and classified. Often, they then use their expertise to arrive at a considered judgment about the wisdom or significance of past decisions and events.

Distinguishing statements of fact, inference, and judgment may at first seem difficult to do. That is because they are often closely woven together. It takes a special and conscious effort to distinguish between these three types of communication. But the effort will be rewarded because it will make reading history (or any subject) more interesting to you. And it will help develop your critical thinking abilities by enabling you to distinguish information from opinions.

Practice this skill on the following excerpt from the textbook. For each of the numbered statements in the excerpt circle F for fact, I for inference, or J for judgment on the answer grid that follows the excerpt.

---

(1) Seeing no future in the Carolinas and unwilling to vegetate at Wilmington, (2) Cornwallis marched north into Virginia, where he joined forces with troops under Benedict Arnold. . . .

(3) General Clinton ordered Cornwallis to establish a base at Yorktown, where he could be supplied by sea. . . .

(4) It was a terrible mistake. (5) The British navy in American waters far outnumbered American and French vessels, but . . . (6) the French had a fleet in the West Indies under Admiral François de Grasse and another squadron at Newport, Rhode Island, where a French army was stationed. (7) In the summer of 1781, Washington, de Grasse, and the Comte de Rochambeau, commander of French land forces, designed and carried out with an efficiency unparalleled in eighteenth-century warfare a complex plan to bottle up Cornwallis.

(8) The British navy in the West Indies and at New York might have forestalled this scheme had it moved promptly and in force. (9) But Admiral Sir George Rodney sent only part of his Indies fleet. (10) As a result, (11) De Grasse, after a battle with a British fleet . . . won control of the Chesapeake and cut Cornwallis off from the sea.

(12) The next move was up to Washington, and this was his finest hour as a commander. (13) He desperately wanted to attack the British base at New York, but at the urging of Rochambeau he agreed instead to strike at Yorktown. . . . (14) He soon had nearly 17,000 French and American veterans in position.

(15) Cornwallis was helpless. (16) He held out until October 17 and then asked for terms [of surrender]. . . .

1. F I J	5. F I J	9. F I J	13. F I J
2. F I J	6. F I J	10. F I J	14. F I J
3. F I J	7. F I J	11. F I J	15. F I J
4. F I J	8. F I J	12. F I J	16. F I J

4: The American Revolution

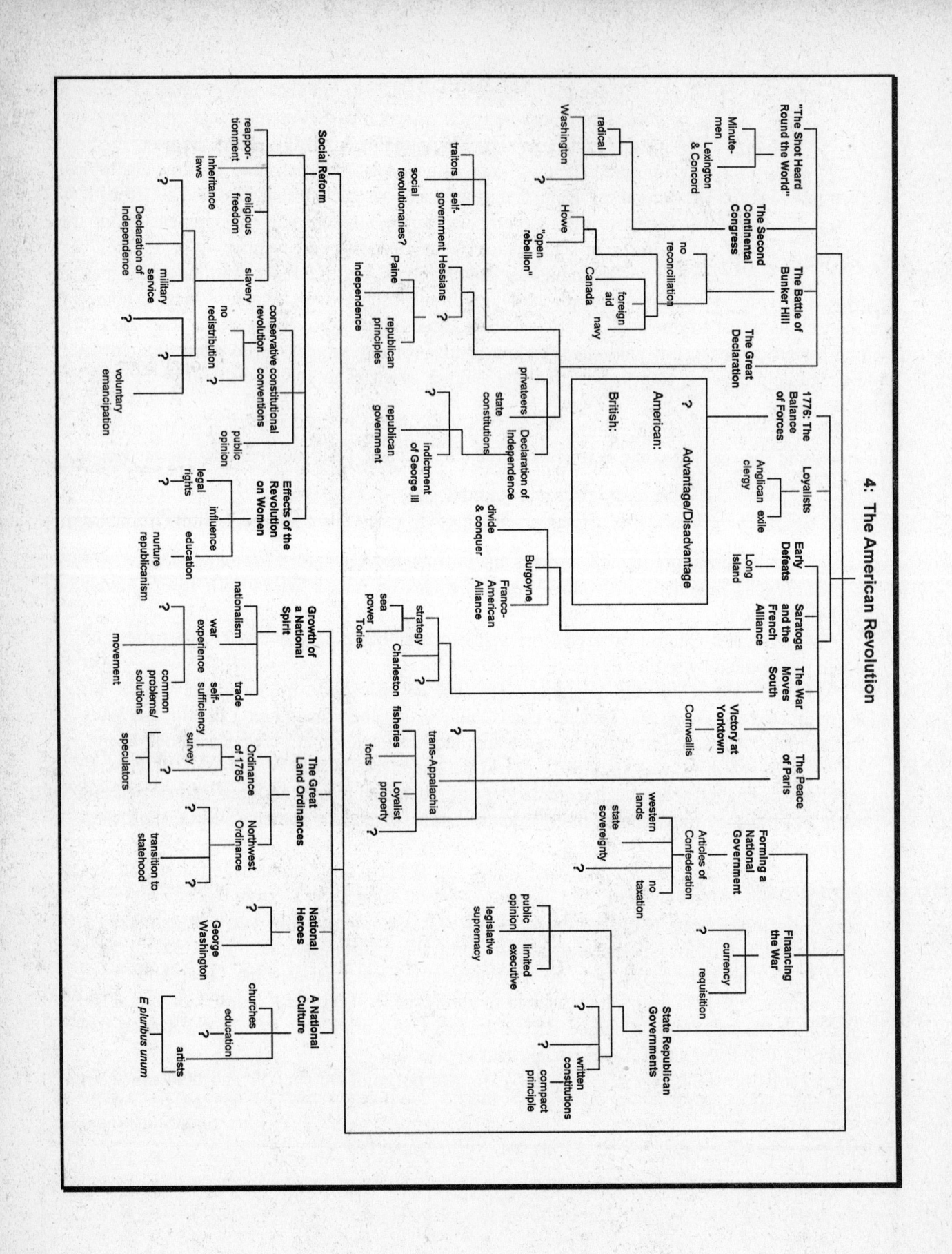

- "The Shot Heard Round the World"
  - Lexington & Concord
  - Minute-men
- The Second Continental Congress
  - Washington
  - radical ?
  - Howe
  - "open rebellion"
  - no reconciliation
    - foreign aid
    - Canada
    - navy
- The Battle of Bunker Hill
- The Great Declaration
  - traitors
  - self-government Hessians
  - social revolutionaries ?
  - Paine
  - independence
  - republican principles
  - republican government
  - Declaration of Independence
    - privateers
    - state constitutions ?
    - indictment of George III
- 1776: The Balance of Forces
  - Advantage/Disadvantage
    - American: ?
    - British:
  - Loyalists
    - Anglican clergy
    - exile
  - Early Defeats
    - Long Island
  - Saratoga and the French Alliance
    - Burgoyne
    - divide & conquer
    - Franco-American Alliance
- The War Moves South
  - strategy
    - sea power
    - Tories
  - Charleston
- Victory at Yorktown
  - Cornwallis
- The Peace of Paris
  - trans-Appalachia
    - fisheries
    - forts
    - Loyalist property ?
- Forming a National Government
  - Articles of Confederation
    - western lands
    - state sovereignty
    - no taxation
- Financing the War
  - requisition
  - currency ?
- State Republican Governments
  - public opinion
  - limited executive
  - legislative supremacy
  - written constitutions
  - compact principle
  - ?
- The Great Land Ordinances
  - Ordinance of 1785
    - survey
    - ?
  - Northwest Ordinance
    - transition to statehood
    - ?
- Growth of a National Spirit
  - nationalism
    - war experience
    - trade
    - self-sufficiency
  - ?
  - common problems/ solutions
  - speculators movement
- National Heroes
  - George Washington
  - ?
- A National Culture
  - churches
  - education
  - artists
  - E pluribus unum
- Effects of the Revolution on Women
  - legal rights ?
  - influence education
  - nurture republicanism
- Social Reform
  - religious freedom
    - Declaration of Independence
  - slavery
    - no redistribution
    - conservative revolution
    - constitutional conventions
    - public opinion
    - military service ?
    - voluntary emancipation ?
  - reapportionment
  - inheritance laws

Chapter 5

The Federalist Era: Nationalism Triumphant

Learning Objectives

After reading Chapter 5 you should be able to:

1. Explain how the Articles of Confederation Congress failed as a national government for the new United States.
2. State the goals and describe the work of the Philadelphia Convention.
3. List the terms of Hamilton's financial program and state his intentions for it.
4. Explain the origins of the party system in American politics, and compare and contrast the views of the Federalists and Republicans.
5. Trace the conduct of American diplomacy in the 1790s and describe how it influenced domestic politics.

Overview

Border Problems

Despite the Treaty of Paris, the British continued to occupy a string of forts in the Northwest, intrigue with the Indians, and trade in furs. In the Southwest, the Spanish first closed the Mississippi River to American commerce, then imposed a tariff on American goods. America was too weak in the 1780s to challenge either European power.

Foreign Trade

America's release from British mercantilism was a mixed blessing. Congress successfully negotiated commercial treaties with Continental powers and the Far East. But southern rice, tobacco, naval stores, and indigo producers were damaged by British postwar policies. For the same reason, northern merchants and fishermen lost the West Indies market, and New England shipbuilding slumped.

America continued to have an unfavorable balance of trade as British merchants dumped low-priced manufactured goods on the U.S. market. This aggravated the economy at a time of postwar depression. Congress's inability to find money to pay its debts undermined public confidence, but efforts to empower Congress to impose tariffs failed.

The Specter of Inflation

The depression and unfavorable balance of trade compelled many states to print paper money and adopt debtor-friendly stay laws. The result was rampant inflation and a further weakening of public confidence. Rhode Island's effort to compel creditors to accept depreciated currency in payment for debts was ruled unconstitutional.

Daniel Shays's "Little Rebellion"

In Massachusetts, bad times, high taxes, and deflation led to foreclosures on western farms and the crowding of debtors prisons. Daniel Shays and his followers rebelled against the state government's insensitivity to the farmers' plight. Congress was unable to respond to the state's plea for help. Throughout the colonies, many were alarmed that liberty had become license and they insisted that the national government must have more authority.

The Road to Philadelphia

The 1786 Annapolis Convention, which was called to discuss common problems of trade, was poorly attended. But Alexander Hamilton, a procentralizing "nationalist" from New York, proposed another convention to address constitutional reforms. Congress endorsed this Philadelphia Convention, and all states except Rhode Island sent delegates.

The Great Convention

The Founding Fathers were politically experienced, pragmatic, and optimistic about America's future. They agreed that the nation ought to have a federal system of republican government. They also agreed that people were selfish by nature, property must be protected, and no single state, section, or group should be allowed to predominate. Power, they thought, had to be balanced and divided. They met in secrecy, scrapped the Articles, and decided to draft an entirely new frame of government.

The Settlement

The Philadelphia delegates agreed to establish a national government of three branches with the power to tax, regulate trade, and use armed force. The quarrel over representation in the national government was resolved in the Great Compromise that created the House of Representatives where representation was proportional, and the Senate where each state had equal representation. Secondly, delegates divided over slavery. Northerners demanded that slaves be counted for taxation, and southerners insisted that slaves be counted for determining representation in the House. This dispute was resolved in the Three-Fifths Compromise—three-fifths of the slaves would be counted for both purposes.

The Constitution gave the president remarkable administrative, military, diplomatic, appointive, and veto powers. The president was to be elected by a cumbersome electoral college system that was designed to throw the election into the House of Representatives. While the Constitution greatly expanded the power of the national government, it limited the exercise of that power with an ingenious system of checks and balances.

Ratifying the Constitution

To get the direct endorsement of the people and to bypass the hostile state legislatures, the framers submitted the Constitution to special state ratifying conventions. Federalists, who supported ratification, were more interested in orderly and efficient government than in safeguarding freedom of choice. Antifederalists believed that free choice was more important than power. They feared the new Constitution would destroy state sovereignty and that centralized republican government could not function well in a large country—a thesis destroyed by James Madison. When Federalists agreed to add amendments to protect civil liberties and states' rights, most opposition to ratification disappeared. Supporters wrote the *Federalist Papers* to try to persuade the vital New York convention to ratify the new Constitution.

Washington As President

Washington was the nation's first, and—acutely aware that his every action set a precedent—one of its more cautious, presidents. He took the separation of powers seriously and believed that the veto could be used only when he considered congressional legislation to be unconstitutional. Although he respected the opinions of his highly competent advisors, Washington was a strong president who made his own decisions.

Congress Under Way

Congress created the executive departments, established the federal courts, and proposed the Bill of Rights to protect individual civil liberties and states' rights from the power of the national government.

Hamilton and Financial Reform

The new nation had a large debt, shaky credit, and an uncertain economic future. Alexander Hamilton, a self-made realist who distrusted the common people, dedicated himself to strengthening the national government by establishing its public credit. He called for funding the national debt at par and for federal assumption of the state debts. He proposed chartering a national bank to hold government funds and issue bank notes. In each case his proposals were deliberately intended to attract the wealthy to support of the national government.

Hamilton faced strong opposition to his bank proposal from Thomas Jefferson who questioned its constitutionality. But the funding, assumption, and bank proposals were adopted and all were very successful. However, Congress rejected his call for government economic planning and national economic self-sufficiency gained through protective tariffs and subsidies to manufacturers.

The Ohio Country: A Dark and Bloody Ground

As Americans migrated into the upper Ohio River Valley, they found trouble. Indians fiercely defended their territory, and settlers blamed the British for inciting them to violence. Westerners grew resentful of a federal government that seemed insensitive to their interests, and they detested the new national government's excise tax on whiskey. Hamilton, however, was determined to enforce the new tax law.

The New Revolution: France

When war broke out between Britain and France in 1793, the United States ignored its moral obligation under the 1778 alliance to aid France. Instead, Washington issued a proclamation of neutrality. "Citizen" Genet, a French representative, was warmly welcomed by the American public, but was coolly dismissed by Washington who objected to Genet's recruiting activities in America. Both the British and the French ignored America's neutral rights on the high seas, but the powerful British navy made British violations more numerous and more costly. In an attempt to avoid war, President Washington sent John Jay to negotiate a settlement with England.

Federalists and Republicans: The Rise of Political Parties

The strengthening of the national government created a need for political machinery that would focus discussion on national issues and nominate candidates for national offices. Jefferson's Republican party and Hamilton's Federalist party sprang to life in the dispute over the national bank, and the controversy over the French Revolution and the resulting war between Britain and France widened the partisan split. Republicans admired the French revolutionaries, while the Federalists idealized the British as defenders of order. Still, both Jefferson and Hamilton endorsed Washington's proclamation of neutrality.

1794: Crisis and Resolution

Federal agents found it impossible to collect the whiskey tax in western Pennsylvania. But the Whiskey Rebellion had disintegrated by the time federal troops arrived. Meanwhile, General Anthony Wayne's victory over the Indians in the Battle of Fallen Timbers opened Ohio to settlement.

Jay's Treaty

In the treaty John Jay negotiated with the British in 1794, England agreed to evacuate the northwest forts and compensate American merchants for ships seized in the West Indies. However, the British made no concessions to American neutral rights. Jay also assented to restrictions on American trade with the French West Indies, and to an arrangement that prevented the U.S. from placing discriminatory duties on British imports.

1795: All's Well That Ends Well

Objectionable as it was, Washington endorsed the Jay Treaty and its few but valuable benefits—reconciliation of Anglo-American relations and evacuation of the northwest forts. As an unexpected bonus, the treaty persuaded the Spanish to conclude the Treaty of San Lorenzo (Pinckney's Treaty) which gave Americans free navigation of the Mississippi River, the right of deposit at New Orleans, and a favorable settlement of the Florida boundary dispute.

Washington's Farewell

Although he usually sided with Hamilton, Washington feared party rivalry. In his Farewell Address, he deplored the baneful effects of partisanship. He also urged Americans to avoid both passionate attachments to foreign countries and permanent alliances.

The Election of 1796

Vice-President Adams narrowly defeated Jefferson in the 1796 presidential election. But, because of electoral chicanery by Hamilton which backfired, Jefferson was elected vice-president. Both Adams and Jefferson disliked Hamilton.

The XYZ Affair

Adams' mission to the French government to discuss its violations of American neutrality was a fiasco. French commissioners (X, Y, & Z) demanded a prenegotiation bribe that bruised America's sense of national honor. Congress ended the French alliance; Adams and Congress mobilized the armed forces; and the public demanded war.

The Alien and Sedition Acts

Conservative Federalists saw the war hysteria as an opportunity to smash the Republicans. The Federalist-controlled Congress passed several acts designed to intimidate recent immigrants from France and to limit their political activity. The Sedition Act was an attempt to silence Republican newspapers. Unlike the alien acts, the Sedition Act was vigorously enforced.

The Kentucky and Virginia Resolves

Jefferson believed that the Alien and Sedition Acts violated the Bill of Rights. In resolutions adopted by the Kentucky and Virginia legislatures, Jefferson and Madison argued from the compact theory of government that states could declare an act of Congress unconstitutional.

Adams made a second attempt at negotiations with the French and, much to the dismay of a warmongering Hamilton, the two nations negotiated the Convention of 1800. It ended the war scare and terminated the 1778 alliance, but nothing was said of French violations of American neutral rights.

People, Places, and Things

Define the following:

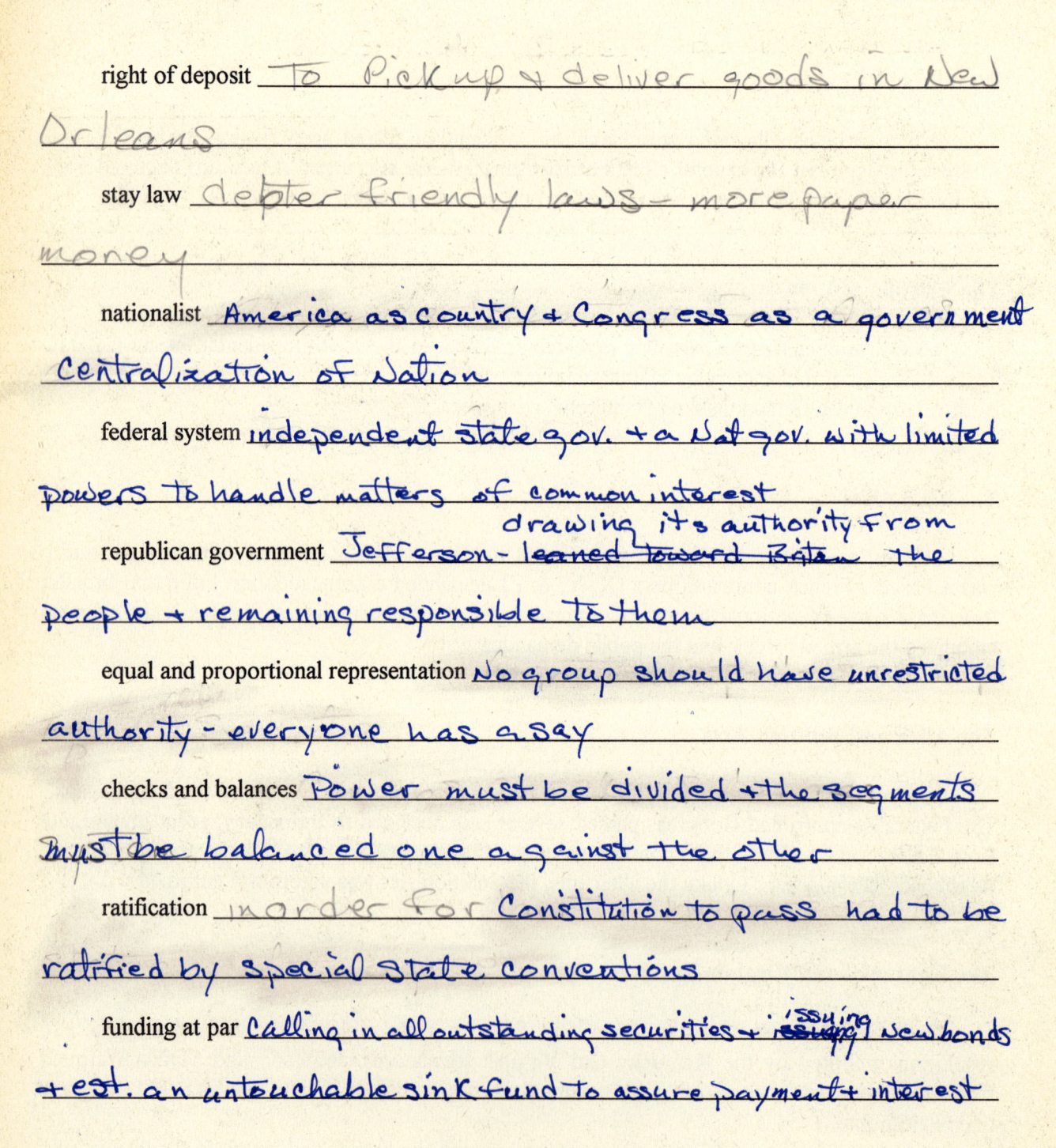

right of deposit _To pickup & deliver goods in New Orleans_

stay law _debter friendly laws - more paper money_

nationalist _America as country & Congress as a government Centralization of Nation_

federal system _independent state gov. + a Nat gov. with limited powers to handle matters of common interest_

republican government _Jefferson - drawing its authority from the people + remaining responsible to them_

equal and proportional representation _No group should have unrestricted authority - everyone has a say_

checks and balances _Power must be divided + the segments must be balanced one against the other_

ratification _in order for Constitution to pass had to be ratified by special state conventions_

funding at par _Calling in all outstanding securities + issuing new bonds + est. an untouchable sink fund to assure payment + interest_

72

implied powers _Federalist felt constitution should have implied powers._

elastic/necessary and proper clause _Jefferson - granting Const. right to pass all laws which shall be necessary + proper_

strict and loose construction _Strict - Anti feds_
loose - Federal

Rule of 1756 _British regulation stating - Neutrals couldn't trade in war time with ports closed to them in peace times_

Describe the following:

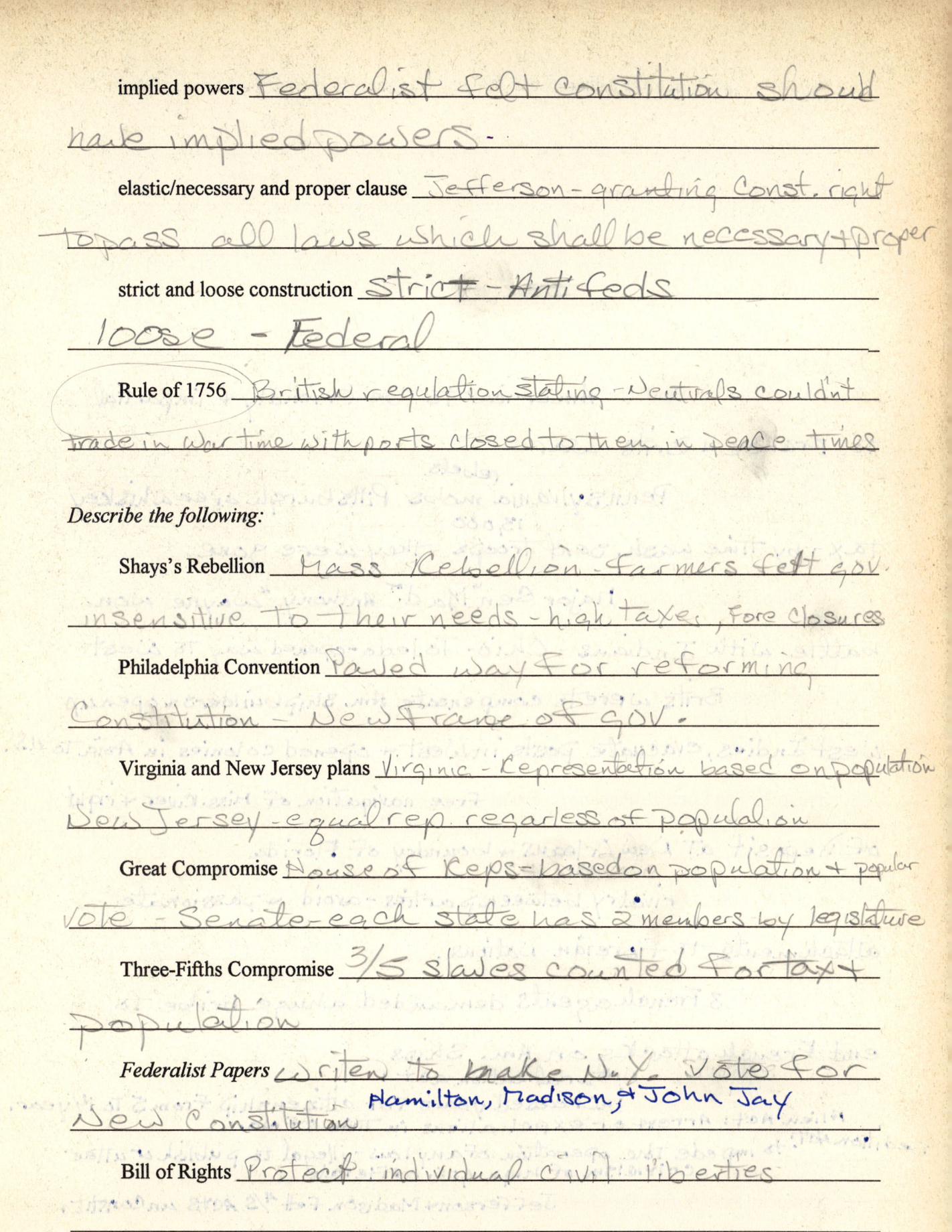

Shays's Rebellion _Mass Rebellion - Farmers felt gov. insensitive to their needs - high taxes, Fore closures_

Philadelphia Convention _Paved way for reforming Constitution - New frame of gov._

Virginia and New Jersey plans _Virginia - Representation based on population New Jersey - equal rep. regardless of population_

Great Compromise _House of Reps - based on population + popular vote - Senate - each state has 2 members by legislature_

Three-Fifths Compromise _3/5 slaves counted for tax + population_

Federalist Papers _Written to make N.Y. vote for New Constitution_ — Hamilton, Madison & John Jay

Bill of Rights _Protect individual civil liberties_

73

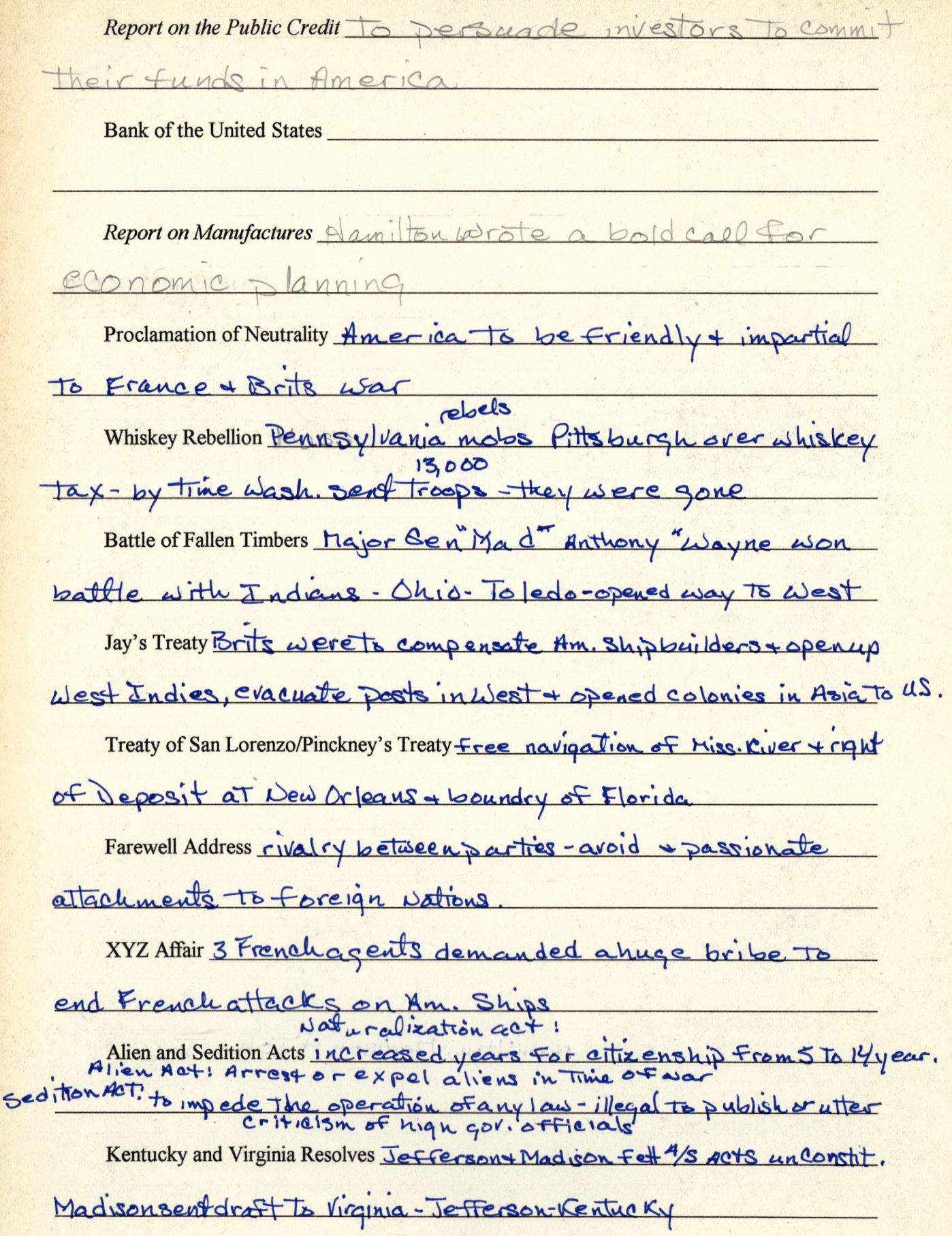

Report on the Public Credit _To persuade investors to commit their funds in America._

Bank of the United States _____

Report on Manufactures _Hamilton wrote a bold call for economic planning_

Proclamation of Neutrality _America to be friendly + impartial to France + Brits war_

Whiskey Rebellion _Pennsylvania rebels mobs Pittsburgh over whiskey tax - by time Wash. sent 13,000 troops - they were gone_

Battle of Fallen Timbers _Major Gen "Mad" Anthony Wayne won battle with Indians - Ohio - Toledo - opened way to West_

Jay's Treaty _Brits were to compensate Am. shipbuilders + open up West Indies, evacuate posts in West + opened colonies in Asia to US._

Treaty of San Lorenzo/Pinckney's Treaty _Free navigation of Miss. River + right of deposit at New Orleans + boundry of Florida_

Farewell Address _rivalry between parties - avoid + passionate attachments to foreign nations._

XYZ Affair _3 French agents demanded a huge bribe to end French attacks on Am. ships_

Alien and Sedition Acts _Naturalization act: increased years for citizenship from 5 to 14 year. Alien Act: Arrest or expel aliens in time of war. Sedition Act: to impede the operation of any law - illegal to publish or utter criticism of high gov. officials_

Kentucky and Virginia Resolves _Jefferson + Madison felt A/S Acts unconstit. Madison sent draft to Virginia - Jefferson - Kentucky_

74

Convention of 1800 _Ended war scare with France abrogating Franco-Am. treaties of 1778. Nothing said about damaged Am. ships by French._

Identify the following:

Daniel Shays _leader of Shays rebellion_

Alexander Hamilton _delegate from N.Y. lawyer_

Founding Fathers _Politically experienced, pragmatic & optimistic about America's future_

James Madison _Key figure at Great Convention & kept most complete notes & influenced writing of Const. crafted the ~~Adm~~ amendments - Bill of Rights_

John Adams _2nd President_

Thomas Jefferson _Third President - Republican_

Electoral College _Elected pres._

Federalists and Antifederalists _Feds for Const. Antifeds against_

Federalist party _high class - merchants, Planters - Britan_

Republican party _more for common people & French Rev._

75

"Citizen" Genet *a French representative*

John Jay *Washington sent him to England to seek treaty — Jay Treaty*

Thomas Pinckney *American envoy to Spain — Pinckney's treaty*

Self-Test

Multiple-Choice Questions:

1. The Articles of Confederation government did NOT
   A. establish a federal bureaucracy
   B. negotiate foreign trade agreements
   C. establish a federal land policy
   D. end the postwar economic depression

2. After the Revolutionary War, New England merchants were hard hit by being excluded from trade with the
   A. southern states
   B. French
   C. British West Indies
   D. Spanish southwest

3. State stay laws were designed to help
   A. immigrants
   B. debtors
   C. blacks
   D. women

4. To many who opposed it, Shays's Rebellion was a reminder that
   A. the possibility of a military coup was always present
   B. slaves could not be trusted
   C. the national government was too weak
   D. the states must be allowed to handle their own problems

5. Most of those who attended the Philadelphia Convention were
   A. nationalists
   B. states' rightists

C. Antifederalists
D. Loyalists

6. The major controversy at the Philadelphia Convention involved the question of
   A. representation in the national government
   B. slavery in the new republic
   C. domestic rebellion in the states
   D. paper currency issued by the states

7. Delegates to the Philadelphia Convention did NOT agree that
   A. the United States should have a federal system of government
   B. the national government should be republican in form
   C. government should protect property
   D. slavery should be abolished

8. The original Philadelphia Constitution did NOT specifically provide that
   A. Congress could regulate interstate trade
   B. the president could veto acts of Congress
   C. states could issue paper currency
   D. states could tax their citizens

9. Opponents of the Philadelphia Constitution objected to the absence of a
   A. provision for popular ratification
   B. specific list of powers of the national government
   C. guarantee of individual civil liberties
   D. provision for proportional representation

10. In New York, ratification of the Constitution was obtained after its supporters promised
    A. commercial favoritism for the port of New York
    B. larger representation for the state in Congress
    C. the first vice-presidency for the state's governor
    D. a bill of rights amended to the Constitution

11. The *Federalist Papers* were written
    A. by Hamilton as a platform for his new Federalist party.
    B. by Madison and Jefferson as a critique of Federalist policies.
    C. by Madison, Jay, and Hamilton in support of the ratification of the Constitution.
    D. by the Virginia delegates to the Philadelphia Convention in support of a federal system of government.

12. The initial source of public revenue enacted by the first session of Congress was a tax on
    A. whiskey
    B. imports
    C. personal incomes
    D. real estate

13. Hamilton's plan for funding the national debt assumed that people were primarily motivated by
    A. a concern for the welfare of the less fortunate
    B. a keen sense of justice and fair play
    C. religious conviction
    D. economic self-interest

14. Madison and Jefferson agreed to Hamilton's assumption program in return for a promise involving the
    A. sale of western lands
    B. location of the national capitol
    C. levying of excise taxes
    D. adoption of the Bill of Rights

15. For Hamilton to get a national bank, he had to argue in favor of
    A. a "strict" view of the Constitution
    B. the concept of "balanced government"
    C. the "due process" clause of the Constitution
    D. the doctrine of "implied powers"

16. Which one of the following is LEAST related to the other three?
    A. General Anthony Wayne
    B. Rule of 1756
    C. Fallen Timbers
    D. Treaty of Greenville

17. In Jay's Treaty, Jay got the British to agree to all of the following EXCEPT
    A. evacuation of northwest forts
    B. recognition of America's neutral rights
    C. compensation for ships seized in the West Indies
    D. opening British colonial ports in Asia

18. Spain agreed to allow American's use of the Mississippi River and the right of deposit in New Orleans in the
    A. Treaty of San Ildefonso
    B. Jay-Gardoqui Treaty
    C. Treaty of San Lorenzo
    D. Jay Treaty

19. In his Farewell Address, Washington warned Americans against the dangers of foreign alliances and
    A. political parties
    B. a national bank
    C. "implied powers"
    D. trade agreements

20. In which pair of items are the two items LEAST related to each other?
   A. Rule of 1756—Farewell Address
   B. XYZ Affair—undeclared war with France
   C. Alien and Sedition Acts—Kentucky and Virginia Resolves
   D. Convention of 1800—Franco-American treaty

Essay Questions

1. State what of real significance the Articles of Confederation Congress achieved between 1781 and 1787, and explain why it essentially failed as a national government.
2. List the major areas of agreement and disagreement among the delegates at the Philadelphia Convention. Explain how their key disagreements were resolved.
3. Explain why there was a need for Hamilton's financial program, what the program contained, what he intended for it to do, and why it provoked opposition.
4. Compare and contrast the principles and public policy positions of the Federalist and Republican parties in the 1790s.
5. Show how foreign policy issues in Washington's and Adams' administrations influenced partisan politics in the United States.

Critical Thinking Exercise

Compare and Contrast

In Chapter 2 you completed a compare-and-contrast matrix on the New England and southern colonies. As you saw, it was an effective way to organize useful information from throughout the chapter, and it helped you improve your understanding of both the New England colonies and the seventeenth-century South.

Chapter 5 devotes considerable space to the political principles and public policies of Alexander Hamilton and the Federalists, one of the two new political parties that emerged in the 1790s. The other party, the Jeffersonian Republicans, is introduced in this chapter, but its political principles and views on public policy are more fully developed in Chapter 6.

You can begin the following compare-and-contrast exercise with your reading of Chapter 5 and complete it when you have read Chapter 6. It requires you to read each of the two chapters carefully to glean information you can include in the matrix. For those places where there is no direct statement from the text about the position of Hamilton and the Federalists, or Jefferson and the Republicans, it is permissible for you to *infer* their position and include it in the matrix. Some blocks have been filled in as examples.

PRINCIPLES AND POSITIONS OF REPUBLICANS AND FEDERALISTS		
	FEDERALISTS	**REPUBLICANS**
VIEWS ON . . .		
human nature	*selfish*	*selfish, but improvable*
common people	*disparaged*	
blacks		
constitutional interpretation		*strict*
government power		
states' rights		
majority rule		
judicial review	*Supreme Court authority*	
military preparedness		
POSITIONS ON . . .		
funding the national debt		*retire the debt*
assumption of state debts		
National Bank		
Proclamation of Neutrality	*endorsed*	
French Revolution		*enthusiasm, excused excesses*
Whiskey Rebellion	*vigorously suppress*	
Jay's Treaty		
XYZ Affair		
Kentucky and Virginia Resolves		
Louisiana Purchase		*constitutionally troublesome, but good for the future*
Embargo Act		

5: The Federalist Era: Nationalism Triumphant

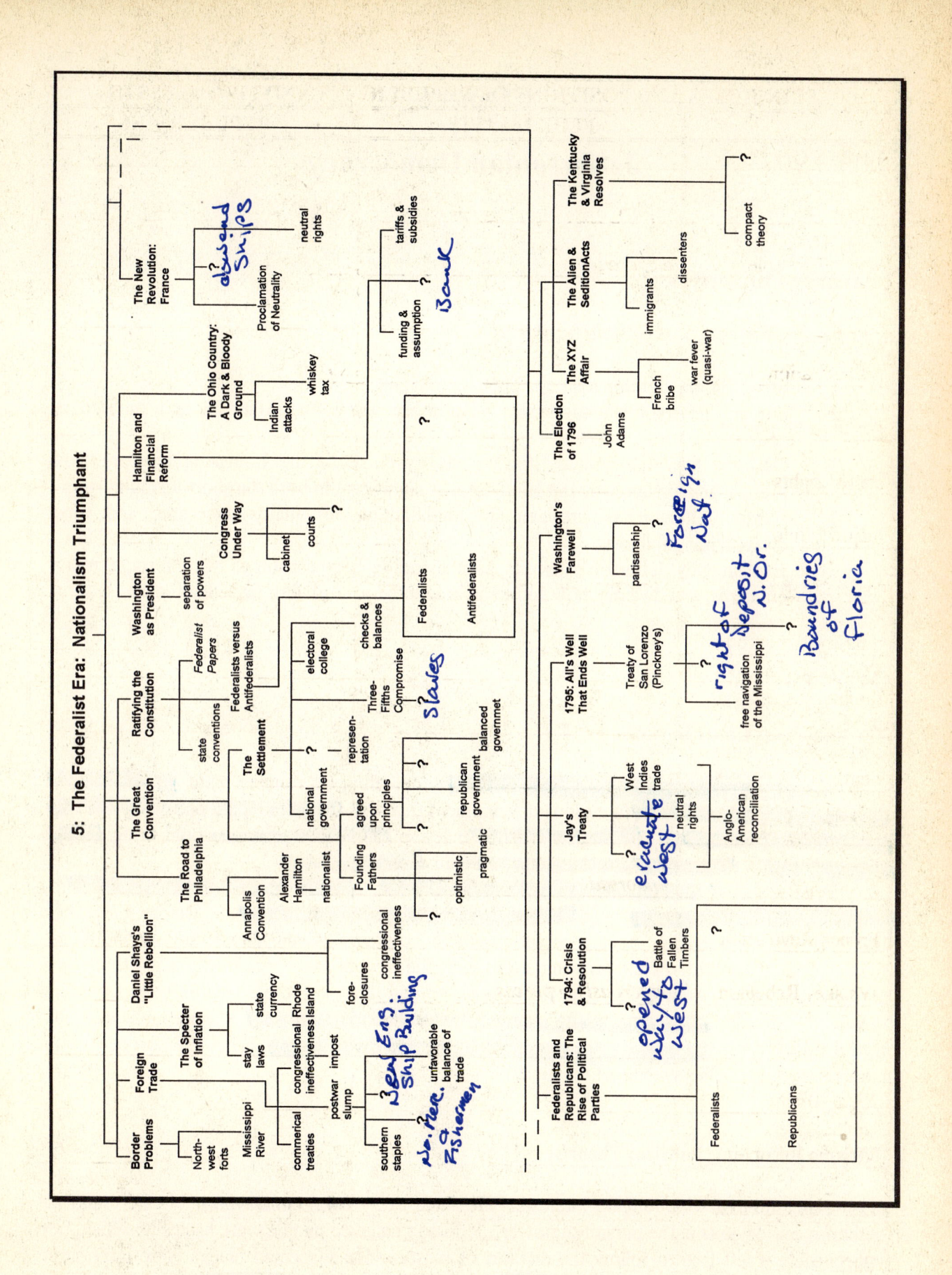

A hierarchical outline/tree diagram of the chapter with the following branches:

Border Problems
- Northwest forts
- Mississippi River
  - commercial treaties

Foreign Trade
- The Specter of Inflation
  - stay laws
  - state currency
  - congressional Rhode ineffectiveness Island
  - impost
- postwar slump
  - southern staples [no mer. fishermen]
  - [New Eng. Ship Building]
  - unfavorable balance of trade

Daniel Shays's "Little Rebellion"
- foreclosures
- congressional ineffectiveness

The Road to Philadelphia
- Annapolis Convention
- Alexander Hamilton — nationalist
- Founding Fathers
  - optimistic
  - pragmatic

The Great Convention
- The Settlement
  - national government
  - agreed upon principles
    - ? — republican government
    - ? — balanced government

Ratifying the Constitution
- state conventions
- Federalist Papers
- Federalists versus Antifederalists
  - electoral college
  - checks & balances
  - representation
    - Three-Fifths Compromise [slaves]
- Federalists
- Antifederalists — ?

Washington as President
- separation of powers

Congress Under Way
- cabinet
- courts — ?

Hamilton and Financial Reform
- The Ohio Country: A Dark & Bloody Ground
  - Indian attacks
  - whiskey tax
- funding & assumption [Bank] — ?
- tariffs & subsidies

The New Revolution: France
- Proclamation of Neutrality [seized ships] — ?
- neutral rights

Federalists and Republicans: The Rise of Political Parties
- 1794: Crisis & Resolution
  - Battle of Fallen Timbers [opened up to west] — ?
- Jay's Treaty
  - West Indies trade
  - neutral rights [evacuate west] — ?
  - Anglo-American reconciliation
- 1795: All's Well That Ends Well
  - Treaty of San Lorenzo (Pinckney's) — ?
  - free navigation of the Mississippi [right of deposit N. Or.] [Boundries of Florida]
- Washington's Farewell
  - partisanship [Foreign Nat] — ?

The Election of 1796
- John Adams

The XYZ Affair
- French bribe
- war fever (quasi-war)

The Alien & Sedition Acts
- immigrants
- dissenters

The Kentucky & Virginia Resolves
- compact theory — ?

- Federalists
- Republicans

81

Chapter 6

Jeffersonian Democracy

Learning Objectives

After reading Chapter 6 you should be able to:

1. State Thomas Jefferson's key political principles.
2. Explain Jefferson's antagonistic relationship with John Marshall and the federal courts.
3. Describe how the United States came to purchase the Louisiana territory from France, and explain why the purchase was significant in both the short and long runs.
4. Assess Jefferson as president by highlighting his major successes and most disappointing failures.
5. Explain why Jefferson's second administration was consumed with foreign policy concerns, and describe how Jefferson attempted to deal with these matters.

Overview

The Federalist Contribution

Thomas Jefferson won the election of 1800 by defeating his running mate, Aaron Burr, in the House of Representatives (a curious development that was prevented from occurring again by the Twelfth Amendment). Federalists worried that the Republican victory would bring radical social reforms, a weakened national government, and economic decline.

Federalists had strengthened the national government, established a sound financial system, tried to diversify the economy, and sought an accommodation with Britain. Before 1798 they had acted with moderation, posing no serious threat to states' rights, democracy, or individual freedom. But their fear of the growing strength of the Republican opposition pushed them into antilibertarian excesses in 1798. The Republicans routed them in the election of 1800 as voters delivered a mandate for individual freedom and limited national power. The Republicans took power peacefully, demonstrating the usefulness of the two-party system. They then proceeded to confirm the great achievements of the Federalist era.

Thomas Jefferson: Political Theorist

Jefferson had wide-ranging interests. He shied away from controversy, but he could be stubborn and devious in the pursuit of power. Jefferson believed people were basically selfish, but improveable if left free to follow the dictates of reason. He suspected blacks were inferior to whites, yet he was a champion of democracy, limited-government, and individual freedom.

Jefferson objected to Hamilton's effort to commercialize and centralize the country. He thought commerce would bring the growth of cities, complicate society, and require government regulation. He wanted America to remain a society of small farmers because he believed that city workers were easy prey for demagogues. He objected to Hamilton's pro-British orientation because he thought of England as immoral, decadent, and corrupt. He was delighted to see the French Revolution strike a blow against monarchy and tyranny, and persisted in excusing the excesses of that revolution.

Jefferson As President

Jefferson's presidency brought a change in style, but it was moderate and he was sensitive to minority rights. He opposed foreign alliances, but was in favor of limited government, paying off the national debt, and cooling partisan passions. His administration repealed the Federalist's excise taxes, including the infamous Whiskey Tax, and cut military spending in order to reduce the debt and balance the budget. The Alien and Sedition acts were allowed to lapse.

Jefferson played down the ceremonial aspects of the presidency. His egalitarianism was reflected in his pell-mell policy at White House functions. He was a superb politician, and a skillful communicator, but he was also a partisan Republican who demanded party discipline in Congress and used his patronage power to reward his friends.

Attacking the Judiciary

In part owing to their aggressive enforcement of the Alien and Sedition acts, Jefferson held a strong distrust of Federalist judges. Lame-duck Federalists compounded this sentiment when they shamelessly passed the Judiciary Act of 1801, expanding the number of federal judges. Adams appointed Federalist "midnight justices" to these new positions in the waning hours of his presidency. The new Republican Congress repealed the act and Jefferson refused to allow several commissions of appointment to be delivered. As a result, appointee William Marbury sued in the Supreme Court. In *Marbury* v. *Madison*, Chief Justice John Marshall ruled that Marbury should receive his appointment, but that the court could not issue a writ of mandamus to require Secretary of State Madison to do so because the Judiciary Act of 1789 in which Congress had empowered the Supreme Court to issue such writs was unconstitutional. The significance of the case lies in Marshall's establishing the power of the Supreme Court to determine the constitutionality of congressional acts.

Jefferson then pursued the removal of Federalist judges through impeachment. One, John Pickering, was impeached and removed, but a similar effort failed to remove justice Samuel Chase from the Supreme Court. Chase's actions had been outrageous in enforcing the Alien and Sedition Acts, but were not "high crimes and misdemeanors," the constitutional standard for removal by impeachment.

The Barbary Pirates

Presidents Washington and Adams had followed international convention by paying tribute (annual protection money) to Barbary pirates in the Mediterranean in order to protect American commerce there. Jefferson dispatched a naval squadron to the Mediterranean, but little was accomplished and the United States continued to make payments until 1815.

The Louisiana Purchase

The major achievement of Jefferson's first term was the purchase of Louisiana territory from France--a quite unexpected opportunity. Because access to the Mississippi River and New Orleans was vital to America's economic growth, Jefferson was alarmed when Spain transferred its Louisiana territory to Napoleonic France in 1800. Napoleon saw Louisiana as a breadbasket for valuable French West Indian sugar plantations.

Jefferson sent James Monroe to Paris with an offer to buy New Orleans and Florida. Meanwhile, French efforts to capture Saint Dominique in the West Indies failed, thereby reducing Napoleon's interest in Louisiana. Napoleon also needed money for a new campaign against the British in Europe.

Thus, Napoleon offered to sell Louisiana to the United States. The deal was struck for $15 million, but there was a catch: the Constitution made no specific allowance for the purchase of foreign territory or the extending of citizenship to its inhabitants by executive act. Jefferson reluctantly abandoned his strict constructionist view of the Constitution, embraced Hamilton's "implied powers," and urged Congress to ratify the Louisiana Purchase Treaty. The popular Louisiana Purchase doubled the size of United States, assured Jefferson's reelection, and dealt a heavy blow to the fortunes of the Federalist party.

Federalism Discredited

The addition of new western states from the Louisiana Territory would eventually reduce New England's influence in national affairs. This realization pushed the Essex Junto of die-hard Federalists to consider secession. They looked to Aaron Burr for help, but Burr lost the race for governor of New York--partly due to Hamilton's opposition. The secession movement failed, and Burr and Hamilton settled their differences when Burr killed Hamilton in a duel.

Lewis and Clark

Jefferson commissioned Lewis and Clark to lead an expedition to explore Louisiana. He was interested in the flora and fauna of the region and the possibility of developing the fur trade. He also had an imperialistic vision of an expanding America. The expedition began in 1804, moved up the Missouri River Valley, crossed the Continental Divide, and traveled on to the Pacific. By the time they returned in 1806, Lewis and Clark had located several passes through the Rockies, established friendly relations with several Indian tribes, and obtained a wealth of information about the country. Later expeditions by Thomas Freeman and Zebulon Pike were less productive.

Jeffersonian Democracy

Jefferson stood midway between the skeptical democracy of the colonial period and the rampant democracy of the Jacksonians. He was deeply committed to majority rule, but he hoped the majority would continue to be independent property-owning farmers. Jefferson's presidency demonstrated that a democratic egalitarian could establish and maintain a stable government. He calmed the fears of those who had thought him a radical. He accepted Federalist ideas on public finance, admitted that manufacturing and commerce were vital to national prosperity, and adopted the view that the federal government should protect and promote economic development. He even learned to live with Hamilton's bank. Thus, he achieved orderly government, security, and prosperity without resort to heavy taxation or placing limits on individual liberty.

Flies in the President's Ointment

Jefferson's second term was less successful than the first. On the one hand, the lack of Federalist opposition weakened party discipline and encouraged fragmentation of the Republicans. On the other hand, the renewal of war in Europe entangled Jefferson's second administration in frustrating controversies over neutral rights. Jefferson's flexibility did not set well with rigid defenders of Republican party principles. John Randolph, for example, was an unyielding defender of states' rights who constantly opposed any departure from principle.

The Burr Conspiracy

Jefferson found another troublesome Republican in Aaron Burr. The president was vindictive toward Burr following the election fiasco in 1800. For his part, Burr flirted with treason in an empire-building scheme in the West. He was arrested and tried for treason, but despite Jefferson's efforts on behalf of the prosecution, Burr was acquitted. The incident was a blow to Jefferson's prestige and left him even more embittered toward the federal judiciary.

Napoleon and the British

Renewal of the war between Britain and France in 1803 stimulated the American economy. The two belligerents needed American goods and American shipping. By 1807, however, the two sides were stalemated, Napoleon controlled Europe and Britain ruled the seas. Because neither nation could strike directly at the other, they resorted to commercial warfare with the intention of disrupting each other's economy. Napoleon's Berlin and Milan decrees and his Continental System made all ships doing business with Britain subject to seizure, and was designed to deny Britain access to the Continent's markets. British orders in council blockaded continental ports and charged customs duties on all goods going to the Continent.

Clever American merchants found loopholes in the restrictive Rule of 1756 and greatly expanded their West Indies trade. In the *Essex* case (1806), however, the British outlawed this re-export trade. American commerce and the nation's prosperity were severely threatened.

The Impressment Controversy

American pride was dealt a blow by the cruel indignities of the British practice of impressment. This age-old policy empowered British naval commanders to forcibly "draft" British subjects into service in time of emergency. The problem was that British subjects often worked on neutral vessels like those of the United States, and the British also refused to recognize the naturalization laws of the United States. Jefferson conceded the right of the British to impress legitimate British subjects from American merchant vessels, but he was irritated when naturalized Americans were seized, and he was outraged when even native-born Americans were taken by impressment.

Frustrated as he was by impressment, the *Essex* decision, and harassment of neutral shipping, Jefferson nevertheless hated the thought of war. He refused to build a navy powerful enough to protect American commerce.

The Embargo Act

America's frustration was compounded in 1807 when the British impressed three American sailors from the naval frigate *Chesapeake*. When the American captain protested, his vessel was fired upon. This was a clear violation of international law and the incident stirred war sentiment in the United States.

Jefferson's response was the Embargo Act. It prohibited all exports from the United States. Jefferson hoped to keep merchant ships off the seas, safe from seizure or impressment. He also hoped to increase pressure on the British and French by denying them access to American goods and the American market—a tactic that had worked during the crises that preceded the Revolution. Instead, the Embargo Act sharply reduced New England's commerce, the nation's prosperity, and Jefferson's popularity.

Americans found ways to violate the embargo. Goods were smuggled in and out of Canada. At first Jefferson tried to vigorously enforce the hated law, then finally gave up. In 1809, Congress repealed the Embargo Act and replaced it with the Nonintercourse Act that forbade trade only with Britain and France. Thus, Jefferson's political career ended on a sour note.

People, Places, and Things

Define the following:

writ of mandamus _a petition to the court (we order) to get a commission_

impressment _Any able-bodied man could be drafted into Brits Navy in emergency_

Describe the following:

Election of 1800 <u>Republicans won - Jefferson + Burr tied House of Reps broke tie</u>

Twelfth Amendment <u>Provided separate balloting in electoral college for President + Vice President</u>

Judiciary Act of 1801 <u>Created six new circuit courts, presided over 16 new Fed. judges, attorneys, marshals + clerks</u>

Marbury v. Madison <u>Chief Justice Marshall ruled Marbury should receive his commission, but couldn't issue w/ man. because of unconstitutional J/A of 1789</u>

Judiciary Act of 1789 <u>Empowered Supreme Court to issue writs of mandamus</u>

Louisiana Purchase <u>Louisiana terr. bought from France about $15 million</u>

Continental System <u>All ships doing business with Britain subject to seizure (French law)</u>

Chesapeake incident <u>3 Am. impressed from ship - ship was fired upon by Brits</u>

Embargo Act <u>Prohibited all exports from US - keep merchant ships off seas, safe from seizure (French) or impressment (Brits)</u>

Nonintercourse Act <u>forbade trade only with Great Britain + France</u>

Identify the following:

Aaron Burr Vice Pres. - tried for Treason - Killed Alex. Hamilton

Thomas Jefferson 3rd Pres of Am. - Republican

John Marshall Chief Justice of Supreme Court

John Pickering District Judge Jefferson had impeached

Barbary pirates No African Arab states - Morocco, Algiers, Tunis + Tripoli made a business of Piracy + ransom

Napoleon Bonaparte Greatest military Genius of that time ruler of France

Essex Junto _____

Lewis and Clark Explorers of Louisiana + beyound

Sacajawea Shoshone woman

Zebulon Pike Explorer - Mississippi Valley + Colorado region Pikes Peak

Self-Test

Multiple-Choice Questions

1. After the election of 1800, the Constitution was amended to change
   A. the suffrage requirements for voting in national elections
   B. the date of the presidential inauguration
   C. voting procedures in the Electoral College
   D. the laws regarding political parties

2. A major contribution of the Federalists was their
   A. leadership skill in organizing the national government
   B. toleration of their political opponents
   C. strict neutrality toward the European war
   D. equal concern for the interests of northern merchants and southern planters and farmers

3. Thomas Jefferson did NOT believe that
   A. humans were selfish by nature
   B. blacks were an inferior race
   C. manufacturing was the key to national prosperity
   D. the majority should rule

4. Thomas Jefferson did NOT favor
   A. states' rights
   B. individual freedom
   C. military preparedness
   D. limited government

5. President Jefferson's first administration was responsible for all of the following EXCEPT
   A. repealing the Whiskey Tax
   B. reducing the national debt
   C. revoking the National Bank's charter
   D. cutting appropriations for national defense

6. Jefferson's presidency was characterized by all of the following EXCEPT
   A. philosophical consistency
   B. practical compromises
   C. stability and prosperity
   D. casual informality

7. The legal precedent for the Supreme Court's authority to declare acts of Congress unconstitutional was established when
   A. the House impeached federal judge John Pickering
   B. the *Marbury* v. *Madison* ruling was handed down in 1803
   C. Congress repealed the Judiciary Act of 1801
   D. a federal court acquitted Aaron Burr of treason charges

8. The case of *Marbury* v. *Madison* concerned
   A. foreign alliances
   B. "high crimes and misdemeanors"
   C. "midnight justices"
   D. the National Bank

9. President Jefferson's first foreign policy decision was to
   A. purchase Louisiana from the French
   B. send a naval squadron to the Mediterranean
   C. remove the British from northwest forts
   D. purchase Florida from Spain

10. In a secret treaty with Spain in 1800,
    A. the United States purchased Louisiana
    B. the Mississippi River was opened to American trade
    C. the United States acquired Florida
    D. France acquired Louisiana

11. Which one of these Caribbean islands played a key role in the Louisiana Purchase?
    A. Barbados
    B. St. Croix
    C. St. Dominique
    D. Martinique

12. What is the correct time order of A) Louisiana Purchase, B) Election of 1800, C) *Marbury* v. *Madison*, D) Burr conspiracy?
    A. A, B, C, D
    B. B, C, A, D
    C. C, A, D, B
    D. A, D, C, B

13. The Lewis and Clark Expedition was commissioned to explore the
    A. Red River Valley
    B. Spanish Southwest
    C. Louisiana Territory
    D. Trans-Appalachian West

14. Jefferson's presidency was characterized by all the following EXCEPT
    A. national prosperity
    B. territorial growth
    C. international peace
    D. Republican popularity

15. John Randolph of Roanoke was notable as
    A. the leader of the Essex Junto
    B. a co-conspirator with Aaron Burr

C. a staunch defender of states' rights
D. the man who negotiated the Louisiana Purchase Treaty

16. After the Battle of Trafalgar in 1805, the war between Britain and France became a war of
    A. guerrilla tactics
    B. prolonged siege
    C. economic attrition
    D. trench warfare

17. In the *Essex* case in 1806, a British court found the United States in violation of the
    A. Embargo Act
    B. Rule of 1756
    C. Milan Decree
    D. Naturalization Act

18. The *Chesapeake* affair involved flagrant use of
    A. the Rule of 1756
    B. judicial review
    C. the Continental System
    D. impressment

19. Thomas Jefferson's political career "ended on a sour note" because of the failure of the
    A. Lewis and Clark Expedition
    B. Louisiana Purchase
    C. Republican effort to purge the federal courts of Federalists
    D. Embargo Act

20. In the following pairs the two items are directly related to each other in each case EXCEPT
    A. Continental System—impressment
    B. *Marbury* v. *Madison*—Judiciary Act of 1789
    C. *Chesapeake* affair—Embargo Act
    D. Election of 1800—Twelfth Amendment

Essay Questions

1. List Thomas Jefferson's political principles and show how they relate to his position on such public policy matters as national finance, economic development, territorial expansion, and foreign policy.
2. State the significance of the *Marbury* v. *Madison* decision and describe how it was arrived at.
3. Explain why the United States purchased Louisiana from France. State what the terms of the purchase were, what it accomplished, and what problems it presented to Jefferson.
4. Evaluate Jefferson as president. What of real significance did he achieve, and what would you count among his failings? Why?
5. Explain how the European war affected the United States during Jefferson's

presidency, and assess Jefferson's conduct of foreign policy in response to the war.

Critical Thinking Exercise

Compare and Contrast

Complete the compare-and-contrast matrix in Chapter 5.

6: Jeffersonian Democracy

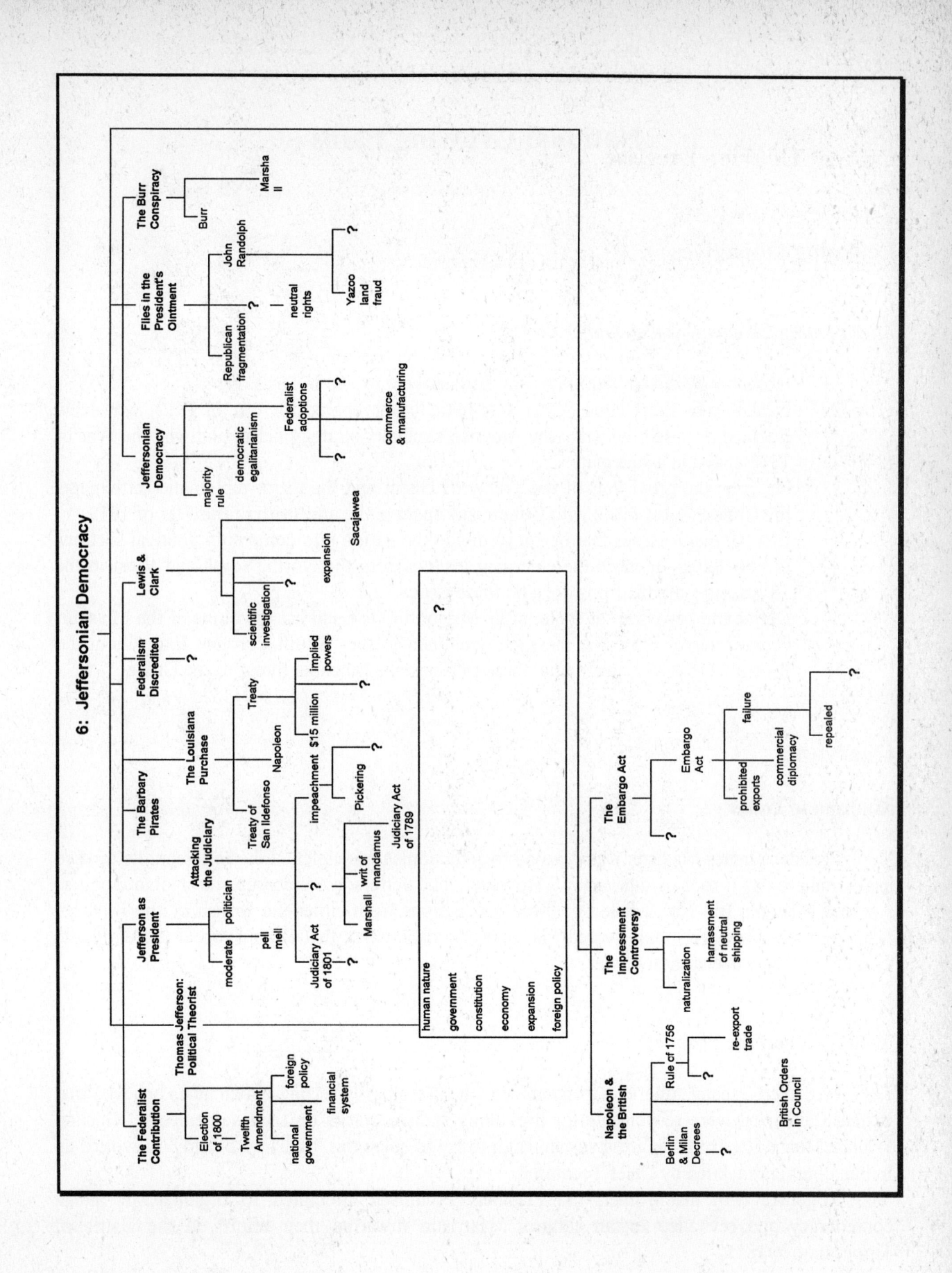

- **The Federalist Contribution**
  - Election of 1800
  - Twelfth Amendment
  - national government
  - financial system
  - foreign policy

- **Thomas Jefferson: Political Theorist**
  - human nature
  - government
  - constitution
  - economy
  - expansion
  - foreign policy
  - ?

- **Jefferson as President**
  - moderate
  - pell mell
  - politician

- **Attacking the Judiciary**
  - Judiciary Act of 1801 — ?
  - Judiciary Act of 1789
  - Marshall — writ of mandamus
  - impeachment — Pickering
  - ?

- **The Barbary Pirates**

- **The Louisiana Purchase**
  - Treaty of San Ildefonso
  - Napoleon
  - Treaty — $15 million
  - implied powers — ?

- **Federalism Discredited** — ?

- **Lewis & Clark**
  - scientific investigation — ?
  - expansion
  - Sacajawea

- **Jeffersonian Democracy**
  - majority rule
  - democratic egalitarianism
  - Federalist adoptions
    - ?
    - commerce & manufacturing
    - ?

- **Files in the President's Ointment**
  - Republican fragmentation — ?
  - neutral rights
  - John Randolph — Yazoo land fraud — ?

- **The Burr Conspiracy**
  - Burr — Marshall

- **Napoleon & the British**
  - Berlin & Milan Decrees — ?
  - Rule of 1756
    - re-export trade
    - ?
  - British Orders in Council

- **The Impressment Controversy**
  - naturalization
  - harrassment of neutral shipping

- **The Embargo Act**
  - ?
  - Embargo Act
    - prohibited exports
    - commercial diplomacy
    - failure — repealed — ?

93

Chapter 7

National Growing Pains

Learning Objectives

After reading Chapter 7 you should be able to:

1. Explain why the United States and Britain went to war in 1812.
2. Explain why the United States was initially unprepared for war in 1812, why New England opposed the war, why America's military strategy failed, and why the War of 1812 ended in a stalemate.
3. Describe the provisions of the Treaty of Ghent and the major diplomatic settlements the United States made with Britain and Spain in the aftermath of the War of 1812
4. List the major issues that began to divide the nation into competing political sections in the 1820s. Identify the emerging leaders from the North, South and West in the 1820s and state their positions on these issues.
5. Define the key issues at stake in the Missouri Crisis and list the terms of the Missouri Compromise. State the message contained in the "South Carolina Exposition and Protest" (1828). Explain how these two posed a potential threat to the Union.

Overview

Madison in Power

President James Madison was devoted to Jeffersonian principles. Like Jefferson, he tried to use commerce as a tool of diplomacy. However, like Jefferson's embargo, the Nonintercourse Act and Macon's Bill No. 2 failed to force concessions from either the British or the French. Napoleon was, however, maneuvered Madison into demanding that Britain repeal the Orders in Council or face a declaration of war.

Tecumseh and the Prophet

Incorrectly, many American frontiersmen who were busily seizing Indian lands believed that British Canadians were responsible for provoking Indian attacks on their settlements. General William Henry Harrison's aggressive campaign to try to solve this "Indian problem," provoked an Indian counterattack led by Chief Tecumseh.

Together with his brother, the Prophet, Tecumseh attempted to organize an Indian confederacy and revitalize Indian culture. Harrison thwarted their efforts in the Battle of Tippecanoe in 1811.

Depression and Land Hunger

The falling prices of agriculture goods threw the West's economy into depression. American commercial restrictions and poor transportation were the major causes of these conditions, but western farmers blamed their problems on British violations of American neutral rights.

Many westerners demanded war with Britain in hopes it would result in America's acquisition of British Canada and Spanish Florida. Further, Madison saw a conquered Canada as a hostage the United States could use to compel the British to respect America's neutral rights. Finally, western "War Hawks" demanded a war with Britain as the only way to uphold the nation's honor and secure true independence.

Resistance to War

Many New England Federalists opposed war with Britain for partisan reasons and because they feared the damage war would do to New England's commercial economy. Also, the two nations had strong cultural and economic ties. Nevertheless, although Napoleonic France, rather than Great Britain, posed the greater potential danger to American interests and ideals, on June 18, 1812, Congress declared war on Great Britain.

The War of 1812

The United States was poorly prepared to obtain its military objectives in 1812. A handful of naval frigates and scores of commissioned privateers performed well in isolated engagements with the powerful British Navy early in the war, but by 1813 American ships were bottled up in port by the powerful British navy.

Poor military leadership doomed the United States to an overly complicated and unsuccessful invasion of Canada in 1812: a three-pronged invasion resulted in defeats at Detroit, the Niagara River, and Montreal. In 1813, Americans were more successful, winning a naval battle on Lake Erie, and General Harrison's troops were victorious at the Battle of the Thames where Tecumseh was killed. Still, Americans were no closer to a conquest of Canada at year's end and the British navy freely harassed New England ports and shipping.

Britain Assumes the Offensive

With their defeat of Napoleon in early 1814, the British were able to expend a greater effort on their war with the United States. The British strategy for 1814 called for a three-pronged attack: full-scale invasion from Montreal; skirmishes and raids on Washington, D.C., and Baltimore in the Chesapeake; and an attack on New Orleans to bottle up the American west. This strategy was little more successful for the British than was America's invasion of Canada, although Washington, D.C., was raided and burned.

"The Star Spangled Banner"

The British were repelled at Fort McHenry (Baltimore) where Francis Scott Key penned "The Star Spangled Banner." The attempted invasion from Montreal was turned back at the Battle of Plattsburg in New York. That left only the British assault on New Orleans.

The Treaty of Ghent

Negotiations to end the War of 1812 began in Ghent, Belgium, in the summer of 1814. Because they expected their strategy to be successful, the British were at first unwilling to make any concessions. British military failures resulted in an agreement to end the hostilities and reestablish the *status quo ante bellum*. Since the Napoleonic War was over as well, the problems of neutral rights and impressment were now moot. The Treaty of Ghent was signed on Christmas Eve, 1814.

The Hartford Convention

From its beginning, New England had opposed the War of 1812. Federalist-controlled state administrations refused to allow state militia to participate in the fighting, and discouraged banks from making loans to the federal government to pay for the war. New England merchants conducted an illegal trade with British Canada throughout the war. The Federalist party was rejuvenated in New England by the war and some encouraged New England's secession from the Union. The Hartford Convention, however, settled for a statement of states' rights and a series of constitutional amendment proposals designed to serve New England's economic and political interests. These Federalists' proposals were discredited when news of the war's end reached Washington, D.C.

The Battle of New Orleans

The defense of New Orleans was entrusted to the tough, hot-tempered Indian fighter, Andrew Jackson—"Old Hickory." With a well-conceived order of battle, Jackson's forces repelled the British invasion with withering fire in early January 1815.

Fruits of "Victory"

The War of 1812 was a standoff. Americans, nevertheless, assumed that Jackson's victory in New Orleans meant they had won the war. Relieved, they believed the war had completed their independence and affirmed their republican system of government. The antiwar Federalist party was discredited and disappeared in the wake of postwar patriotism.

With the end of the Napoleonic War in Europe, the United States now was freed from foreign involvement and the domestic conflict it had nourished. Peace, prosperity, patriotism, and an end to partisan bickering were the fruits of victory.

Anglo-American Rapprochement

Gradually the United States and Britain found their way to friendship. In the Rush-Bagot Agreement in 1817 the two nations agreed to naval arms limitations on the Great Lakes. In the Convention of 1818, they negotiated a boundary settlement from the Lake of the Woods to the Rocky Mountains, agreed to a joint occupation of the Oregon Country, and settled a dispute over the use of Canadian fisheries.

The Transcontinental Treaty

In a spirit of intimidation, rather than friendship, the United States settled outstanding issues with Spain. Secretary of State John Quincy Adams initiated negotiations for the American acquisition of Florida in 1819. In the resulting Transcontinental Treaty, Spain relinquished Florida as part of a larger settlement that established the western boundary to America's Louisiana Purchase Territory and extended the nation's territorial claims to the Pacific coast.

The Monroe Doctrine

America's withdrawal from Europe was completed by the Monroe Doctrine in 1823. The doctrine came in response to Russia's threat to colonize along the Pacific coast and to the threat of several European nations to recolonize the newly independent Latin American republics. In the Monroe Doctrine the United States unilaterally asserted that the Western Hemisphere was no longer open to new colonization, that the United States opposed any European nation's interference in Latin America's political affairs, and that the United States would refrain from involvement in strictly European affairs. Although the United States was too weak at the time to enforce these pronouncements, the Monroe Doctrine perfectly expressed the wishes of the American people.

The Era of Good Feelings

Less a figure than his predecessors, President James Monroe nevertheless came to embody American nationalism, and he presided over the brief postwar Era of Good Feelings. One reason for the harmony during his first term was that Republicans had come to accept most of the economic policies earlier advocated by the Federalists. A Republican-controlled Congress created a new national bank, passed America's first protective tariff, and appropriated federal aid for transportation improvements. The Jeffersonians had successfully struck a balance between individual liberty and responsible government. Soon, however, national expansion would threaten the postwar spirit of unity.

New Sectional Issues: Protection, Western Lands, Banking, Slavery

Like other issues in the Era of Good Feelings, the tariff controversy was agitated by both the War of 1812 and the Panic of 1819. The Tariff Act of 1816 was enacted to protect America's industries and jobs. Except for the commercial interests of New England, high tariffs were supported in every section of the country. In time, the South and Southwest turned against protective tariffs concluding that they increased the costs of imports and inhibited the export of cotton.

The national bank's charter was not renewed in 1811. Some opponents questioned its constitutionality; others opposed its competition with state banks. The absence of a national bank during the War of 1812 complicated war financing and lowered the value of bank notes. In response, Congress created a new Second Bank of the United States in 1816. The new bank was badly managed at first and was endangered by the Panic of 1819. New management and tighter credit policies saved the bank, but at the expense of public favor. All sections were split over the desirability of having a new bank, and westerners in particular opposed its tight money policies during the Panic of 1819.

The liberal land acts of 1800 and 1804 reduced the price of public land and the minimum unit for sale. Public land sales boomed until 1818. Then, agricultural prices fell as foreign markets shrank and the Panic of 1819 destroyed many farms. The West strongly favored a cheap land policy while the North feared it would drain off cheap labor. The South worried about competition from cotton producers in the virgin lands of the Southwest. Westerners were also most enthusiastic for federally financed internal improvements like the National Road.

The most divisive sectional issue was slavery. This issue generated surprisingly little controversy from 1789 to 1819. Slave importations increased in he 1790s, but the foreign slave trade was quietly abolished in 1808. Free and slave states entered the Union in equal numbers (11 each in 1819). Southerners ardently defended slavery while most northerners, to the extent they took a position, opposed it. Many westerners, especially native southerners, also supported slavery.

Northern Leaders

Monroe's secretary of state, John Quincy Adams, was the North's best-known political leader in the 1820s. Originally a Federalist like his father, Adams converted to the Republican party after 1800. Adams was capable, ambitious and intelligent, but he was inept in personal relationships and was a demanding perfectionist. He was a committed nationalist; open-minded toward tariff policy and supportive of federally funded internal improvements.

Daniel Webster was a congressional leader. He was a skillful constitutional lawyer and a remarkable orator. Webster had a powerful mind, but, though a nationalist, he was slavishly devoted to serving New England's business interests. He opposed the War of 1812, protective tariffs, the bank, cheap land, and internal improvements.

The North's most masterful politician was Martin Van Buren, the affable leader of New York's Albany Regency. Van Buren seldom took a strong position on any of the key issues of the day. To him, issues were merely means of winning elections.

Southern Leaders

Georgia's William H. Crawford, a spokesman for southern planters, was the South's most prominent leader. Tending toward states' rights, Crawford nevertheless endorsed moderately protective tariffs. The other major southern leader was South Carolina's John C. Calhoun. Before 1825 he was an ardent nationalist.

Western Leaders

Kentuckian Henry Clay was one of the most charming political leaders of his generation. Intellectually inferior to Adams and Calhoun, Clay nevertheless used his charisma and skill at arranging compromises to carry him far in national politics. He authored the American System of protective tariffs and internal improvements to meld the economic interests of the East and West. He disliked, but tolerated slavery.

Another western leader was the colorful expansionist, Thomas Hart Benton. He supported homestead legislation and internal improvements, but strongly opposed all banks. He was the champion of small western farmers. Military heroes William Henry Harrison and Andrew Jackson were emerging political leaders in the West.

The Missouri Compromise

The Panic of 1819 worsened tension among the sections and growing sectionalism repeatedly influenced the politics of the 1820s. The most sharply divisive event was the Missouri Crisis of 1819-1820. Many of Missouri Territory's settlers were native southerners who owned slaves, and they petitioned for Missouri's admission as a slave state. But New York Congressman James Tallmadge's amendment called for the gradual abolition of slavery in the proposed new state—the first attempt to restrict the expansion of slavery since the Northwest Ordinance of 1787.

The debate generated by the Tallmadge Amendment did not deal with the morality of slavery or the rights of blacks; what was at stake was political influence. Northerners complained of the advantages the South gained from the Three-Fifths Compromise and also feared having to compete with slave labor.

Henry Clay's Missouri Compromise admitted Missouri as a slave state and Maine as a free state, and the Thomas Amendment barred slavery north of 36° 30' latitude in the old Louisiana Purchase Territory. Southerners accepted these terms since they believed the banned territory was environmentally hostile to slavery anyway. Clay also worked out a compromise when the Missouri constitution tried to ban free blacks from migrating into the new state. The Missouri Crisis warned of the potential divisiveness of the slavery issue.

The Election of 1824

Internal improvements also proved to be a divisive, though less disruptive, issue. And Southerners strongly opposed a new protective tariff law that was equally strongly supported by the North and West. The old two-party system was breaking down by 1824; Republicans were factionalized and in disarray; and political leaders concentrated on positioning themselves for the presidency. Consequently, the presidential fight in 1824 was waged over personalities, not issues. The electoral college vote was split between Adams, Jackson, Crawford, and Clay. Clay's support helped Adams, who was elected president by the House of Representatives. Calhoun won the vice-presidency.

John Quincy Adams As President

Adams hoped to make his presidency a tribute to nationalism. Yet the boldness of his program exceed his political ability to make it happen. He often appeared insensitive to public feelings, and he failed to use his power to build support for his programs. Scrupulously honest, he nevertheless was dogged by charges that he and Clay had struck a "corrupt bargain" to gain Adams the presidency in 1824.

Calhoun's "South Carolina Exposition and Protest"

As the North and West grew more favorable toward high tariffs, the export-conscious South grew more antitariff. Outraged by the record high Tariff of Abominations in 1828, southerners turned to Calhoun who now reached a turning point in his career. In his "South Carolina Exposition and Protest" (1828), he repudiated his earlier nationalism and emerged as the states' rights spokesman of southern interests. He argued that a state could interpose its authority to nullify any act of Congress it found to be in violation of the Constitution. Thus was born the doctrine of nullification.

The Meaning of Sectionalism

Postwar prosperity produced national growth that in turn produced sectional conflict. Nationalists like Henry Clay hoped federal action could make sectional difference work for the benefit of everyone. Another unifying influence was the postwar patriotism of Americans and their pride in their unique system of government.

People, Places, and Things

Define the following:

privateer *Merchant ships lashed canons on deck & went off to attack British ships*

status quo ante bellum *everything was to go back as it was before war*

rapprochement *America & Britain found their way to friendship* protective tariff __Tariff act of 1816 - because of 1812 War + Panic of 1819__

sectionalism __North wanted protection - South No., West was divided - slavery was coming up.__

internal improvements __roads, bridges - Federal projects__

states' rights __has right to interpose its authority__

factionalism __Republicans had divided into different groups of thought__

nullification __A state could nullify any act of Congress if found in violation of Constitution__

Describe the following:

Macon's Bill No. 2 __removed all restrictions / Permitted Am ships to go anywhere but closed Am ports to Briton + France warships__

Battle of Tippecanoe __disillusioned Indians + shattered their confederation__

Treaty of Ghent __Negotiations to end war - Brits agreed Back to status quo...__

Hartford Convention __New England was going to secede from Union__

Battle of New Orleans __American Gen Jackson won this after treaty of Ghent.__

101

Rush-Bagot Agreement U.S & Britan agreed to Naval arms limitations on the Great Lakes

Transcontinental Treaty U.S. settled outstanding differences with Spain - got Florida, extended U.S. to Pacific Coast & Est. boundry of Louisiana Terr.

Monroe Doctrine Western Hemisphere closed to further colonization

Panic of 1819 Agricultural prices fell as foreign markets shrank + destroyed many farms.

Tariff of 1816 was inacted to protect America's industries + jobs.

Second Bank of the United States the absence of a Nat Bank during (1812) War. complicated war financing + lowered value of bank notes

Albany Regency Political machine in New York Headed by Martin Van Buren

American System Protective tariffs + internal improvements to meld the economic interests of the East + West

Tallmadge Amendment Prohibited further introduction of slavery + Provided all slaves born in Missouri after it became state were to be free at age 25

Thomas Amendment forever prohibited slavery in all other parts of Louisiana Purchase No of 36° 30 No latitude

Missouri Compromise Missouri was Slave + Maine was Free to preserve balance in the Senate

"corrupt bargain" by making Henry Clay Sec. of State. People felt Adams + Clay had made a deal

Tariff of Abominations High duties on raw wool, hemp, flex fur + liquor

"South Carolina Exposition and Protest" S. Carolina - unfair + unconstitutional Calhoun - provided defense of the right of the people of a state to reject a law of Congress

Identify the following:

James Madison 3rd American President

William Henry Harrison Western Political Leader

Tecumseh Indian War Leader + preached Anti-White doctrine

"War Hawks" Westerners demanded war with Brits as only way to uphold Nations honor + secure true Independence.

Andrew Jackson Won battle of New Orleans - Western Leader - Great Am. General

John Quincy Adams Sec of State under Monroe, Senator from Mass., Am. minister to Netherlands + Prussia

James Monroe 4th U.S Pres. & served 2 Terms - Nationalist Gov. of Va., U.S. Senator + cabinet member

Daniel Webster Lawyer + Orator served in Congress during 1812 War

Martin Van Buren Senator from New York - Albany Regency was his Pol. machine

William H. Crawford _Most Prominent Southern leader - Sec. of Treasury_

John C. Calhoun _Southerner So. Carolina - Sec. of War_

Henry Clay _Western Leader - Seeing Nat. Needs from broad perspective - American System_

Locate the following places: Write in both the place name and its map location number.

1. The three places where the British attempted to implement their three-pronged attack on the United States in 1814.

   _____ _____

   _____ _____

   _____ _____

2. The Great Lake on which American naval forces achieved an important victory over the British in 1813.

   _____ _____

3. The area to which the United States acquired joint occupation rights with Great Britain in 1818.

   _____ _____

4. The western and eastern termini of the United States-Canadian boundary negotiated in 1818.

   eastern _____ _____

   western _____ _____

5. The Louisiana Purchase boundary line negotiated between the United States and Spain in 1819. (Name the treaty.)

   _____ _____

104

6. The territory whose "purchase" by the United States was negotiated with Spain in 1819.

   _____ _____

7. The battle where forces commanded by William Henry Harrison broke the back of Tecumseh's bid to forge a formidable Indian confederacy in the West in 1811.

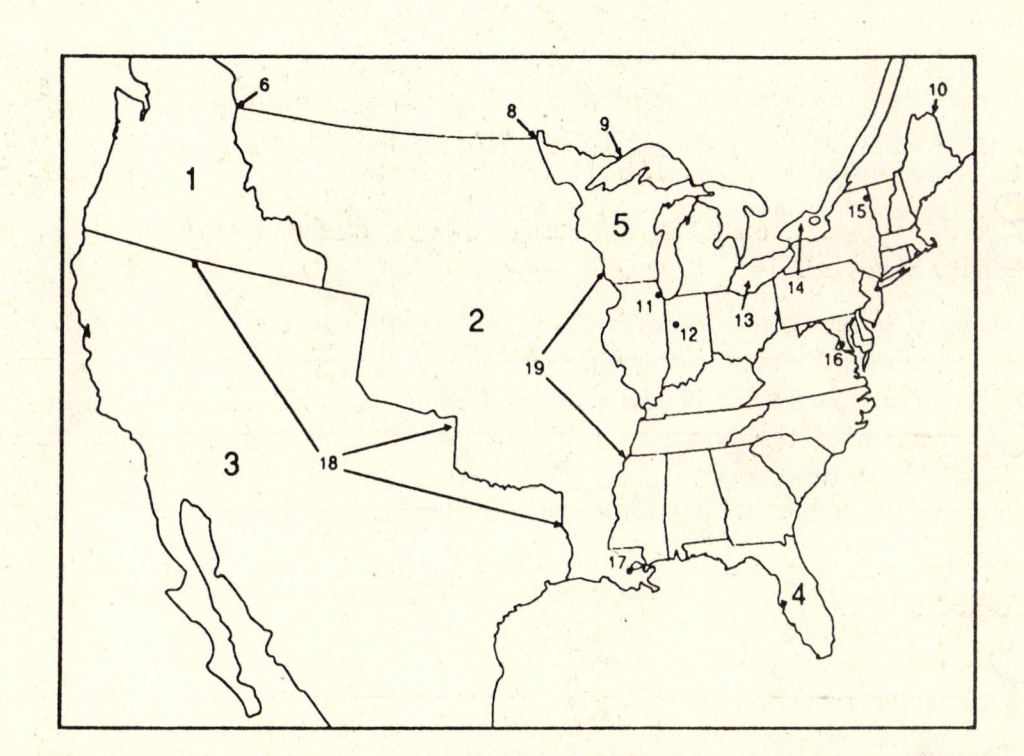

   _____ _____

Self-Test

Multiple-Choice Questions

1. Like Jefferson, President Madison attempted to use _____ as a way to force Britain and France to recognize America's neutral rights.
   A. secret alliances
   B. espionage
   C. foreign trade
   D. military preparedness

2. The "War Hawks"
   A. expressed the war sentiments of New England
   B. supported Madison's commercial retaliation as a means of conducting diplomacy with Britain and France

105

C. feared that Madison's diplomacy was costing the nation its honor and, potentially, its independence
D. opposed the plan for an invasion of Canada

3. All of the following issues helped Americans justify their declaration of war against Great Britain in 1812 EXCEPT
A. recognition that Britain, not Napoleon, posed a greater threat to the United States
B. nonrecognition of neutral rights and the policy of impressment
C. British provocation of Indians in the Old Northwest
D. vindication of national honor and pride

4. In the Treaty of Ghent ending the War of 1812, the British agreed to
A. the creation of an Indian buffer state in the Old Northwest
B. stop the impressment of American sailors
C. several territorial concession to the United States
D. stop the fighting

5. Delegates to the Hartford Convention in 1814-1815
A. endorsed a secession ordinance
B. proposed a number of constitutional amendments
C. denounced the principles embedded in Madison and Jefferson's Kentucky and Virginia Resolves
D. adopted a resolution to form a New England confederation

6. The attitudes of most Americans in the immediate aftermath of the War of 1812 included all of the following EXCEPT
A. self-confidence
B. faith in republicanism
C. national patriotism
D. strident partisanship

7. The United States and Britain agreed to limit naval armaments on the Great Lakes in the
A. Transcontinental Treaty
B. Treaty of Ghent
C. Rush-Bagot Agreement
D. Monroe Doctrine

8. In an agreement with Great Britain in 1818 the United States acquired
A. joint responsibility for defending the Western Hemisphere
B. joint occupation rights in the Oregon Country
C. a new western boundary to the Louisiana Purchase Territory
D. possession of Florida

9. The Louisiana Purchase boundary with Spanish territories in North America was first clearly defined in the
A. Rush-Bagot Agreement, 1817
B. Treaty of Ghent, 1814

C. Transcontinental Treaty, 1821
D. Monroe Doctrine, 1823

10. The Monroe Doctrine did NOT intend to prevent
    A. the founding of new European colonies in the Western Hemisphere
    B. America intervening in the affairs of Europe
    C. European nations interfering in the political affairs of Latin American republics
    D. the United States acquiring any new territories in the Western Hemisphere

11. After the War of 1812 many Republicans were convinced that the United States needed all of the following EXCEPT
    A. a new national bank
    B. to abolish slavery
    C. a protective tariff
    D. federal aid to improve transportation

12. Supporters of a protective tariff act in 1816 argued that it would do all of the following EXCEPT
    A. promote the textile industry in the South
    B. advance America's national economic self-sufficiency
    C. help lead to the abolition of slavery
    D. create an urban market for western agricultural goods

13. The primary argument of those who opposed the rechartering of the original Bank of the United States in 1811 was that it was
    A. poorly managed
    B. unconstitutional
    C. controlled by powerful state banks
    D. responsible for causing economic depressions

14. Henry Clay's American System was primarily designed to promote
    A. military preparedness
    B. the centralization of political power
    C. territorial expansion
    D. national economic self-sufficiency

15. If enacted, the Tallmadge Amendment would have
    A. prohibited any restrictions on Missouri's admission as a slave state
    B. gradually abolished slavery in Missouri
    C. banned slavery north of 36°30' latitude in the old Louisiana Territory
    D. abolished slavery in all states north of 36°30' latitude

16. The Missouri Compromise did NOT result in
    A. admitting Missouri as a slave state
    B. banning slavery north of 36°30' latitude in the old Louisiana Territory
    C. banning slavery in all states north of 36°30' latitude
    D. maintaining the balance in the number of slave and free states in the Union

17. The 1824 presidential election featured
    A. an unusually heavy turnout of voters
    B. a tie between two vice-presidential candidates
    C. the choice of president made by the House of Representatives
    D. the election of a president and vice-president from opposing political parties

18. President John Quincy Adams was
    A. a strong nationalist
    B. a skillful politician
    C. a brilliant orator
    D. well attuned to public sentiment

19. John C. Calhoun was moved to write his "South Carolina Exposition and Protest" in response to congressional legislation on
    A. land policy
    B. internal improvements
    C. slavery
    D. tariff policy

20. John C. Calhoun's nullification theory argued that
    A. a state had the constitutional right to secede from the Union
    B. a state could declare an act of Congress unconstitutional
    C. slavery was a positive good and morally defensible
    D. slavery could not be banned from U.S. territories

Essay Questions

1. Which one of the following do you think was the primary cause of the War of 1812: neutral rights, Indian provocation, economic depression, land hunger, the "War Hawks"? Evaluate the importance of each issue, then justify your choice.
2. Compare and contrast the military strategies of the British and the Americans in the War of 1812, then explain why the war ended in a stalemate.
3. Explain why the United States was so remarkably successful in the conduct of its diplomacy between 1815 and 1823 when it had been so unsuccessful before 1815.
4. Explain why each of the following issues tended to be politically controversial after 1815: protective tariffs, internal improvements, public land sales, the national bank.
5. Explain what was at stake in Missouri's admission to the Union. Evaluate the text authors' claim that it was "one of the . . . most critical" of the sectional questions.

Critical Thinking Exercise

Cause and Effect

In Chapter 3 you were introduced to the importance of cause-effect relationships to historical study. You completed an exercise involving causal chains. Chapter 7 presents events in the early nineteenth century, including the War of 1812, that were the effects of several contributory causes. Again, *contributory causes* are causes that act and interact simultaneously to produce an effect.

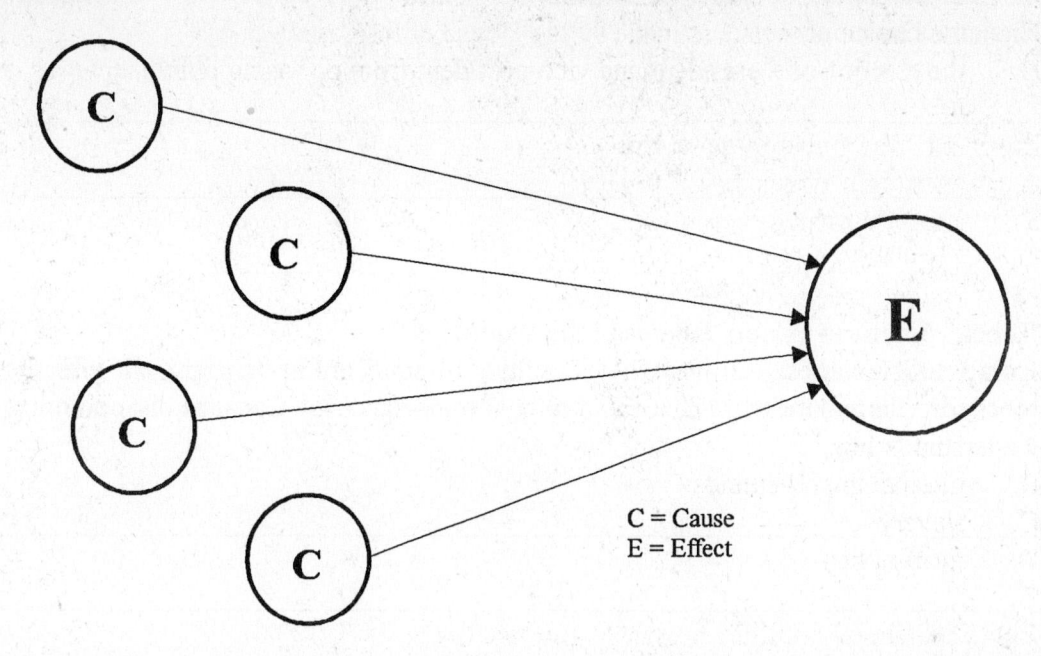

C = Cause
E = Effect

Each of the groups below is identified by an effect, followed by a list of items that may have been contributory causes to that effect. Your task is to line out those items from the list that were *not* contributory causes of the stated effect, then write a sentence that express the relationship between the remaining causes and the effect. (Note: Any number of causal items in each group *may be* correct). The first group has been completed as an example.

X. Effect: Economic depression on western farms
Contributory causes: American commercial restrictions, ~~lack of cultivable land~~, ~~British boycott of American goods~~, poor transportation facilities, ~~bad weather~~

<u>The depression that hit western farming was the consequence of both American commercial restrictions and a slow and cumbersome transportation system.</u>

1. Effect: The War of 1812
Contributory causes: land hunger, sense of national honor, British rescinding the Orders in Council, agricultural depression, violations of neutral rights

_____

_____

_____

2. Effect: Federalists oppose the War of 1812
   Contributory causes: impressment of merchant sailors, Madison's refusal to invade Canada, partisan advantage, belief that Madison provoked war, concern for the health of New England's economy

3. Effect: American military failures in the War of 1812
   Contributory causes: an inept navy, refusal of state militia to fight, an effective British blockade, the failure to realize the strategic importance of Canada, disappointing military leadership

4. Effect: Pronouncement of the Monroe Doctrine
   Contributory causes: Russian colonization of the Pacific coast, concern over Spanish expansion in the Caribbean, the threat of European recolonization in Latin America, British interest in commercial opportunities in Latin America, fear that the United States would be drawn in Latin American revolutions.

5. Effect: Dawning of an Era of Good Feelings
   Contributory causes: "victory" in the War of 1812, economic prosperity, proposals from the Hartford Convention, Republican adoption of Federalist programs, Monroe's presidential style

6. Effect: Crisis over the admission of Missouri to the Union
   Contributory causes: Tallmadge amendment, Three-Fifths Compromise, the morality of slavery, the North controlled the House of Representatives, the rights of African-Americans, Missouri was located north of the Ohio River

   _____

   _____

   _____

7: National Growing Pains

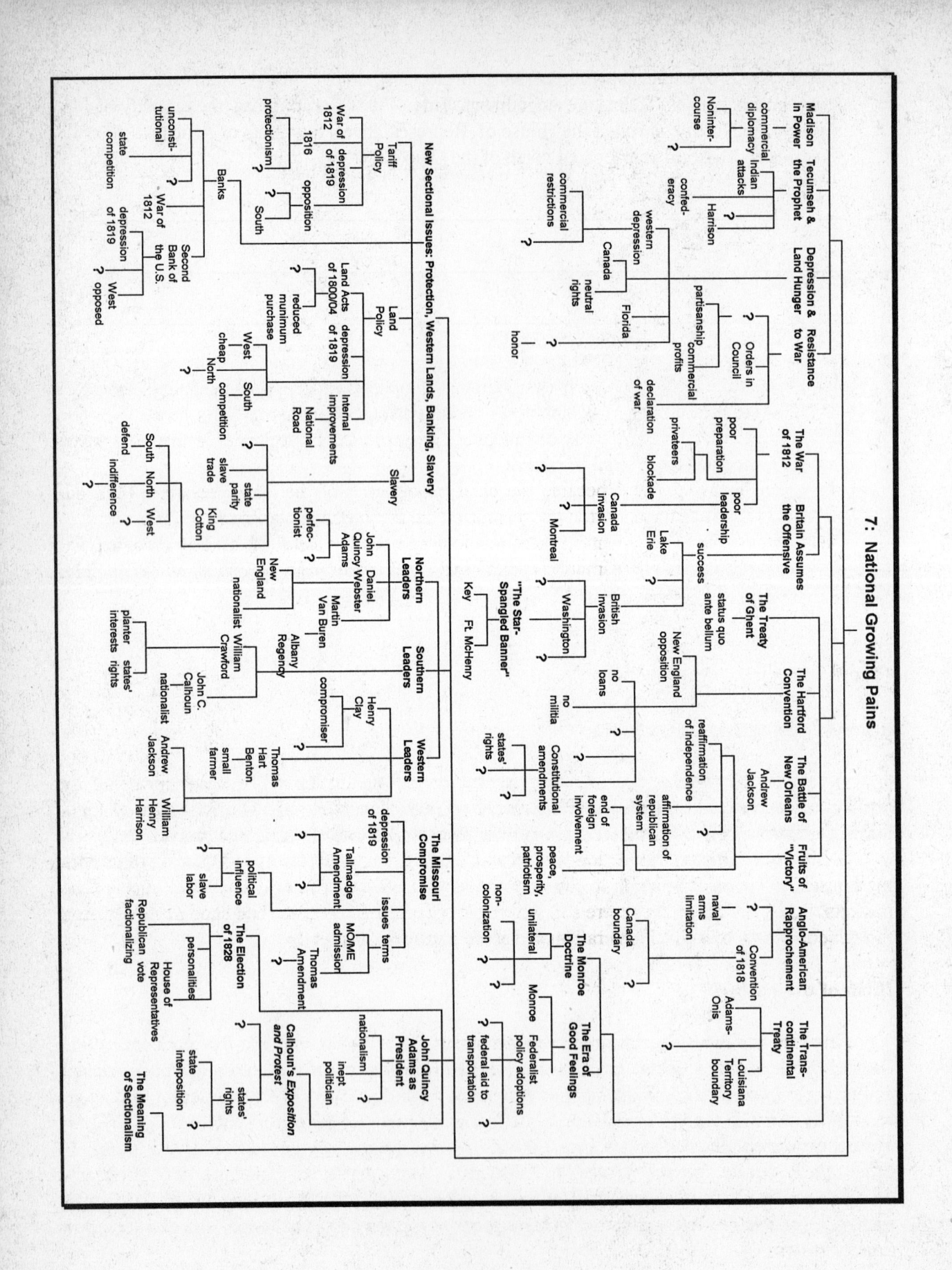

Madison in Power
- Tecumseh & the Prophet
  - Noninter-course
  - commercial diplomacy
  - Indian attacks — ? — confederacy — Harrison
- Depression & Resistance to Land Hunger to War
  - commercial restrictions — ?
    - western depression — Canada
    - neutral rights — Florida
  - partisanship — ?
    - commercial profits — Orders in Council
    - honor — ?
    - declaration of war

The War of 1812
- Britain Assumes the Offensive
  - poor preparation — privateers
  - poor leadership — blockade
  - success — ? — Canada invasion
    - Lake Erie
    - Montreal
  - status quo ante bellum — British invasion
    - Washington
    - "The Star-Spangled Banner" — Key, Ft. McHenry

The Treaty of Ghent
- New England opposition
- no loans
- no militia
- states' rights — ?
- Constitutional amendments — ?

The Hartford Convention
- reaffirmation of independence
- end of foreign involvement
- affirmation of republican system — ?

The Battle of New Orleans — Andrew Jackson

Fruits of "Victory"
- peace, prosperity, patriotism
- Anglo-American Rapprochement
  - Canada boundary
  - naval arms limitation — ?
  - Convention of 1818
  - Adams-Onis
- The Trans-continental Treaty
  - Louisiana Territory boundary — ?
- The Era of Good Feelings
  - Federalist policy adoptions
    - federal aid to transportation
- The Monroe Doctrine
  - non-colonization
  - unilateral — ?
  - Monroe

New Sectional Issues: Protection, Western Lands, Banking, Slavery
- Tariff Policy
  - War of 1812 — 1816
    - protectionism — ?
    - opposition — South
  - Banks
    - unconstitutional — War of 1812 — Second Bank of the U.S.
    - state competition — depression of 1819 — ? — West opposed
- Land Policy
  - Land Acts of 1800/04 — depression of 1819 — ?
    - reduced minimum purchase
    - West cheap — North competition
    - South
  - Internal improvements — National Road
- Slavery — ?
  - state parity — King Cotton
  - South defend
  - North indifference — ?
  - West

Northern Leaders
- John Quincy Adams — ? — perfectionist
- Daniel Webster — New England nationalist
- Martin Van Buren — Albany Regency

Southern Leaders
- William Crawford — states' rights
- John C. Calhoun — nationalist
- Henry Clay — compromiser

Western Leaders
- Thomas Hart Benton — small farmer
- Andrew Jackson
- William Henry Harrison

The Missouri Compromise
- depression of 1819
- political influence — ?
- slave labor
- Tallmadge Amendment
- issues — admission — MO/ME
- terms — Thomas Amendment

The Election of 1828
- personalities
- House of Representatives
- Republican vote factionalizing — ?

John Quincy Adams as President
- nationalism — ?
- inept politician — ?
- states' rights

Calhoun's *Exposition and Protest*
- state interposition

The Meaning of Sectionalism

- planter interests
- states' rights

112

Chapter 8

Toward a National Economy

Learning Objectives

After reading Chapter 8 you should be able to:

1. Trace the origins and early development of the factory system in the United States.
2. List the sources of early nineteenth-century America's industrial labor force.
3. Explain why a class-conscious industrial proletariat did not appear in the early stages of America's industrial revolution.
4. Explain why cotton became the chief export crop of the South between 1815 and 1840, and how the cotton gin revitalized the institution of slavery after 1800.
5. Define the government-business relationship in early nineteenth-century America, and show how "internal improvements" and other government action at all levels aided economic growth.

Overview

America's Industrial Revolution

The growth of American industry required certain technological advances including the factory system, interchangeable parts, the steamboat, and the cotton gin. The Bank of the United States provided an important source of credit for financing America's industrial revolution.

America's industrial revolution was slow in coming. Except in the manufacturing of textiles, the household system continued to thrive in the early nineteenth century, usually to supply local markets. Most urban workers were still self-employed artisans. Yet, hat and shoe manufacturing, though conducted by household craftsmen, served a national market

Birth of the Factory

Innovations in textile machinery were imported from Britain after the Revolutionary War. Samuel Slater, defying British laws, memorized the construction of the cotton spinning machine and brought it to America where he built the nation's first factory in 1790. By paying low wages to child workers to tend the machines, Slater's factory was profitable from the start. The factory system expanded when Francis Cabot Lowell and the Boston Associates used water power to drive their textile power looms in Waltham, Massachusetts. There, Lowell's Boston Manufacturing Company combined machine production, efficient management, large-scale operation, and centralized marketing to mass produce a standardized product—the essence of the factory system.

An Industrial Proletariat?

As the importance of skilled labor declined, skilled workers became either employers or wage-earning employees, and the gap between owners and workers widened. Workers made some collective efforts to protect their interests, but more remarkable was the relative absence of a self-conscious working class solidarity. This has been variously attributed to a number of things: the availability of a frontier to which dissatisfied workers could escape; the racial and ethnic differences among workers that inhibited recognition of their common interests; or the continuous flow of immigrants willing to work for low wages who could easily replace dissatisfied employees. Significantly, the expanding economy offered workers opportunity to rise out of the working class, and, anticipating this, workers never developed strong class feelings.

Employment in industry usually meant an improvement in conditions of labor and living standards for wage earners. Most early factory workers were women and children. Compared to farm labor, factory work was relatively easy for children, and it provided their families with extra income.

Francis Cabot Lowell's Waltham System

Instead of hiring children, the Boston Associates adopted the "Waltham System" of employing single young women in their mills. Their work and leisure-time activities were both strictly supervised, but the women were relatively well paid and most enjoyed the camaraderie with other women. Wage reductions and work speedups eventually destroyed their idyllic conditions, and by 1830 mill owners were turning to Irish immigrants to operate their machines.

Strangers at the Door

The doubling of America's population from 1790 to 1820 was almost entirely due to natural increase. But immigration from Europe, especially from Ireland and Germany, reached flood-tide proportions after 1830. Most immigrants were attracted by economic opportunity, but the promise of political and religious freedom and the chance to escape harsh conditions at home drew others. Some immigrants migrated on to the West, but most Irish immigrants settled in eastern cities. This massive influx of poor and culturally distinct immigrants temporarily depressed living standards and increased social tensions, but generally their labor was a stimulus to the American economy.

Technological Advances

Few people in the 1820s realized how profoundly the factory system would affect their lives. Yet, increasingly larger and more efficient machine processes slowly moved into many areas of consumer goods production including woolens, iron products, nails, paper, glass, pottery, and canned food.

Corporations

Mechanization of production required substantial capital investment, and capital was in chronically short supply in early nineteenth-century America. Because Americans, including many businessmen, tended to associate corporations with monopoly, corruption, and the undermining of individual enterprise, the corporate form of business organization was slow to develop in America. But as the volume of foreign commerce fell after 1812, capital was transferred from commerce to industry—attracted by high profits and the growing prestige of manufacturing. The growth of manufacturing further reduced America's dependence on foreign commerce, but augmented nationalist and isolationist sentiment. Manufacturing also stimulated commercial agriculture as farmers found markets for their goods in the growing size and increasing number of manufacturing cities.

Cotton Revolutionizes the South

The booming textile industries of Britain and New England created a growing demand for raw cotton. Eli Whitney's invention of the cotton gin in 1797 made the profitable production of upland cotton possible throughout the South, and cotton soon became the nation's major export crop. Northerners profited from the cotton trade by handling the transportation, insurance, and final disposition of the cotton crop. Western farmers profited from the sale of their surplus corn and hogs to feed southern slaves. Cotton was the major expansive force in the national economy between 1815 and 1840.

Revival of Slavery

The cotton gin stimulated cotton production and the booming cotton culture revitalized slavery in the South. The libertarian beliefs of the Revolutionary generation were tempered by their racial prejudices and respect for private property, and their fear of slave revolt. Many opponents of slavery came to see the deportation of freed slaves back to Africa as an answer to America's racial problem. Most blacks—who had no memory of Africa—opposed colonization, but paternalistic whites were convinced both races would be better off if they were separated.

The American Colonization Society was founded in 1817. It established the African colony of Liberia, but few blacks migrated. As cotton production expanded, the growing need for labor in the South acted as a brake on the colonization movement. To supply the great demand for slaves in the new cotton lands of the Southwest, slave traders evaded state laws against the interstate sale of slaves. Slaves from the Upper South were increasingly sold off to the cotton boom states along the Gulf coast.

Free blacks in the North were little better off than those in the South. Most were denied the right to vote, education, and decent housing and employment. Racial segregation was the rule. Free blacks employed the tactic of peaceful persuasion to try to improve their lot.

Roads to Market

The spread of settlement into the Mississippi Valley created challenges that required technological advances if they were to be met. Most were related to the westerners' major problem: transportation improvements that would increase land values and stimulate trade. The natural trade pattern was between East and West, so much attention was given to road construction over the Appalachian Mountains. The first trans-Appalachian road--between Philadelphia and Lancaster, Pennsylvania--was opened in 1794.

Transportation and the Government

Most of the improved highways were built by private investors who charged tolls for the use of their turnpikes. Local, state, and national governments often bought stock in these companies, or financed construction of their own turnpikes. Thus, a mixture of public and private capital developed these financially risky, but socially desirable enterprises. The federal government financed the Old National Road, but political sectionalism prevented the undertaking of a comprehensive internal improvements program. Overland transportation continued to be an expensive way to transport goods to market.

"Organs of Communication"

The efforts of John Fitch, John Stevens, and Robert Fulton gradually produced an efficient steamboat to ply the western rivers and thereby enrich the economy of the Mississippi Valley. Freight rates between New Orleans, Louisville, Cincinnati, and Pittsburgh plummeted, and the Old Northwest became part of the national market economy. Steamboats became luxurious travel vessels and made New Orleans one of the world's major ports.

The Canal Boom

Although their construction was expensive and posed formidable engineering problems, canals held great promise for reducing transportation costs between the east coast and the western interior. DeWitt Clinton convinced the New York state legislature to pioneer the effort, resulting in the state-financed construction of the Erie Canal. Unlike many subsequent canal projects it inspired, the Erie Canal proved to be an enormous financial success.

The Emporium of the Western World

By initiating regular freight and passenger service to England, and by reforming the system of import sales, New York City merchants had established that city's premier role in domestic and foreign commerce. The Erie Canal cemented the city's position as the national metropolis. New England, Pennsylvania, and Maryland tried, but failed to match New York's Erie Canal connection with the western heartland. Western states and private investors often faced financial loss in their effort to provide feeder line canals connecting western farms with the Great Lakes and, via the Erie Canal, New York City. Nevertheless, the canal boom substantially lowered East-West transportation costs and benefited both western farmers and the national economy.

Government Aid to Business

Both the national and state governments were active in promoting economic development. Federal banking, tariff, and land legislation all influenced economic growth. States adopted general incorporation laws to standardize the issue of charters, and continued to issue special corporate charters as well. Manufacturers also benefited from state tax breaks, federal patent laws, and the courts' hostility toward labor unions.

The Marshall Court

Chief Justice John Marshall was a strong nationalist and held a Hamiltonian view of the Constitution. His decisions consistently favored manufacturing and business interests, advanced economic development, and established the supremacy of national legislation over state laws. In several opinions, the Marshall Court upheld the sanctity of contracts and the precedence of federal power over state authority. In *McCulloch* v. *Maryland* (1819) the Court affirmed the constitutionality of the Second Bank of the United States, thereby legitimizing the doctrine of implied powers.

In 1837, Chief Justice Roger Taney's ruling in the Charles River Bridge case declared that public convenience superseded the interests of a particular company, further advancing economic development.

People, Places, and Things

Define the following:

factory system _____

_____

household system _____

_____

proletariat _____

_____

Waltham System _____

_____

corporation _____

_____

upland cotton _____

_____

cotton gin _____

_____

turnpike _____

_____

general incorporation law _____

_____

interstate commerce _____

_____

Describe the following:

American Colonization Society _____

_____

Clermont _____

_____

Erie Canal _____

_____

Sturges v. *Crowninshield* New York bankruptcy law unconstitutional

_____

Dartmouth College v. *Woodward* charter granted by state was a contract & not to be canceled or altered without consent

McCulloch v. *Maryland* Maryland tried to tax Bank - since Bank was legal unconstitutional to tax

Gibbons v. *Ogden* State can ~~tax~~ regulate commerce that begins & ends in its Terr. but not when transaction crosses state line

Charles River Bridge case ~~State had no~~ right to place comfort & convenience over rights co.

Identify the following:

Samuel Slater Skilled mechanic made first cotton thread machine
* First Factories in America

Boston Associates ~~deve~~ group of Merchants headed by Francis Cabot Lowell

Francis Cabot Lowell revolutionized Textile Production & set up Waltham System - (unmarried women workers)

Eli Whitney Built first Cotton Gin

Robert Fulton Built first operating Steam boat

DeWitt Clinton Mayor of NewYork had Erie canal built

John Marshall Cheif Justice - Supreme Court

Roger Taney New Chief Judge (Justice)

119

Self-Test

Multiple-Choice Questions

1. In the United States the industrial revolution began with major technological innovations in

    A. shoe and boot manufacturing
    B. the steel industry
    C. textile manufacturing
    D. the machine tool industry

2. Because they were poor, most Irish immigrants to America in the early nineteenth century settled in

    A. eastern cities
    B. midwestern farms
    C. the South
    D. frontier areas.

3. It would be LEAST accurate to say that most early nineteenth-century immigrants to America
    A. came from northwestern European countries
    B. settled in the Northeast and Middle West
    C. migrated for economic reasons
    D. were middle-class Protestants

4. Most early nineteenth-century factory workers
    A. felt a keen sense of class consciousness
    B. quickly joined national labor unions to look out for their interests
    C. expected to eventually rise out of the working class
    D. felt a close and personal relationship to their employer

5. The Waltham System employed _____ as factory laborers in the textile industry.
    A. poor children
    B. young single women
    C. Irish immigrants
    D. apprentices

6. The factory system in America
    A. quickly replaced the household system of production
    B. was initiated by Francis Cabot Lowell and the Boston Associates
    C. was tied to the mass production of machine-made goods
    D. required little capital investment in its early years

7. Much of the early investment capital in manufacturing in America came from
    A. northeastern merchants
    B. the federal government

C. southern planters
D. the savings of workers

8. The corporation as a form of business organization was slow to develop in America primarily because
    A. state governments refused to charter them
    B. general incorporation laws were too prohibitive
    C. they were not an efficient means of raising venture capital
    (D.) there was a strong popular bias against them

9. America's most profitable export item in the early nineteenth century was
    A. corn
    (B.) cotton
    C. textiles
    D. machinery

10. The early nineteenth-century South's prosperity depended on all of the following EXCEPT
    (A.) agricultural diversity
    B. slave labor
    C. cotton production
    D. foreign trade

11. The movement to colonize blacks back to Africa was unsuccessful primarily because
    A. it was opposed by the nation's most respected leaders
    B. northern free blacks opposed it
    (C.) there was an increasing demand for slave labor in the South
    D. most northern whites opposed segregation of the races

12. The major application of steamboats for transporting goods in America was on
    A. New England streams
    (B.) western rivers
    C. the Great Lakes
    D. the Gulf of Mexico

13. The first dramatic decline in freight rates in the East-West trade occurred with the construction of
    A. turnpikes
    B. bridges
    (C.) canals
    D. railroads

14. The Erie Canal was the brainchild of
    A. Eli Whitney
    B. Samuel Slater
    (C.) DeWitt Clinton
    D. Oliver Evans

15. _____ was the primary beneficiary of the Erie Canal, while _____ was the primary beneficiary of the steamboat.
    A. New York City; New Orleans
    B. Philadelphia; Louisville
    C. Baltimore; New Orleans
    D. New York City; Cincinnati

16. The Supreme Court cases of *Sturges* v. *Crowninshield* and *Dartmouth College* v. *Woodward* both had to do with
    A. federal power and national banking
    B. local ordinances and voting rights
    C. state power and private contracts
    D. states' rights and slavery

17. The most helpful ruling the Marshall Court rendered to the doctrine of implied powers came in its decision in
    A. *Dartmouth College* v. *Woodward*
    B. *McCulloch* v. *Maryland*
    C. *Marbury* v. *Madison*
    D. *Gibbons* v. *Ogden*

18. John Marshall's famous legal dictum that "the power to tax involves the power to destroy" came in his decision in
    A. *Gibbons* v. *Ogden*
    B. Charles River Bridge case
    C. *McCulloch* v. *Maryland*
    D. *Dartmouth College* v. *Woodward*

19. Generally, Chief Justice John Marshall's decisions had all of the following effects EXCEPT
    A. encouraging economic development
    B. sanctifying property rights
    C. increasing the authority of the national government
    D. encouraging business monopolies

20. The case of *Gibbons* v. *Ogden* involved the question of
    A. a state's right to legalize slavery
    B. a state's right to regulate interstate commerce
    C. the federal government's authority to tax private business
    D. the federal government's power to collect customs duties

Essay Questions

1. Explain why the Industrial Revolution with its factory system of production was slow developing in the United States. Refer especially to technology, competing systems of production, and capitalization.

2. Describe the process whereby America, a land of farmers and artisans, created an industrial labor force. Where did the workers come from; how did these working-class employees relate to their employers; and why did they become a self-conscious working class?
3. Explain the relationship between Eli Whitney's cotton gin, the emergence of the cotton culture in the South, and the revival of slavery after 1800.
4. Evaluate the colonization movement as an antislavery effort. Define its goals, its assumptions, and its means of dealing with the slavery issue. Explain why it failed.
5. Trace the evolution of America's transportation revolution. Assess the importance of turnpikes, canals, and steamboats to the opening of the West and the creation of a national market economy.
6. Demonstrate how local, state, and national governments, by legislation and court decisions, promoted economic development in early nineteenth-century America.

Critical Thinking Exercise

Facts, Inferences, and Judgments

In Chapter 4 you were introduced to the importance of distinguishing between the historian's use of facts, inferences and, judgments. In the narrative below, determine which of the numbered statements is a fact, an inference, or a judgment. Circle your choice in the answer grid that follows.

---

(1) The most important legal advantages bestowed on businessmen in the period were the gift of Chief Justice John Marshall. (2) Historians have tended to forget that he had six colleagues on the Supreme Court, (3) and that is easy to understand. (4) Marshall's particular combination of charm, logic, and forcefulness made the Court . . . remarkably submissive to his view of the Constitution. (5) Marshall's belief in a powerful central government explains his tendency to hand down decisions favorable to manufacturing and business interests. (6) He also thought that "the business community was the agent of order and progress" (7) and tended to interpret the Constitution in a way that would advance its interests. . . .

(8) Marshall's decisions concerning the division of power between the federal government and the states were even more important. (9) The question of the constitutionality of a national bank . . . had not been submitted to the courts during the life of the first Bank of the United States. (10) By the time of the Second Bank there were many state banks, (11) and some of them felt that their interests were threatened by the national institution. (12) Responding to pressure from local banks, (13) the Maryland legislature placed an annual tax of $15,000 on "foreign" banks. (14) The Maryland branch of the Bank of the United States refused to pay, whereupon the state brought suit against its cashier, John W. McCulloch. (15) *McCulloch* v. *Maryland* was crucial to the Bank, (16) for five other states had levied taxes on its branches, (17) and others would surely follow suit if the Maryland law were upheld.

1. F I J	5. F I J	9. F I J	13. F I J
2. F I J	6. F I J	10. F I J	14. F I J
3. F I J	7. F I J	11. F I J	15. F I J
4. F I J	8. F I J	12. F I J	16. F I J
			17. F I J

8: Toward a National Economy

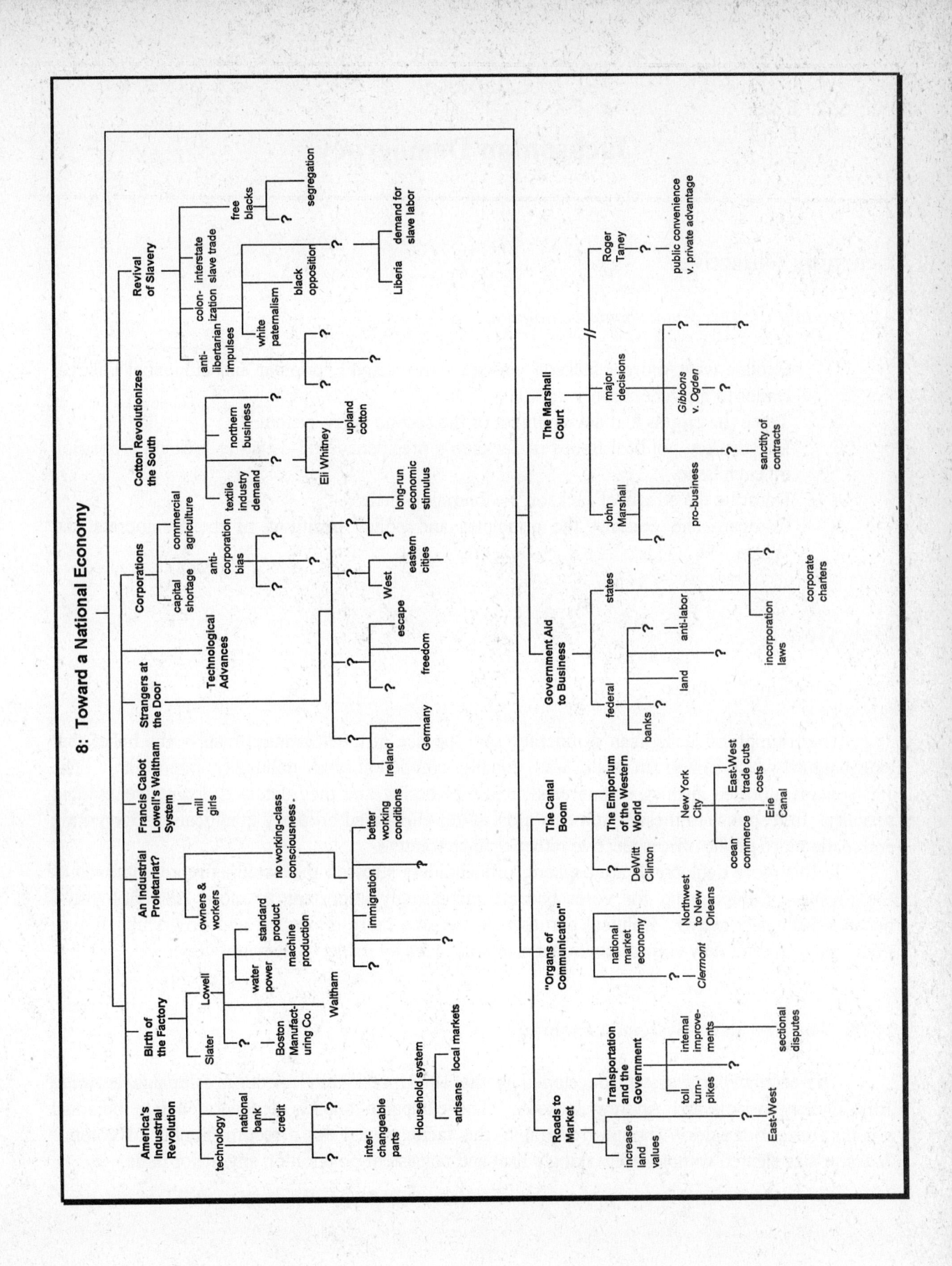

- **America's Industrial Revolution**
  - technology
    - national bank credit
    - ?
    - interchangeable parts
  - Household system
    - artisans
    - local markets

- **Birth of the Factory**
  - Slater
    - ?
    - Boston Manufacturing Co.
  - Lowell
    - water power
    - standard product
    - machine production
  - Waltham

- **An Industrial Proletariat?**
  - owners & workers
  - no working-class consciousness
    - ?
    - better working conditions
    - immigration
      - ?

- **Francis Cabot Lowell's Waltham System**
  - mill girls

- **Strangers at the Door**
  - Technological Advances
    - ?
    - Ireland
    - Germany
    - ?
    - escape freedom
    - ?
    - West
    - eastern cities
    - ?
    - long-run economic stimulus

- **Corporations**
  - capital shortage
  - commercial agriculture
  - anti-corporation bias

- **Cotton Revolutionizes the South**
  - textile industry demand
  - northern business
    - ?
  - Eli Whitney
    - upland cotton

- **Revival of Slavery**
  - anti-libertarian impulses
    - ?
  - white paternalism
    - colonization
    - interstate slave trade
    - free blacks
      - ?
      - segregation
    - black opposition
      - ?
      - Liberia
      - demand for slave labor

- **Roads to Market**
  - Transportation and the Government
    - toll turnpikes
      - ?
      - increase land values
      - East-West
    - internal improvements
      - ?
      - sectional disputes

- **"Organs of Communication"**
  - national market economy
    - ?
    - *Clermont*
    - Northwest to New Orleans

- **The Canal Boom**
  - DeWitt Clinton
  - The Emporium of the Western World
    - New York City
      - ocean commerce
      - Erie Canal
      - East-West trade cuts costs

- **Government Aid to Business**
  - federal
    - banks
    - land
  - states
    - anti-labor
      - ?
    - incorporation laws
      - corporate charters

- **The Marshall Court**
  - John Marshall
    - pro-business
    - ?
  - major decisions
    - *Gibbons v. Ogden*
      - ?
      - ?
    - sanctity of contracts
      - ?
  - Roger Taney
    - public convenience v. private advantage

125

Chapter 9

Jacksonian Democracy

Learning Objectives

After reading Chapter 9 you should be able to:

1. Explain why Andrew Jackson was such an unusually popular and influential political leader to his generation.
2. Trace the origins and development of the second party system.
3. List the key political issues of Jackson's presidency and describe Jackson's position on each issue.
4. Describe the effects of Jackson's economic policies.
5. Compare and contrast the principles and policy positions of the Democrats and Whigs.

Overview

"Democratizing" Politics

The triumph of Jacksonian democracy saw the rise of the "common man"—the belief that every adult white American male was equally competent and politically important. The Jacksonians glorified instinct, ordinariness, and mediocrity, and they detested distinctiveness and servility. In response to these sentiments most states eliminated property qualifications for voting and made more public offices elective rather than appointive.

In this more democratic atmosphere, officeholders stressed their role as representatives of the people. Campaigning for votes became increasingly important as more "common men" became politically active. Political parties now became more important and powerful. It was their role to recruit new voters in national elections, even by resort to demagoguery.

1828: The New Party System in Embryo

The second party system developed in the 1828 presidential election campaign between John Quincy Adams and Andrew Jackson. The campaign quickly degenerated into personal attacks from both sides. Though deplorable, this tactic turned out a record number of voters. Jackson was elected without ever taking a firm and consistent position on any major issue.

The Jacksonian Appeal

When he was elected president, Jackson was a wealthy planter, land speculator, and slaveowner. But, as a relatively rough-hewn and poorly educated westerner, Jackson was a perfect symbol of the new democratization of American life. Jackson epitomized many American ideals: self-madeness, patriotism, generosity, morality, tenacity, and equal opportunity. He was both an average and ideal American and was thereby able to draw voters' support from every section and social class.

The Spoils System

Jackson quickly adopted a system for replacing federal officeholders with his own supporters, a system his supporters called rotation and his opponents derisively dubbed the spoils system. Rotation, which illustrated the Jacksonians' contempt for expert knowledge, was intended to inhibit the development of an entrenched bureaucracy and allow more citizens to participate in the tasks of government—a democratic concept, but not one calculated to produce efficiency in government. The fact is, most of Jackson's appointees were not "common men," but were drawn from the same social and intellectual elite as those they replaced.

President of All the People

Jackson turned to an unofficial Kitchen Cabinet of close friends to advise him. He saw himself as the direct representative of all the people and willingly used his authority on their behalf. He vetoed more congressional bills than all his predecessors combined. He expanded the powers of the presidency, but, as a Jeffersonian, he favored limited powers for the national government. Jackson was a poor administrator, had strong prejudices, and held contempt for expert advice, but he was a strong and popular leader.

Sectional Tensions Revived

Jackson tried to steer a moderate course through sectional differences over tariff, public land, and internal improvements policies. At the time, low-tariff southerners were attempting to forge a sectional alliance with westerners who favored cheap public lands. Daniel Webster rose to defend northeastern interests in the Webster-Hayne debate and, in his second reply to Hayne, he denounced the states' rights doctrine, defended the Union, and effectively prevented a West-South alliance.

The Bank: "I Will Kill It!"

Under its president, Nicholas Biddle, the Second Bank of the United States was well managed and acted as a central bank, controlling the lending policies of state banks which, if left unregulated, caused inflation and exaggerated the business cycle. The Bank's stabilizing policies won it many supporters, but it did have opponents—hard-money advocates who feared paper money, and many state banks that disliked its regulating authority. To some it smacked of special privilege because it held a monopoly of public funds yet was governed by a handful of rich investors.

Jackson's Bank Veto

Jackson was a hard money man, suspicious of all commercial banking and paper money. Henry Clay and his National Republican party sought to use the Bank issue to undermine Jackson's popularity. Congress passed a bill to recharter the Bank in 1832, but Jackson vetoed it. He insisted the Bank was unconstitutional and an undemocratic, specially privileged institution with too many foreign investors. Jackson considered his reelection in 1832 as a mandate to destroy the Bank. At Jackson's request, Treasury Secretary Roger Taney withdrew all government funds from the Bank and deposited them in several politically sympathetic, but sound, "pet" state banks.

Jackson Versus Calhoun

John C. Calhoun was Jackson's first vice-president and he hoped to succeed Jackson to the presidency. But the two men were clashing personalities and the Peggy Eaton affair and revelations of Calhoun's criticism of Jackson's invasion of Florida in 1818 caused Jackson to question Calhoun's loyalty and honor. Nevertheless, Calhoun and Jackson were not far apart ideologically; they both believed in government economy, distributing federal treasury surpluses to the states, and limiting the power of the national government, and Jackson often took the states' rights view.

Indian Removals

Jackson was a states' rightist on Indian policies. He viewed Indians as savages who refused to adopt the white man's ways, and who could best be dealt with by removal from the path of western settlement. His removal policy led to the government purchase of tribal lands and relocation of the Indians to the Trans-Mississippi West. Many tribes were removed peacefully, but the Sac and Fox and Seminoles resisted. The Cherokees sought to escape removal by adopting white ways. They established an independent Cherokee Nation within Georgia, though Georgia refused to recognize it. In *Worcester* v. *Georgia* the Supreme Court ruled that the state of Georgia had no constitutional authority to govern the Cherokees. Jackson backed Georgia who ignored the Court, and thousands of Cherokee were removed along the "Trail of Tears" to the West. Jackson's defiance of the Court encouraged extreme states' rights southerners.

The Nullification Crisis

In 1832, southerners were dissatisfied with the new Tariff of 1832, sensitive to the rise of antislavery sentiment in the North, and fearful of slave rebellion. They felt that the tariff and slavery issues symbolized the tyranny of a northern majority, and they turned to Calhoun's doctrine of nullification for defense. South Carolina nullified the 1832 tariff. Jackson's response to this threat to the Union was twofold: He labeled the nullifiers as treasonous and called for military preparations to occupy South Carolina, but he also asked congressional leaders for a downward revision of the tariff. Other southern states did not rally to South Carolina's defense, and with an invasion threatened, Calhoun and the South Carolinian radicals settled for a compromise tariff that gradually reduced tariff rates. South Carolina withdrew its Nullification Ordinance, then embarked on a crusade to unify the South behind the states' rights doctrine.

Boom and Bust

An increase in the nation's stock of gold and silver specie encouraged the now unregulated state banks to offer easy credit, especially for land speculation. Alarmed by the speculative mania that ensued, Jackson issued the Specie Circular that required public land to be paid for in gold and silver. The paper money-fed land boom ended and banks were forced to suspend specie payments on their paper notes. Jackson's combative Bank War and his ill-considered Specie Circular contributed to a retraction of the economy.

Jacksonianism Abroad

Jackson was an exaggerated patriot. Nevertheless, his forceful yet unnecessarily blustering diplomatic style finally opened the British West Indies to American merchants and forced France to pay compensation for damages dating back to the Napoleonic wars.

The Jacksonians

By 1836, Jacksonian politics had produced a fairly cohesive Democratic party. Diverse in its make-up, the party loyal nevertheless agreed on some underlying principles: suspicion of special privilege and business monopoly, equal economic opportunity, limited national government, political freedom, and faith in the common man. Democrats generally endorsed states' rights, public education, and social equality among whites.

Rise of the Whigs

Jackson's opponents were less cohesive. Clay's National Republican party was simply anti-Jackson. But, as Jackson's second term ended his opponents began to coalesce into a new Whig party. It attracted those with a Hamiltonian view of national economic development, advocates of a strong central government, intellectuals, and fierce Jackson haters. The Whigs also appealed to ordinary people who were frightened by the excesses of individualism in Jacksonian America. But the Whig's "favorite son" nominating tactic failed in 1836, and Martin Van Buren succeeded Jackson to the presidency.

Martin Van Buren: Jacksonianism Without Jackson

Van Buren was Jackson's vice-president and a devoted Jacksonian Democrat. He opposed the National Bank, favored state-sponsored internal improvements, and equivocated on the tariff. He was preeminently a practical politician. Van Buren took office as the Panic of 1837 began, but recovery was swift. Then, in 1839, a general depression set in when cotton prices collapsed and several state governments defaulted on internal improvements debts. To the dismay of activist Whigs, Van Buren assumed a hands-off approach to the depression. Van Buren's primary maneuver was to withdraw public funds from the state banks and deposit government specie in an independent treasury. Heavy agricultural exports, foreign investment capital, and the California gold rush maintained a supply of specie in the economy.

The Log Cabin Campaign

For the 1840 presidential election the Whigs adopted Jacksonian campaign tactics and nominated a noncontroversial military hero, William Henry Harrison. They contrasted Harrison's simple, brave, honest public spiritedness with Van Buren's "aristocratic" ways. The Whig's log cabin and hard cider campaign was too much for Van Buren who tried to campaign on the issues. A huge turnout of voters elected Harrison. Harrison had little stomach for strong presidential leadership and Whig leaders Henry Clay and Daniel Webster anticipated congressional control of the administration. But Harrison died shortly after his inauguration and Vice-President John Tyler's elevation to the presidency confronted congressional Whigs with unanticipated problems.

People, Places, and Things

Define the following:

common man _Ordinary white male citizens made mediocrity a virtue_

Jacksonian democracy _was more attitude than of practice. Said people knew what was right by instinct._

disestablishment _____

equality of opportunity _every American could become anything given the opportunity._

spoils system ~~the victor~~ Jacksons' people who filled gov. jobs

rotation Jackson replaced federal office holders with his own supporters

distribution _____

removal removed Indians + sent out west

Describe the following:

Election of 1828 Jackson won - smear campaine on both sides

Webster-Hayne debate Hayne (West + South - low Tariffs + cheap land - states rights - Webster - Northern interests 2 days + blocked vote - All Americans said No - took floor

Peggy Eaton affair wife of Sec of War had affair before marriage with Eaton while married to another, snubbed by Calhoun's wife - Jackson took offense

Maysville Road veto the road in Kentucky + it was up to state to fund + build

Worcester v. Georgia Supreme Court ruled Georgia had no constitutional right to govern the Cherokees

Trail of Tears thousands of Cherokees removed to west 4,000 many died from starvation + exposure

Nullification Crisis S. Carolina nullified was going to Tariff of 1832 (Calhoun's doctrine of nullification) Because of slavery + High Tariff Jackson - said it was treasonous + was going to send troups.

131

Bank War _Fight between Jackson + ~~Taney~~ Biddle over the lending of money_

"pet" banks _Favored state banks that received fed. funds._

Specie Circular _Purchasers of public land had to pay in gold or silver_

Panic of 1837 _every bank in country had to suspend specie payments. Speculators couldn't get rid of land + people panicked + tryed to get money out of banks._

Independent Treasury Act _All payments made to government had to be made in hard cash_

Election of 1840 _Log Cabin Campaign - Harrison died_

Identify the following:

Andrew Jackson _Pres. of U.S., Indian fighter - liked common + ordanary_

John C. Calhoun _1st Vice Pres. under Jackson_

Denmark Vesey _ex-slave organized revolt in Charleston 1822 - But was discovered_

Nat Turner _uprising of slaves in Virginia led by Nat Turner in 1831_

Nicholas Biddle _President of Nat Bank of America from Philadelphia - wanted "sound" banking_

[handwritten at top: withdrew all gov. funds from bank + put in "pet" banks / state]

Roger Taney — *former Sec. of Treasury seceeded John Marshall as Supreme Court Justice 1836*

Jacksonian Democrats — *included all people, suspicous of Bank, Co's freedom of economic opportunity, political freedom*

Whigs — *Henry Clay's Republican party - against Jackson joined with others who wanted strong gov. for bank - intellectuals + fierce Jackson haters*

Martin Van Buren — *Vice Pres. under Jackson*

William Henry Harrison — *Hero of Tippecanoe - son of Benjamin H. signer of Dec. of Independence*

Self-Test

Multiple-Choice Questions

1. An important political change of the 1820s was that
   A. senators began to be elected by popular vote rather than by state legislatures
   B. issues became the key subjects of political campaigns rather than personalities
   C. free blacks and women were allowed full political freedom
   (D.) most states removed the property qualification for voting from their constitutions

2. Andrew Jackson's popularity as a presidential candidate in 1828 was in large part due to his
   A. determination to take a clear and consistent stand on controversial issues
   B. dislike for political parties and popular campaigning
   (C.) image as a strong-willed, self-made man of the people
   D. devotion to reason and expert advice in the making of public policy

3. Which one of the following is LEAST related to the other three?
   A. political appointment
   B. the spoils system
   (C.) disestablishment
   D. rotation

4. In the Webster-Hayne debate, Daniel Webster
   (A.) attacked the doctrine of states' rights
   B. introduced the possibility of distributing federal treasury surpluses to the states

    C.   blamed Jackson for the suffering along the Trail of Tears
    D.   urged Jackson to veto the Maysville Road Bill

5. Of the following, the BEST example of Jackson's advocacy of limited federal government was his
   A. action during the Nullification Crisis
   B. issuing the Specie Circular
   C. veto of the Maysville Road Bill
   D. adoption of the rotation system of federal appointment

6. Indian removal was an example of President Jackson's usual endorsement of
   A. protectionism
   B. nullification
   C. states' rights
   D. internal improvements

7. In *Worcester* v. *Georgia* the Supreme Court ruled that
   A. the Second Bank of the United States was constitutional
   B. a state could not nullify an act of Congress
   C. Indian tribes were independent of federal authority
   D. Indian tribes could not be governed by states

8. The Nullification Crisis of 1832 involved a dispute over
   A. distribution of federal surpluses
   B. protective tariffs
   C. internal improvements
   D. public land policy

9. The Tariff of 1832 was declared null and void by
   A. the South Carolina state legislature
   B. the governor of South Carolina
   C. a state convention in South Carolina
   D. the South Carolina state Supreme Court

10. President Jackson viewed South Carolina's Ordinance of Nullification
    A. as treasonous
    B. indifferently
    C. as a legitimate expression of states' rights
    D. as a peaceful means of preserving the Union

11. The Nullification crisis was resolved by all these actions EXCEPT
    A. the Ordinance of Nullification was repealed
    B. other southern states' refusal to support nullification
    C. the 1832 tariff rates were gradually reduced
    D. the U.S. Army temporarily occupied South Carolina and collected the tariffs

12. Andrew Jackson liked
    A. banks
    B. high protective tariffs
    C. Indians
    D. state-financed internal improvements projects

13. The Second Bank of the United States was opposed by all of the following EXCEPT
    A. most hard-money men
    B. Henry Clay
    C. Martin Van Buren
    D. many state banks

14. When he vetoed the recharter bill, Jackson argued that the Second Bank of the United States
    A. overextended financial credit
    B. was too lenient in its loan policies
    C. refused to pay off the national debt
    D. was a privileged monopoly of the rich

15. After his reelection in 1832, Andrew Jackson weakened the Second Bank of the United states by
    A. firing its president, Nicholas Biddle
    B. removing all government deposits from it
    C. revoking its existing charter
    D. moving its headquarters from Philadelphia to New York

16. President Jackson's 1836 Specie Circular
    A. outlawed paper money
    B. required federal funds to be deposited in "pet" banks
    C. directed that public land purchases be paid for in gold and silver
    D. distributed surplus federal funds back to the states

17. Jacksonian Democrats tended to oppose
    A. free public schools
    B. equal economic opportunity
    C. the rise of the common man
    D. central banking

18. In contrast to the Democrats, Whigs
    A. were states' rightists
    B. had no effective congressional leadership
    C. admired the strong presidency
    D. favored federal aid to economic development

19. The Independent Treasury Act of 1840 appealed most to
    A. Whigs
    B. land speculators

C. hard-money men
D. "pet" banks

20. The dominant symbol of the Whig presidential campaign in 1840 was a
    A. gold coin
    B. rifle
    C. bank
    D. log cabin

Essay Questions

1. Account for Andrew Jackson's appeal to ordinary voters in the 1820s and 1830s. Stress especially his personal qualities and his symbolic representation of democracy.
2. Describe the role of Andrew Jackson, Martin Van Buren, Henry Clay, Daniel Webster, and John C. Calhoun in the development of the second party system.
3. Describe the Nullification Crisis' impact on sectional tensions and national harmony. What role did tariff policy, slavery, and southern unity play in its origins and resolution?
4. Explain why Jackson opposed the Second Bank of the United States. What were his motives; what actions did he take; and what effects did they have?
5. Compare and contrast the views of Jacksonian Democrats and the Whigs both on matters of political principles and their positions on public issues.

Critical Thinking Exercise

Compare and Contrast

In earlier chapters you witnessed the common use of comparing and contrasting relationships as a tool historians use to organize information. Chapter 9 discusses the political principles and public policy views of the Jacksonian Democrats and the Whigs—the two major parties of the second party system. In the chart on page 137, indicate with a simple "favored," "opposed," or similar brief notation the position generally or usually taken by each of the two parties on the political principles and public policies indicated. (Note: Starred (*) boxes indicate additional principles and policy views discussed in the chapter on which Democrats and Whigs held views. You are to define these issues and complete these boxes as well.) Try to *infer* a party's position where no direct evidence is presented in the text.

PRINCIPLES AND POLICY VIEWS OF DEMOCRATS AND WHIGS		
	WHIGS	**DEMOCRATS**
Views on . . .		
states' rights		
equal opportunity		
common man		
strong presidency		
*		
*		
Positions on . . .		
distribution of federal surplus		
Indian removal		
protective tariffs		
Specie Circular		
federal internal improvements		
Independent Treasury		
*		
*		

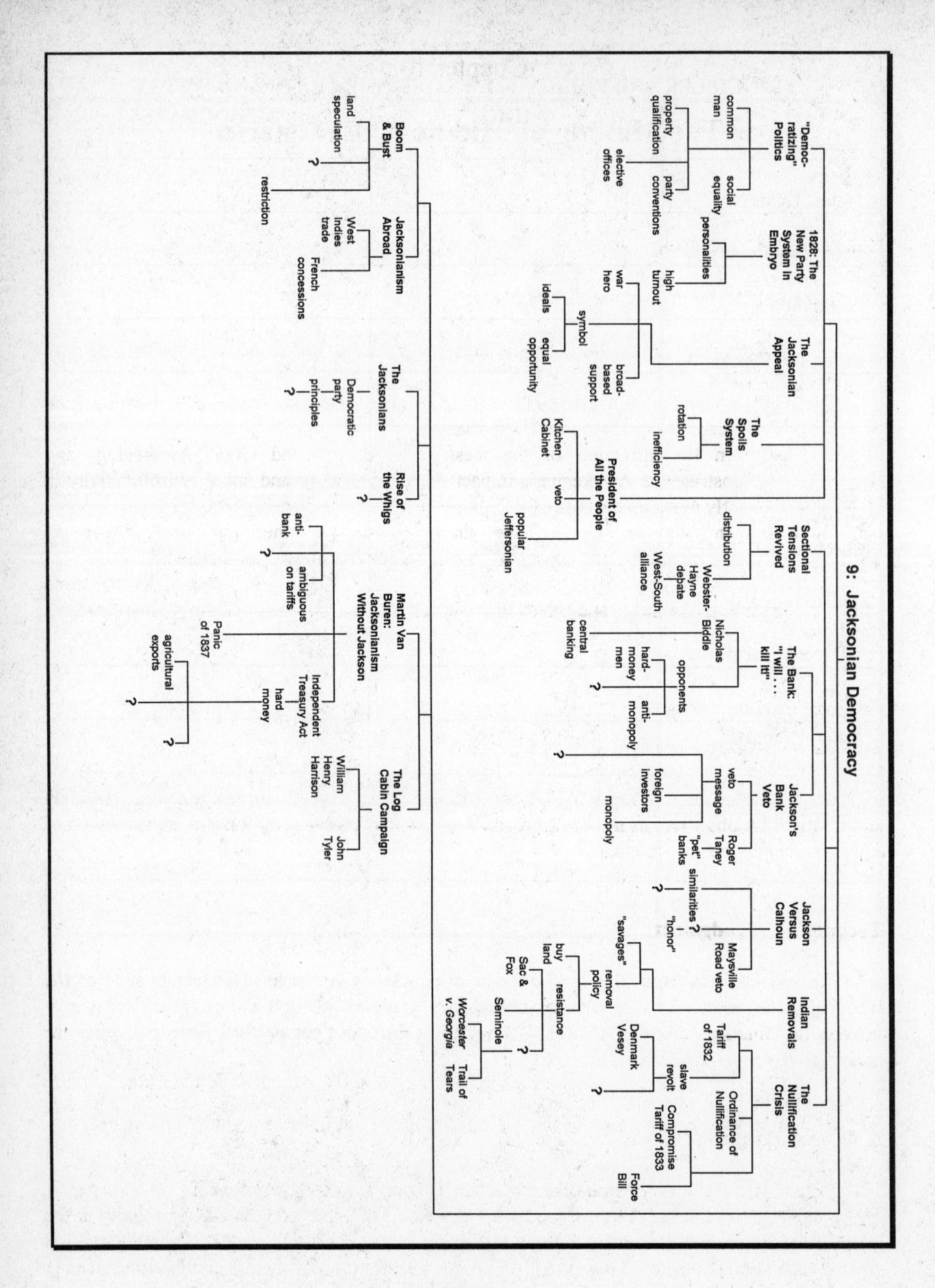

9: Jacksonian Democracy

"Democratizing" Politics
- common man
- property qualification
- elective offices
- social equality
- party conventions
- personalities

1828: The New Party System in Embryo
- high turnout
- personalities

The Jacksonian Appeal
- war hero
- symbol
  - ideals
  - equal opportunity
- broad-based support

The Spoils System
- rotation
- inefficiency

President of All the People
- Kitchen Cabinet
- veto
- popular Jeffersonian

Sectional Tensions Revived
- distribution
- Webster-Hayne debate
- West-South alliance

The Bank: "I will... kill it!"
- Nicholas Biddle
- opponents
  - hard-money men
  - anti-monopoly
- central banking

Jackson's Bank Veto
- veto message
  - foreign investors
  - monopoly
- Roger Taney
- "pet" banks

Jackson Versus Calhoun
- similarities ?
- "honor"
- Maysville Road veto

Indian Removals
- removal policy
  - "savages"
  - buy land
- resistance
  - Sac & Fox
  - Seminole ?
- Worcester v. Georgia
- Trail of Tears

The Nullification Crisis
- Tariff of 1832
- slave revolt
  - Denmark Vesey
- Ordinance of Nullification
- Compromise Tariff of 1833
- Force Bill

Jacksonianism Abroad
- West Indies trade
- French concessions

Boom & Bust
- land speculation ?
- restriction

The Jacksonians
- Democratic party principles ?

Rise of the Whigs
- anti-bank
- ambiguous on tariffs ?

Martin Van Buren: Jacksonianism Without Jackson
- Panic of 1837
  - agricultural exports ?
- Independent Treasury Act
  - hard money ?

The Log Cabin Campaign
- William Henry Harrison
- John Tyler

138

Chapter 10

The Making of Middle-Class America

Learning Objectives

After reading Chapter 10 you should be able to:

1. Summarize Alexis de Tocqueville's observations about early nineteenth-century America.
2. State how early industrialization changed the American family and describe how Americans compensated for these changes.
3. Explain the attraction of the message in the Second Great Awakening, and demonstrate the Awakening's impact on social thought and social reform activity in the early nineteenth century.
4. Explain why so many early nineteenth-century Americans were drawn to communitarianism, and describe some of the peculiarities of communal life.
5. State the origins of early nineteenth-century social reform movements, list the most significant of these, and assess their impact on early nineteenth-century American life.

Overview

Tocqueville and Beaumont in America

In 1831, Frenchman Alexis de Tocqueville toured the new American republic extensively and wrote of his observations in *Democracy in America*, a classic description and interpretation of early nineteenth century America.

Tocqueville in Judgment

Tocqueville was captivated by the theme of equality in America. This was in spite of the fact that there was at the time a wide and growing gap between rich and poor and substantial poverty in American cities. But, from Tocqueville's European perspective, America seemed to be an undifferentiated middle-class society.

A Restless People

Visitors to early nineteenth-century America were struck by the mobility of Americans, partly the result of the high rate of population growth. Many moved to seek opportunity in the West, from which five new states entered the Union in the 1830s and 1840s. Others moved to towns and cities. Population movement from farms to cities produced both spectacular growth in the large cities and the emergence of new towns, especially in the Northeast and Northwest. However, only the perimeter of the South experienced significant urban growth.

Off to Work

Before 1830 most nonagricultural jobs were performed in the household. Even in cities, the typical worker was an artisan—a skilled craftsman or shopkeeper who worked in his own home. In the 1820s and 1830s, household artisans began to take on wage-earning unskilled workers and use economies of scale to expand production. Elaborate rules governing worker behavior replaced the personal relationships of the apprentice system. The growing size of the artisan's business forced its movement out of his home and into factories. This resulted in the segregation of cities into residential and commercial districts.

The Family Recast

The factory system and the growth of cities diminished the importance of home and family as the unit of economic production. More and more breadwinners worked outside the home, and this had an enormous impact on traditional family roles. In the absence of their husbands, middle-class wives and mothers exercised more authority and enjoyed more prestige. Still, the doctrine of "separate spheres" and the "cult of true womanhood" confined middle-class women to the home, where they were expected to tend only to family matters.

The middle class made a conscious effort to limit family size. People married later and the birth rate declined. As families became smaller, relations within them became more caring. Children in the smaller family were lavished with attention and affection by mothers who had little opportunity to direct their attention or passions outside the home and family.

The Second Great Awakening

The growing belief in the innate goodness of children was but one attack on orthodox Calvinist doctrine. A new evangelical revivalism, the Second Great Awakening, also set aside the doctrine of predestination and the arbitrary power of God. Evangelist Charles Grandison Finney urged his followers to take their salvation into their own hands; salvation was available to all. This optimistic message and the entertaining methods of the evangelists enormously increased church membership. Those uprooted by the growth of industry and commerce were attracted to this comforting message of personal salvation. Women, charged with the spiritual education of their children, were also drawn to evangelical revivalism. They founded the Female Missionary Society and even moved outside their homes and paternalistic, authoritarian churches to organize the salvation of anxious souls.

The Era of Associations

Voluntary associations joined the family and church as an institutional pillar of the middle class. These uniquely American associations formed around local issues such as care for orphans or combating drunkenness. Together, they formed a "benevolent empire" of aid and comfort for those without families to provide for them.

Backwoods Utopias

Some reformers tested their reform theories by withdrawing from society and establishing experimental communities. The first of these communitarians were religious reformers such as the Rappites, Shakers, and the Oneida community. The most important religious communitarians were the Mormons. Their unorthodox views, such as polygamy and their sense of being a chosen people, forced them to migrate eventually to the Great Salt Lake where the faith has flourished ever since.

Secular communitarians included the utopian socialists Robert Owen and Charles Fourier. Owen's advocacy of free love and atheism doomed his communes, but Fourier's cooperative phalanxes enjoyed some temporary success.

The Age of Reform

Other reformers assumed the responsibility for caring for the physically and mentally disabled and for the rehabilitation of criminals. These reformers, convinced that people were primarily shaped by their surroundings, established specialized institutions (orphanages, prisons, asylums) for dealing with social problems. Life in these institutions was highly disciplined and aimed toward rehabilitation.

"Demon Rum"

The temperance movement was the most widely supported and successful reform movement of the time. Americans in the 1820s consumed prodigious amounts of alcohol. Men routinely drank at work and in taverns. The American Temperance Union and the Washingtonians conducted educational campaigns against drunkenness—which they considered the root of crime and social decay. Temperance organizers eventually reached beyond exhortation to demand legal prohibition of alcohol. Their major success came in the Maine Law of 1851 that prohibited the manufacture and sale of alcoholic beverages.

The Abolitionist Crusade

The most significant and provocative reform movement was abolitionism—the drive to abolish slavery. In 1831, William Lloyd Garrison began publication of *The Liberator* newspaper where he pronounced himself in favor of immediate abolitionism and racial equality. His radical brand of abolitionism provoked opposition even in the North. Most abolitionists took a more moderate approach, settling for gradual abolition of slavery through political means. This wing of abolitionism founded the Liberty party.

Frederick Douglass, a former slave, was the most visible of the many free blacks who participated in the abolitionist movement. Like Garrison, he demanded the end of slavery and full equality for blacks, but Douglass was willing to work within the political system. Unlike Garrison, but like most other abolitionists, Douglass was not a moral perfectionist and did not denounce the Constitution even though it countenanced slavery.

Women's Rights

The women's rights movement was closely related to abolitionism. Women came to see that, like blacks, they were discriminated against by a social and legal system that subordinated them and prevented them from achieving their full potential. Thus, most women's rights activists began their reform careers as abolitionists, but, faced with sexual discrimination in that movement, they turned their efforts to women's rights. They campaigned for the right to vote, the right to own property, and the opportunity to participate in affairs outside the home. They stated their movement's principles at the Seneca Falls Convention in 1848. Feminists achieved few practical results at the time, but they persevered.

People, Places, and Things

Define the following:

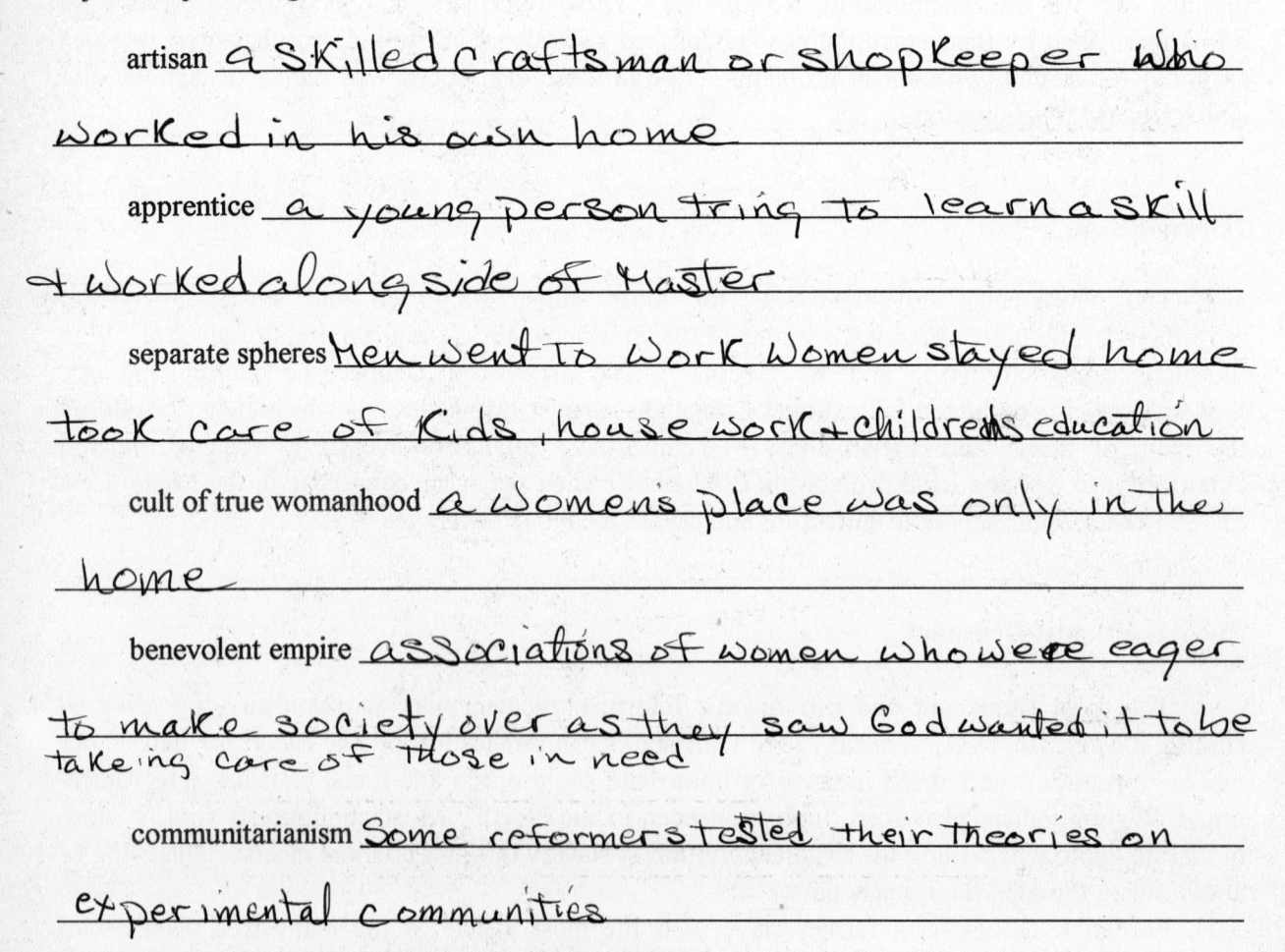

artisan _a skilled craftsman or shopkeeper who worked in his own home_

apprentice _a young person trying to learn a skill & worked alongside of master_

separate spheres _Men went to work Women stayed home took care of kids, housework + childrens education_

cult of true womanhood _a women's place was only in the home_

benevolent empire _associations of women who were eager to make society over as they saw God wanted it to be taking care of those in need_

communitarianism _Some reformers tested their theories on experimental communities_ polygamy _Mormons - having more than one wife_

temperance _Womens' groups to ban liqur - root of crime + decay_

abolitionism _____

Describe the following:

Democracy in America _Tocqueville's Book on America_

Second Great Awakening _New wave of revivalism to set aside predestination, infant damnation, Promise of salvation_

Female Missionary Society _1826 - the start of a Nat. crusade against drunkenness_

American Temperance Union _____

Washingtonians _1840 - organization of reformed drunkards - set out to reclaim alcoholics_

Maine Law _1851 - prohibited the manufacture + sale of alcoholic beverages_

The Liberator _Newspaper in favor of immediate freedom of slaves_

Liberty party _____

Seneca Falls Convention _____

Identify the following:

Alexis de Tocqueville French aristocrats to study America

Charles Grandison Finney Revivalist minister against booze

Rappites formed by George Rapp renounced sex + marriage + took every word in Bible

Ann Lee English women - Mother Ann - saw visions - Crist came back as women + that she was Crist.

Shakers Celibrant, believed end was near - equal work + reward made simple but beautifull furniture

Mormons many wives, exclusivism, chosen people

Joseph Smith Founded mormons - saw visions - murdered by mob

Brigham Young took over leadership took to Salt lake City

Robert Owen Brit. utopian bought the rappite settlement Free love + enlightened atheism

Charles Fourier French - members worked when they wanted + were paid more for repulsive work

Dorthea Dix <u>Pioneer reformer to improve life for insane in U.S.</u>

William Lloyd Garrison <u>Founder + editor of Liberator - leading antislavery publication</u>

Theodore Dwight Weld <u>minister part of Garrison's group - split + formed new group</u>

James G. Birney <u>a Kentucky slaveholder converted to evangelical Christ + abolitionism by Weld - ran for Pres.</u>

Frederick Douglass <u>ex slave effective spokesman against slavery</u>

Sarah and Angelina Grimke <u>began careers in abol. movement leading advocates of womens' rights</u>

Elizabeth Cady Stanton <u>Helped draft Declaration sentiments</u>

Susan B. Anthony <u>reformer - womens' rights</u>

Locate the following places: Write in both the place name and its map location number.

1. America's three largest cities in 1830.

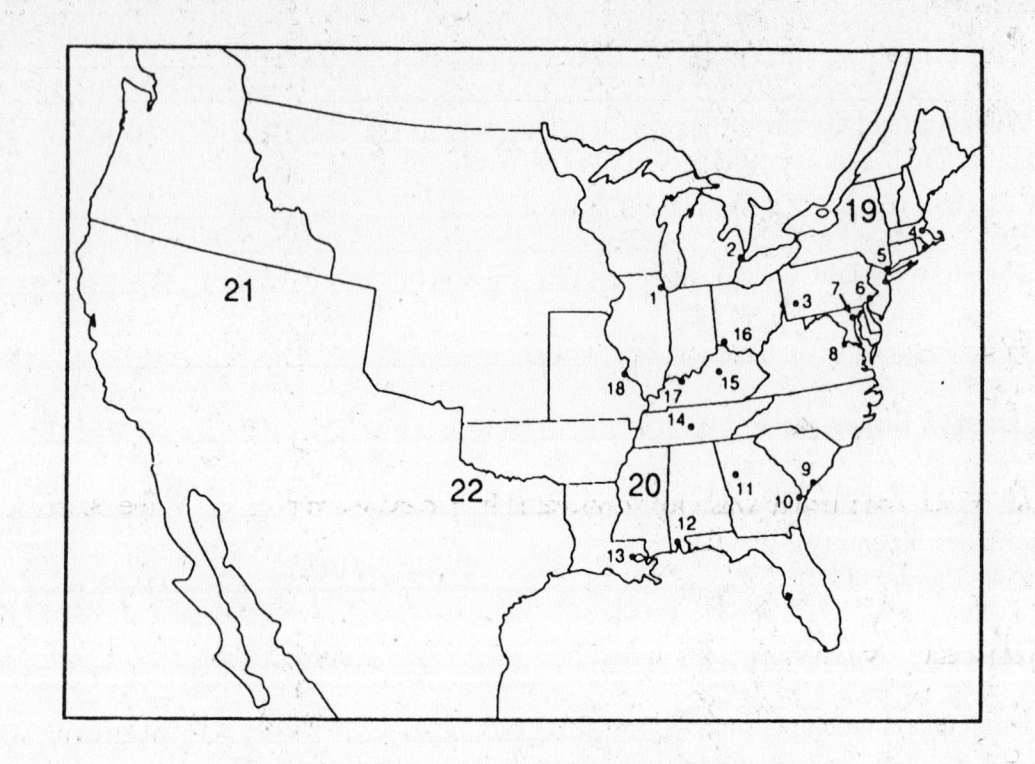

2. Five new towns that developed in the Ohio-Mississippi River Valley as population moved West in the 1820s and 1830s.

_____ _____
_____ _____
_____ _____
_____ _____
_____ _____

3. The five major cities in the South in the 1820s and 1830s.

_____ _____
_____ _____
_____ _____
_____ _____
_____ _____

4. The "burned-over district" evangelized by Second Great Awakening revivalists in the 1820s and 1830s.

   _____   _____

5. Site of the Mormon settlement in the Far West.

   _____   _____

Self-Test

Multiple-Choice Question

1. Alexis de Tocqueville was most captivated by the evidence of _____ he observed in early nineteenth-century America.
   A. racism
   B. poverty
   C. equality
   D. patriotism

2. In early nineteenth-century American cities, inequalities of wealth
   A. were narrowing
   B. were widening
   C. remained stable
   D. began to appear for the first time

3. Most early nineteenth-century Americans moved frequently in search of
   A. peace and solitude
   B. economic opportunity
   C. close and lasting social relationships
   D. a healthier climate

4. All of the following accompanied the industrial revolution in early nineteenth-century America EXCEPT
   A. rapid population growth
   B. growth in the size and number of cities
   C. increase in the size of families
   D. a declining birthrate

5. Household industries in early nineteenth-century America usually involved all the following EXCEPT
   A. work and production in a home
   B. family ownership of the firm
   C. use of apprentice workers
   D. a complex division of labor

147

6. Which one of the following LEAST influenced women's role in early nineteenth-century America?
    A. the doctrine of separate spheres
    B. the women's rights movement
    C. the cult of true womanhood
    D. their economic class

7. The early nineteenth-century's expectations of true womanhood included all of the following EXCEPT
    A. religious education
    B. marital submissiveness
    C. the nurture of children
    D. public service

8. In the early nineteenth century, America's birth rate began to fall for all the following reasons EXCEPT
    A. young people began marrying later
    B. the willful practice of sexual abstinence
    C. the overall slower growth of the population
    D. couples waiting longer to have children

9. The leading evangelist of the Second Great Awakening was
    A. William Lloyd Garrison.
    B. Charles Grandison Finney
    C. James G. Birney
    D. Theodore Dwight Weld

10. The Second Great Awakening evangelists expressed the belief that
    A. each individual could make a personal choice for his or her own salvation
    B. infants were born in innate sin
    C. God predetermined who would receive His grace
    D. God revealed his Word by divine revelation

11. Early nineteenth century middle-class families were becoming all the following EXCEPT
    A. smaller in size
    B. a more intimate and caring group
    C. more a unit of economic productivity
    D. more socially active

12. The "three pillars" of early nineteenth-century American middle-class life included all the following EXCEPT
    A. church
    B. family
    C. voluntary associations
    D. political parties

13. The most important and long-lasting religious communitarian movement of the early nineteenth century was the
    A. utopian socialists
    B. Shakers
    C. Mormons
    D. abolitionists

14. Robert Owen's New Harmony and Charles Fourier's phalanxes were both experiments in
    A. economic classicism
    B. utopian socialism
    C. religious communalism
    D. evangelical revivalism

15. Most early nineteenth-century reformers believed that people's lives were primarily shaped by
    A. predestination
    B. their social environment
    C. human nature
    D. fate

16. The most widely supported and successful reform movement on the early nineteenth century was
    A. temperance
    B. abolition
    C. women's rights
    D. communalism

17. Which one of the following is LEAST related to the other three?
    A. Washingtonian societies
    B. Maine laws
    C. abolitionism
    D. temperance

18. Immediate abolitionists argued that the best way to end slavery was by
    A. persuading Americans that slavery was a moral evil
    B. colonizing freed slaves back to Africa
    C. freeing slaves' children as they reached maturity
    D. compensating slaveowners for freeing their slaves

19. Match the names on the left with their role in abolitionism.

    A. William Lloyd Garrison   1. black abolitionist
    B. Frederick Douglass   2. radical abolitionist
    C. James G. Birney   3. abolitionist financier
                                   4. abolitionist candidate

    A. A-1, B-2, C-3
    B. A-2, B-4, C-1

149

C. A-2, B-1, C-4
D. A-3, B-1, C-2

20. The principles of the women's rights movement that were formulated at the Seneca Falls convention came in a document patterned after the
    A. Magna Carta
    B. Constitution
    C. Declaration of Independence
    D. *The Liberator*

Essay Questions

1. Assess the accuracy of Tocqueville's view of early nineteenth-century America as a land of equality. Cite evidence of unusual equality as well as the absence of equality in various aspects of American life at the time.
2. Assume the role of the head of a middle-class household in the 1820s. Describe how the changes taking place in the national economy affect your family's life and how you are coping with those changes.
3. Explain how evangelical churches and voluntary associations compensated for changes the industrial revolution brought to the American family.
4. Choose one of the communitarian experiments mentioned in the chapter, assume the role as one of its members, and describe a day in your life in the commune.
5. Choose what you think were the two most significant early nineteenth-century reform movements, tell why you chose those two, and assess their importance to American history.

Critical Thinking Exercise

Cause and Effect

In earlier chapters you completed exercises on causal chains and contributory causes to a single effect. Often, however, there will be several *effects* to a given cause or complex of causes.

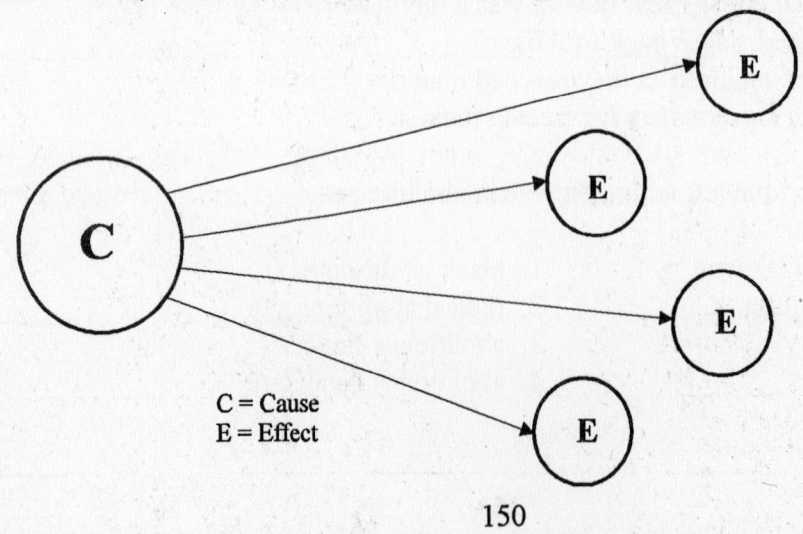

C = Cause
E = Effect

Chapter 10 focuses on the effects of economic change and social reform in the early nineteenth century. In the several groups below, mark out the items that were **not** effects of the stated cause(s), then write a sentence that expresses the cause and effect relationship in each group.

1. Cause: Population mobility
   Effects: transformation of southern society, increase in the number of towns, population growth in the West, reduction in the gap between rich and poor, growth in size of large cities

   _____
   _____
   _____

2. Cause: Emergence of the factory system
   Effects: division of cities into residential and occupational areas, adoption of a wage payment system, growth of the apprenticeship system, decline of household industry, increased opportunities for skilled labor

   _____
   _____
   _____

3. Cause: Growth of industry
   Effects: increased family income, improved living standards, new economic opportunities for women, decline of child labor, emergence of an organized working class

   _____
   _____
   _____

4. Causes: Growth of the factory system and cities
   Effects: overall increase in family size, increased family intimacy, reduced economic importance of the family, ending of the "cult of true womanhood," increased prestige and authority for wives/mothers.

   _____
   _____
   _____

5. Cause: Second Great Awakening
   Effects: mobilization of women to social action, increasing church membership, renewal of the doctrine of predestination, decline of Calvinist theology, heightened hopes for personal salvation

6. Cause: Abolitionist movement
   Effect: caused some to question the morality of slavery, dramatically increased popular commitment to racial equality, provoked controversy among antislavery northerners, softened southern views on slavery, spawned a women's rights movement

9: Jacksonian Democracy

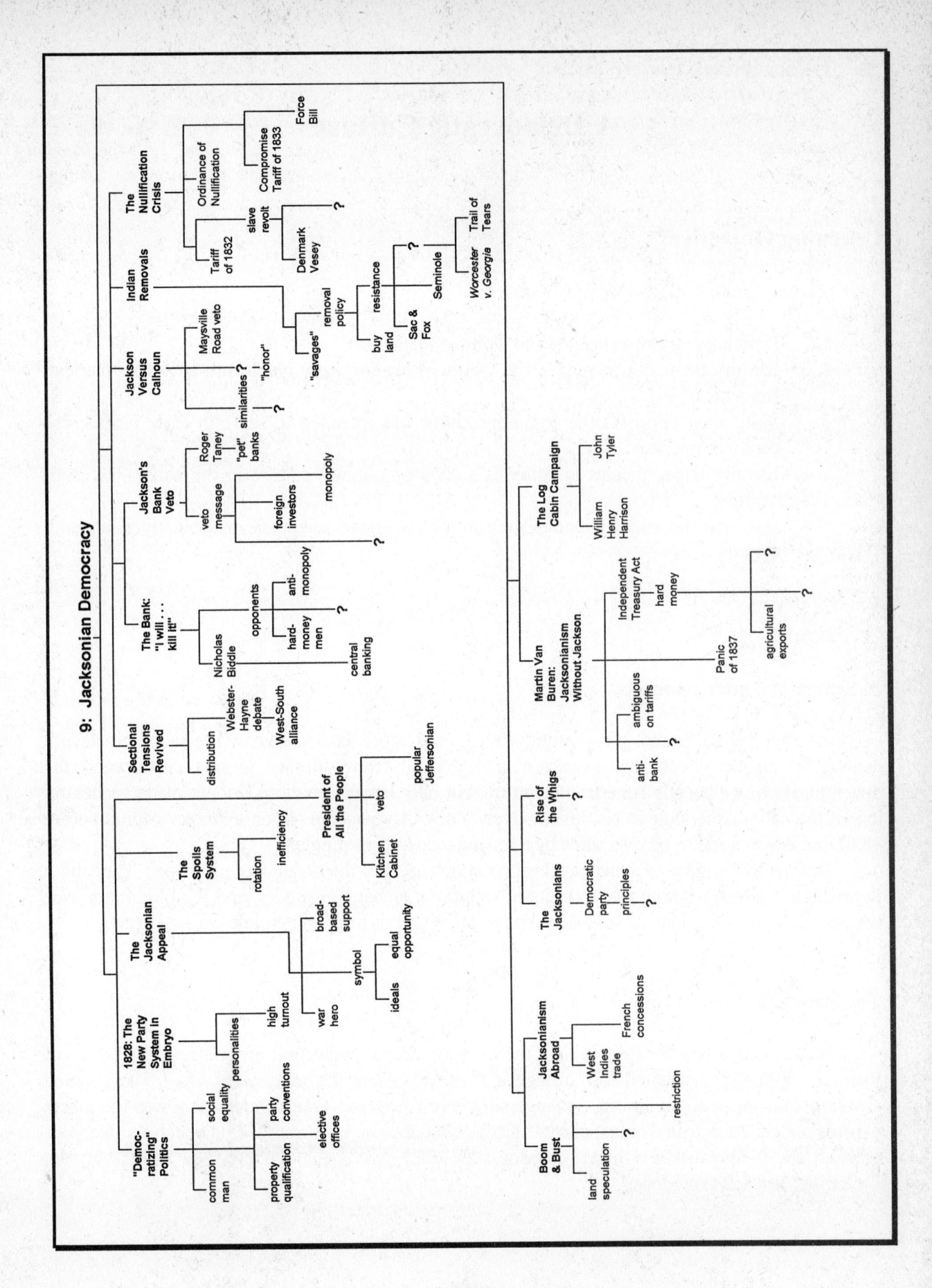

- **"Democ-ratizing" Politics**
  - common man
  - property qualification
    - social equality
    - elective offices
  - party conventions
- **1828: The New Party System in Embryo**
  - personalities
  - high turnout
- **The Jacksonian Appeal**
  - war hero
  - symbol
    - broad-based support
    - ideals
    - equal opportunity
- **The Spoils System**
  - rotation
  - inefficiency
- **President of All the People**
  - Kitchen Cabinet
  - veto
  - popular Jeffersonian
- **Sectional Tensions Revived**
  - distribution
  - Webster-Hayne debate
  - West-South alliance
- **The Bank: "I will . . . kill it!"**
  - Nicholas Biddle
  - opponents
    - anti-monopoly
    - hard-money men
    - ?
  - central banking
- **Jackson's Bank Veto**
  - veto message
  - Roger Taney
  - "pet" banks
  - foreign investors
  - monopoly
  - ?
- **Jackson Versus Calhoun**
  - similarities
  - ?
  - "honor"
  - Maysville Road veto
- **Indian Removals**
  - "savages"
  - removal policy
    - buy land
    - resistance
      - Sac & Fox
      - Seminole
      - ?
      - Worcester v. Georgia
      - Trail of Tears
- **The Nullification Crisis**
  - Tariff of 1832
  - slave revolt
    - Denmark Vesey
    - ?
  - Ordinance of Nullification
    - Compromise Tariff of 1833
    - Force Bill
- **The Jacksonians**
  - Democratic party principles
  - ?
- **Rise of the Whigs**
  - ?
- **Martin Van Buren: Jacksonianism Without Jackson**
  - anti-bank
  - ambiguous on tariffs
  - ?
  - Panic of 1837
    - agricultural exports
    - ?
  - Independent Treasury Act
    - hard money
    - ?
- **The Log Cabin Campaign**
  - William Henry Harrison
  - John Tyler
- **Jacksonianism Abroad**
  - West Indies trade
  - French concessions
- **Boom & Bust**
  - land speculation
  - ?
  - restriction

153

Chapter 11

A Democratic Culture

Learning Objectives

After reading Chapter 11 you should be able to:

1. Define literary romanticism and Transcendentalism.
2. Identify the major themes in the works of leading early nineteenth-century American romantics.
3. State what purposes the common school was intended to serve in early nineteenth-century America.
4. Identify major themes in America's civic or popular culture in the early nineteenth century.
5. Describe the major accomplishments of American scientists in the early nineteenth century.

Overview

In Search of Native Grounds

As the United States grew larger, richer, and more centralized in the early nineteenth century, a distinctly democratic culture emerged. Eastern literary groups encouraged the development of a distinctly American literature, but only James Fenimore Cooper made successful use of the national heritage in his novels. New York City was the nation's literary capital before 1830, but it was soon to be overtaken by a renaissance in New England.

Before 1830 most of America's best painters received their training in Europe. They did a flourishing business painting the portraits of wealthy merchants, planters, and Revolutionary War heroes. Self-trained primitive artists catered to the tastes of rural and middle-class patrons.

The Romantic View of Life

Romanticism was a revolt against the cold logic and intellectual orderliness of the Age of Reason. Romantics believed that change and growth were the essence of life. They valued intuition, individualism, optimism, and ingenuity. New England Transcendentalism was the fullest expression of American romanticism. Transcendentalists subordinated intellect to feelings, stressed the uniqueness and innate goodness of each individual, and glorified nature, human aspiration, and self-confidence.

Emerson and Thoreau

The leading Transcendentalist was the American philosopher Ralph Waldo Emerson. In "The American Scholar" he urged Americans to seek inspiration in America's own natural surroundings. Although he was confident that change would bring progress, he was too much the individualist and idealist to accept the cooperation and compromises required of an active social reformer. His faith in self-reliance made him an opponent of powerful government, but he did admire strong leadership.

Rampant materialism disgusted Henry David Thoreau. Like Emerson, he was a stubborn individualist and objected to social restrictions and strong government. In a hermitlike experiment he tried to demonstrate that man need not depend on society for a satisfying existence. His book, *Walden,* is an indictment of social conformity. In "Civil Disobedience" he justified the right of a citizen to disobey an unjust or immoral law, yet, like Emerson, he refused to participate in organized reform movements.

Edgar Allan Poe

Romantic poet Edgar Allan Poe was haunted by melancholia throughout his relatively short life. His highly imaginative works reveal his fascination with mystery, fright, and the occult. He perfected the detective story, dealt with science fiction themes, and was a master of the horror story. His poem "The Raven" was instantly popular.

Nathaniel Hawthorne

Novelist and short story writer Nathaniel Hawthorne disliked the egoism and bland optimism of the Transcendentalists. He made excellent use of New England history as background, but his works were chiefly concerned with the individual's struggle with sin, guilt, and pride. His *The Scarlet Letter* perfectly reflected these themes.

Herman Melville

Like his friend, Nathaniel Hawthorne, Herman Melville could not accept the pervasive optimism of his day, but he did admire Emerson and, like Emerson, he protested the subordination of human beings to machines. Melville dealt with the dark side of human nature in *Moby Dick,* a subtle and symbolic treatment of good and evil, faith and pride. It is one of the world's finest novels, but, unlike Poe and Hawthorne, Melville's work was little appreciated by his contemporaries.

Walt Whitman

Walt Whitman was the most romantic and authentically American writer of his age. Like Hawthorne, he was politically active, but he greatly admired Emerson and the Transcendentalists, especially their view that inspiration and aspiration, not intellect, were at the heart of all human achievement. His free verse poetry in *Leaves of Grass* reflects his uncritical and undisciplined reliance on natural inclinations.

The Wider Literary Renaissance

Although less profound and original than his famous New England contemporaries, Henry Wadsworth Longfellow's many poems were enormously popular. And he captured the spirit of his times better than any of them. New Englanders also dominated the writing of history. These avidly read histories were written for a popular audience and incorporated romantic themes. Southern literature was even more romantic than that of New England. South Carolina's William Gilmore Simms was the most versatile, influential, and prolific of southern writers.

Domestic Tastes

Charles Bulfinch developed a Federalist style of architecture that gave Boston a unique dignity and charm. The elaborately decorated Gothic style was more suitable to the prevailing romanticism.

Americans of the period were growing increasingly attracted to native American art. The Hudson River school specialized in grandiose pictures of wild landscapes. Art unions formed to encourage native art. They were a boon to many artists and helped introduce art work into middle-class homes. Charming lithographs by Currier and Ives were even more widely popular.

Education for Democracy

The early nineteenth-century common school movement was based on the Jeffersonian belief that the success of a democratic government depended on an educated citizenry. Common schools were free tax-supported schools that were administered statewide and employed professionally trained teachers. New England's Horace Mann, whose faith was in the improvability of the human race through education, became the chief advocate of public schools. By the 1850s every state outside the South provided free elementary schools and supported teacher's colleges.

Common schools were successful for a variety of reasons: employers needed trained and well-disciplined workers; non-English and non-Protestant immigrants needed to be "Americanized"; working-class children needed to be instilled with middle-class values. Most assuredly, common schools were a melting pot of America's increasingly economically differentiated and ethnically diverse population.

Engines of Culture

The growth of an urban middle class increased interest in cultural refinement. Improved printing technology reduced the price of books, magazines, and newspapers, making them more accessible to the public. Highly sentimental "domestic" novels and nondenominational religious literature were best-sellers. Self-improvement and "how-to" books were also very popular.

Philanthropists' support made many educational activities available to all. Mutual improvement societies called lyceums illustrate the new popularity of knowledge and culture. Lyceums established libraries and sponsored lecture series featuring leading scholars of the day.

The State of the Colleges

Early nineteenth-century America had too many colleges for too few students. These private and expensive institutions generally geared their curriculum toward the training of clergymen. In the 1840s some colleges began to introduce more courses in science, economics, and mathematics. Western and southern colleges offered mechanical and agricultural subjects, and some colleges began to allow female enrollments.

Civic Cultures

Boston, Philadelphia, and New York vied for primacy as the cultural center of the United States. In the West, Cincinnati emerged as the center of trans-Allegheny culture. Nevertheless, many cities had literary and natural history societies and were regular stops on the lyceum circuit.

Scientific Stirrings

Progress in scientific development was slow. Tocqueville attributed Americans' indifference to science to their distrust of theory and abstract knowledge. The nation did have active, though usually part-time geologists, naturalists, and physicists. Physiologist William Beaumont became the world's leading expert on the human gastric system.

American Humor

The contrast between American ideals and the reality of American life in the early nineteenth century was often exploited by comic writers. The anti-intellectual Jacksonians were the favorite butt of New England's intellectual satirists. Juxtaposing the genteel and vulgar in American life was also popular in the South and West, as were themes of violence and shady characters.

People, Places, and Things

Define the following:

romanticism _____

_____

Transcendentalism _____
_____

common school _____
_____

lyceum _____
_____

Describe the following:

The Last of the Mohicans _____
_____

Walden _____
_____

"Civil Disobedience" _____
_____

"The Raven" _____
_____

The Scarlet Letter _____
_____

Moby Dick _____
_____

Leaves of Grass _____
_____

Identify the following:

James Fenimore Cooper _____

_____

Washington Irving _____

_____

Benjamin West _____

_____

John Singleton Copley _____

_____

Charles William Peale _____

_____

Gilbert Stuart _____

_____

Ralph Waldo Emerson _____

_____

Henry David Thoreau _____

_____

Edgar Allan Poe _____

_____

Nathaniel Hawthorne _____

_____

Herman Melville _____

_____

Walt Whitman _____
_____

Henry Wadsworth Longfellow _____
_____

William Gilmore Simms _____
_____

Hudson River school _____
_____

Currier and Ives _____
_____

Horace Mann _____
_____

William Beaumont _____
_____

Self-Test

Multiple-Choice Questions

1. The center of American literary romanticism in the 1830s and 1840s was
   A. New York City
   B. New England
   C. the South
   D. the West

2. Transcendentalists believed the key to truth was
   A. reason
   B. intuition
   C. the Bible
   D. formal education

3. Most Transcendentalists believed that the good would prevail if each individual
   A. simply obeyed the law
   B. did what seemed most logical and reasonable
   C. followed the dictates of his or her own conscience
   D. became active in social reform movements

4. America's leading Transcendentalist was
   A. Nathaniel Hawthorne
   B. Herman Melville
   C. Ralph Waldo Emerson
   D. Henry Wadsworth Longfellow

5. Although most literary romantics admired Emerson, they often disagreed with his views on
   A. individualism
   B. powerful government
   C. materialism
   D. social activism

6. Henry David Thoreau's *Walden* was an indictment of
   A. civil disobedience
   B. individualism
   C. conformity
   D. idealism

7. Edgar Allan Poe's works dealt with all the following themes EXCEPT
   A. mystery
   B. horror
   C. science fiction
   D. self-help

8. The New England writer who was most fascinated by the themes of sin, guilt, and pride in America's Puritan heritage was
   A. Nathaniel Hawthorne
   B. Herman Melville
   C. Henry David Thoreau
   D. Edgar Allan Poe

9. Pessimism and the darker side of human nature was a favorite theme in the works of all of the following EXCEPT
   A. Nathaniel Hawthorne
   B. Ralph Waldo Emerson
   C. Edgar Allan Poe
   D. Herman Melville

10. Walt Whitman's poetry is probably best described as
    A. highly intellectual
    B. highly critical

C. undisciplined
D. uninspired

11. The highly talented and popular New England poet who wrote of Paul Revere's famous ride was
    A. Henry Wadsworth Longfellow
    B. James Russell Lowell
    C. William Gilmore Simms
    D. Edgar Allan Poe

12. The Hudson River school of artists specialized in
    A. Gothic architecture
    B. classical themes
    C. portraits
    D. grandiose landscapes

13. Educational reforms in the early nineteenth century did NOT
    A. establish publicly financed elementary schools
    B. restore colleges to the honored place they had enjoyed in the Revolutionary era
    C. create state-administered public school systems
    D. found normal schools to train teachers

14. One of America's chief advocates of public schools in the early nineteenth century was
    A. William Beaumont
    B. Horace Mann
    C. Hosea Biglow
    D. Charles Bulfinch

15. Proponents of common schools did NOT argue that these schools would
    A. save taxpayers money
    B. train and discipline workers
    C. Americanize immigrants
    D. spread middle-class values

16. Most early nineteenth-century popular literature dealt with all the following themes EXCEPT
    A. sentimentality
    B. self-improvement
    C. science
    D. religion

17. Most early nineteenth-century American colleges
    A. maintained strict discipline of their student body
    B. were relatively inexpensive to attend
    C. were overcrowded
    D. were privately endowed

18. Beyond elementary school, most early nineteenth-century American's higher education relied on attendance at
    A. college
    B. high school
    C. lyceum lectures
    D. scientific demonstrations

19. The cultural center of the trans-Allegheny West in early nineteenth-century America was
    A. St. Louis
    B. Pittsburgh
    C. Louisville
    D. Cincinnati

20. A favorite theme of early nineteenth-century American satirists was the contrast between
    A. romanticism and Transcendentalism
    B. ideals and reality
    C. democracy and equality
    D. individualism and freedom

Essay Questions

1. State the values of literary romanticism. Do you agree or disagree with these values? Why or why not?
2. Which of the major romantic authors seems most interesting to you? Why?
3. What arguments were used in support of the establishment of free tax-supported schools in early nineteenth-century America? Which argument sounds most plausible to you? Why?
4. Why do you think American science was unremarkable in the early nineteenth century? What, of scientific value, was accomplished?
5. Compare and contrast the major themes in literary romanticism and the civic or popular culture of early nineteenth-century America.

Critical Thinking Exercise

Classification

In previous chapters you worked with classification matrices to help you gain control of the narrative information presented in the textbook. In those cases, much of the classification matrix was already prepared for you to complete. In the following exercise, you are to prepare your own classification matrix that will identify six major early nineteenth-century authors (Emerson, Thoreau, Poe, Hawthorne, Melville, and Whitman) with their views and the major themes of their writing. The six authors will be listed along one side of the classification matrix. You must decide what themes and views to list along the other side of the matrix, then indicate at proper intersections whether the author's view or treatment of that theme was positive or negative, or whether he treated that theme at all. Carefully read the relevant early sections of Chapter 11 to find useful information.

Your matrix, then, must show each author's views and themes (insofar as the text provides that information). For example, your matrix should show at a glance that Emerson's and Thoreau's views were optimistic (a theme in their writings), but the views and themes of Poe, Hawthorne, and Melville were more pessimistic. There is no direct reference in the text on optimism as a theme in Whitman's work (though one can infer from the text that he was optimistic). Thus, a portion of your chart might look something like this (using "+" as a positive view by the author toward the theme, "-" as a negative view, and "na" as an absence of information.

Views and Themes of Early Nineteenth-Century American Authors						
Theme	Emerson	Thoreau	Poe	Hawthorne	Melville	Whitman
optimism	+	+	-	-	-	(+)

Hint: Some of the themes you might include (try to find about a dozen) are: attitudes toward individualism, materialism, human nature, and so on.

11: A Democratic Culture

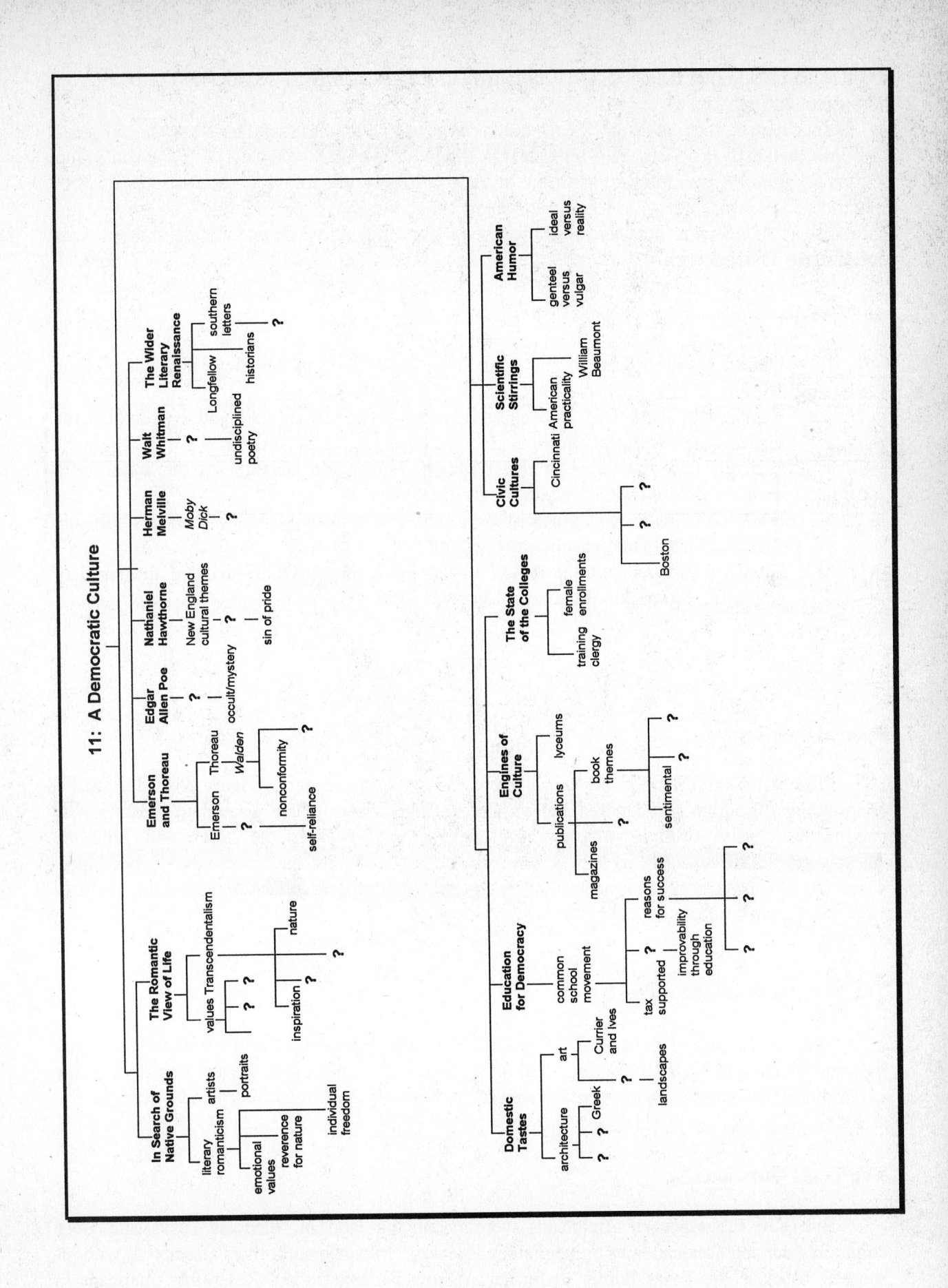

In Search of Native Grounds
- literary romanticism
  - artists
    - portraits
  - emotional values
  - reverence for nature
  - individual freedom

The Romantic View of Life
- values Transcendentalism
  - ?
  - ?
  - inspiration
  - nature
  - ?

Emerson and Thoreau
- Emerson
  - ?
  - self-reliance
- Thoreau
  - *Walden*
  - nonconformity
  - ?

Edgar Allen Poe
- ?
- occult/mystery

Nathaniel Hawthorne
- New England cultural themes
- ?
- sin of pride

Herman Melville
- *Moby Dick*
- ?

Walt Whitman
- ?
- undisciplined poetry

The Wider Literary Renaissance
- Longfellow
- historians
- southern letters
- ?

Domestic Tastes
- architecture
  - ?
  - ?
  - Greek
- art
  - Currier and Ives
  - ?
  - landscapes

Education for Democracy
- common school movement
- tax supported
- reasons for success
  - ?
  - improvability through education
  - ?
  - ?

Engines of Culture
- publications
  - lyceums
  - magazines
  - ?
  - book themes
    - sentimental
    - ?
    - ?

The State of the Colleges
- training clergy
- female enrollments

Civic Cultures
- Cincinnati
- ?
- ?
- Boston

Scientific Stirrings
- American practicality
- William Beaumont

American Humor
- genteel versus vulgar
- ideal versus reality

165

Chapter 12

Expansion and Slavery

Learning Objectives

After reading Chapter 12 you should be able to:

1. Define "manifest destiny" and relate it to the conduct of American diplomacy in the 1840s.
2. Explain why the United States and Mexico went to war in 1846 and explain how the United States won the war.
3. Describe how the terms of the Treaty of Guadalupe Hidalgo set the stage for a renewed debate over slavery in the United States.
4. State the terms of the Compromise of 1850 and explain why it was thought by many to be the final solution to the slavery issue.
5. Compare and contrast the views of national leaders as they debated the issue of slavery in the territories between 1845 and 1850.

Overview

Tyler's Troubles

President John Tyler did not get along well with Whig leaders. Henry Clay designed a congressional program that ignored Tyler's states' rights views. Clay wanted to create a new national bank, raise tariffs, distribute surplus federal funds back to the states, and, with the Preemption Act, legalize the right of squatters to occupy and purchase unsurveyed public land. Tyler vetoed the Bank bill and, once Congress repealed the Distribution Act, signed the Tariff of 1842 raising tariff rates.

The Webster-Ashburton Treaty

Tyler's secretary of state, Daniel Webster, negotiated a settlement of the disputed boundary between Maine and New Brunswick. The popular Webster-Ashburton Treaty was a workable compromise that avoided injury to vital business ties between the United States and Britain.

The Texas Question

By 1830 thousands of Americans were occupying land in Mexican Texas and were commonly defying Mexican laws on religion and slavery. Mexican authorities attempted, without success, to close the Texas border to further American immigration. Resentful Americans in

Texas rose in revolt against President Santa Anna's dictatorship in 1835. After massacres at Goliad and the Alamo, Sam Houston's Texan army defeated Mexican forces, who then retreated across the Rio Grande. President Jackson then recognized the new government of the independent Republic of Texas. Most Texans wanted Texas annexed to the United States, but fear of war with Mexico and concern that it might stir up the slavery controversy delayed the annexation of Texas until 1845.

Manifest Destiny

Since the first colonial founding, Americans had continuously expanded their territorial holdings. By the 1840s Americans were confident that one day America would be a powerful nation stretching from the Atlantic to the Pacific. It was, they thought, the "manifest destiny" of Americans (God's chosen people) to occupy and exploit the entire continent and make it a showcase of democracy and economic opportunity.

Life on the Trail

Pioneers heading west more often faced dangers from accidents, poor sanitation, and exposure than from Indian attack. The demands of westward migration required family self-sufficiency where all labor was shared. Letters and journals reveal that life on the trail was especially taxing for women.

California and Oregon

California and Oregon were the favorite destinations of westward pioneers in the 1840s. "Oregon fever"—a form of land hunger produced by glowing reports of the Willamette Valley—gripped the nation. Thousands of pioneers embarked on the Oregon Trail that stretched from Missouri to the Columbia River. Most pioneers were young families who made the five-month trip as a self-governing community on the march. West Coast harbors also offered economic opportunity to eastern merchants. They were the keys to trade with the Orient. Because Mexico owned California and the British had claims in the Oregon Country, these became items of diplomatic concern to American leaders.

The Election of 1844

But it was Texas that dominated the politics of 1844. Clay and Van Buren wanted to ignore the Texas annexation issue, but the Democrats nominated "dark horse" expansionist James K. Polk who pledged the reannexation of Texas and reoccupation of Oregon. The election was extremely close. The decisive factor was the abolitionist Liberty party's capture of enough votes in New York to deny its Electoral College votes to Clay. Polk's narrow victory was taken as a mandate for expansion, and Congress passed a joint resolution to annex Texas.

Polk As President

James K. Polk was an uncommonly successful president. Congress followed his leadership to lower the tariff, restore the independent treasury, and halt federal funding of internal improvements. He also successfully pursued the acquisition of Oregon and California. Polk's astute diplomacy led to the division of the Oregon country at the 49th Parallel from the Rockies to the Pacific, and gave the United States use of the Strait of Juan de Fuca into Puget Sound.

War with Mexico

In 1846, the expansionists spirit in America would bully proud Mexico into a war for territorial conquest. When Texas was annexed in 1845, Mexico broke diplomatic relations with the United States. Polk sent General Zachary Taylor's army to South Texas to defend the disputed border with Mexico. He then sent John Slidell to Mexico City with an offer to settle the dispute in Texas and buy California. Mexican authorities rejected Slidell; Polk ordered Taylor's army to the Rio Grande; and hostilities began. Taylor's army enjoyed immediate success against a poorly equipped and poorly led Mexican army.

To the Halls of Montezuma

Polk was an effective commander-in-chief, but his top ranking generals were Whigs. This injected divisive partisanship into the conduct of the war. Further, from the outset, Polk faced opposition to the war: many northerners feared the war would lead to the expansion of slavery, and some Whigs alleged that Polk had deceived Congress and provoked an unnecessary war of aggression against Mexico.

The Mexican War saw a continuous series of military victories by American armies in a three-pronged invasion of Mexico. United States forces, with the help of American settlers already there, occupied California. Taylor invaded northern Mexico, and, after a successful amphibious landing at Vera Cruz, General Winfield Scott's army captured Mexico City.

The Treaty of Guadalupe Hidalgo

Polk sent diplomat Nicholas Trist to negotiate a peace treaty in Mexico City. In the Treaty of Guadalupe Hidalgo, Mexico confirmed the Texas boundary at the Rio Grande and ceded New Mexico and California to the United States. The United States agreed to pay Mexico $15 million and assume $3.25 million of Mexican debts owed to American citizens.

The Fruit of Victory

In the Treaty of Guadalupe Hidalgo, the United States acquired an immense amount of new territory at relatively small cost. As a consequence, the wealth of the 1848-1849 gold rush would enhance America's prosperity, not Mexico's. This seemed an ultimate justification of manifest destiny.

Slavery: The Fire Bell in the Night Rings Again

While prosperity came from territorial expansion, sectional harmony did not. Once again the nation had to answer the question, Is slavery to be allowed into the territories of the United States? The Constitution prevented federal control of slavery in the states, but it gave Congress control in the territories. There was where slavery's opponents could combat the institution they deplored.

Congressman David Wilmot opened the debate with a proviso that would have prevented the expansion of slavery into the territory acquired from Mexico. It passed the House, but failed in the Senate where John C. Calhoun argued that Congress had no right to bar slavery from any territory. Others tried to find grounds for compromise between Wilmot and Calhoun. Polk suggested extending the 36° 30' line of the Missouri Compromise to the Pacific coast. Senator Lewis Cass proposed to settle the issue by "popular sovereignty"—organizing the territories without mention of slavery and letting local settlers decide whether theirs would be a free or slave territory. It seemed a democratic way to solve the problem and it allowed Congress to avoid having to make the decision.

The Election of 1848

Neither the Whigs who nominated Zachary Taylor nor the Democrats who backed Lewis Cass took a position on the issue of slavery in the territories in the 1848 campaign. But antislavery Democrats and Liberty party abolitionists formed the Free Soil party to oppose the expansion of slavery. Taylor won the election.

The Gold Rush

Still, the question of slavery in the territories had to be faced. Thousands of Americans flooded into California's gold fields in 1848-1849, creating demands for a territorial government. Taylor proposed to admit California to statehood without the prior organization of a territorial government. Californians submitted an antislavery constitution with their request for admission. Southerners were outraged because the admission of California would give the free states a majority and control of the Senate.

The Compromise of 1850

Once again, Henry Clay rose to offer a compromise. He proposed that California be admitted as a free state; the remainder of the Mexican Cession be organized without mention of slavery; a Texas-New Mexico boundary controversy be settled in New Mexico's favor, but Texas be compensated with a federal assumption of its state debt; the slave trade (but not slavery) be abolished in Washington, D.C.; and a more effective fugitive slave law be enacted and vigorously enforced.

Clay's proposals generated a great debate. Calhoun argued for a federal guarantee for slavery in all territories; Webster backed Clay's proposals; and abolitionist Senator William Seward cited a "higher (moral) law" that bound him to oppose the expansion of slavery. The death of President Taylor broke the deadlock. Senator Stephen Douglas maneuvered the proposals through Congress, including the antilibertarian Fugitive Slave Act that compelled northerners to cooperate in the capture of runaway slaves. The proposals passed one by one. For the time, the Compromise of 1850 preserved the Union.

People, Places, and Things

Define the following:

Manifest Destiny <u>Gods chosen people gave right to strech from Sea to Sea</u>

joint resolution _____

popular sovereignty <u>letting territories decide on slavery</u>

Describe the following:

Distribution Act <u>distribute the proceeds from land sales to the states</u>

Webster-Ashburton Treaty <u>Webster convinced maine & Mass to go with old line & compromise</u>

Treaty of Guadalupe Hidalgo <u>Rio Grande boundary of Texas & Mex + ceded New Mexico & Cal. to US. for $15 mill</u>

Wilmot Proviso <u>No slavery or involuntary servitude to exist in ~~Texas~~ territory except for crime & they had to be convicted</u>

Free Soil party <u>Barnburners & anti slavery Liberty Party joined together</u>

Fugitive Slave Act __Compelled Northerners to cooperate in the capture of runaway slaves__

Compromise of 1850 __Cal. Free - remainder people would have ~~by popular sovereignty~~ say__

Identify the following:

John Tyler __Pres of U.S. states rights southerner against Bank__

Henry Clay __Congressman from Kentucky opposed annexation of Texas. Wanted Nat Bank__

Daniel Webster __Sec. of State - resigned__

Stephen F. Austin __led Americans to Texas to settle land - 1821__

Santa Anna __Mex. President - took 6,000 men No. Alamo__

Sam Houston __Former gov. + congressman from Tenn. Pres. of Texas - then Gov.__

John C. Calhoun __T~~y~~ler appointed him Sec. of State__

James K. Polk __expansionist - Dark horse - victory mandate for expansion__

Zachary Taylor __Polk sent Taylor ~~expansionist~~ to So. Tex. to defend against Mexico__

John Slidell _envoy to Mex - cancel Mex debts for Tex & Rio Grande boundary_

Winfield Scott _Gen. in charge of offense - captured Mexico City_

Nicholas P. Trist _Saw Mexico was disorangnized & did the Treaty of Guadalupe_

David Wilmot _Dem congressman from Penn._

Lewis Cass _Senator from Mich - don't mention slavery - let settlers settle issue - Popular sovereignty_

Barnburners _Van buren wing of Dem party - to call attention to their radicalism._

Martin Van Buren _Free soil candidate_

Stephen A. Douglas _____

Locate the following places: Write in both the place name and its map location number.

1. The state whose boundary was involved in the Webster-Ashburton Treaty.

2. The site of the battle where Texan troops were massacred while attempting to stop a Mexican army invasion of Texas in 1835.

3. Three major Pacific ports acquired by the United States in the 1840s.

4. The river where a military skirmish ignited the Mexican War in 1846.

5. The independent nation annexed by the United States in 1845.

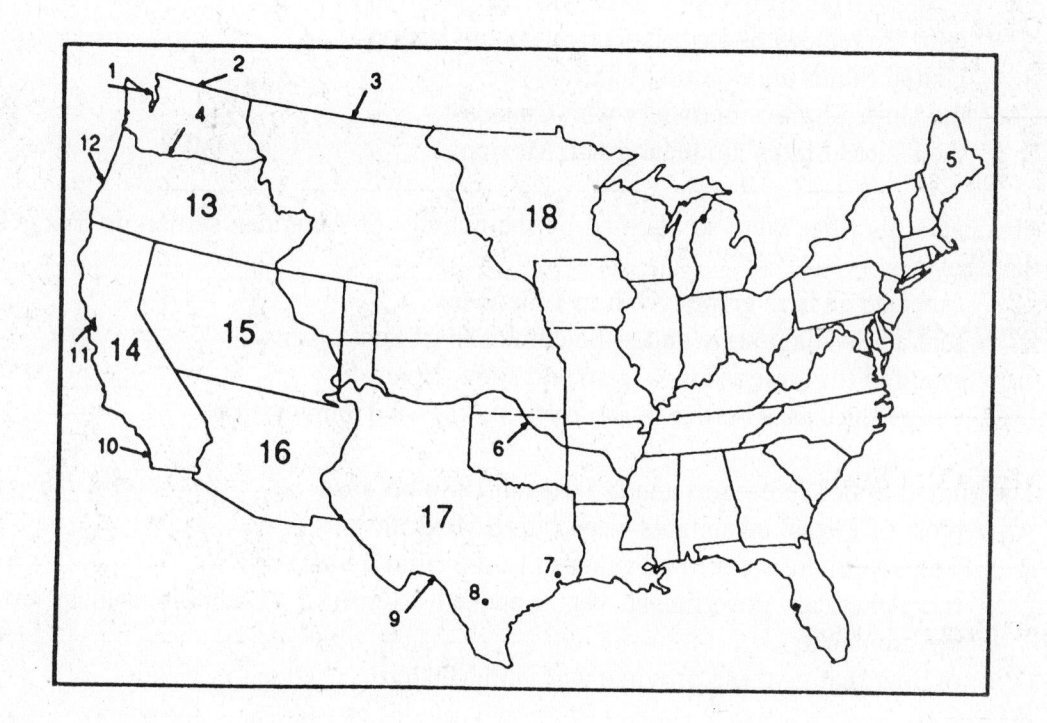

6. The boundary line established in the Oregon Settlement in 1846.

7. The state admitted to the Union as a free state in the Compromise of 1850.

8. The territories where, in the Compromise of 1850, the question of slavery was left open to resolution by popular sovereignty.

173

Self-Test

Multiple-Choice Questions

1. All but one of President Tyler's cabinet members resigned in protest when he vetoed a bill to
   A. distribute surplus federal funds back to the states
   B. establish a new Bank of the United States
   C. allow squatters to occupy and buy unsurveyed public land
   D. prevent the expansion of slavery into any unoccupied territory.

2. The Webster-Ashburton Treaty dealt with the question of
   A. joint United States-British occupation of Oregon
   B. United States annexation of Texas
   C. the United States' boundary with Canada
   D. the United States' boundary with Mexico

3. Mexican authorities were so alarmed by the number of American settlers in Texas by 1830 that they
   A. canceled all land grants given to Americans
   B. sent an invading army under the command of Santa Anna
   C. required the Americans to learn and speak Spanish
   D. closed the Texas border to any further American immigration

4. The United States refused to annex Texas in 1836 because
   A. most of Texas' inhabitants were native Mexicans
   B. Texans did not want to be annexed to the United States
   C. the American government was opposed to armed rebellions against established governments
   D. of fear that it would provoke war with Mexico

5. The phrase "manifest destiny" expressed a popular attitude favoring
   A. the abolition of slavery
   B. evangelical revivalism
   C. slavery
   D. territorial expansion

6. Migration to Oregon in the 1840s was stimulated by
   A. Mormon missionaries who had explored the area
   B. the discovery of gold in the Columbia River
   C. reports of rich agricultural land there
   D. the Hudson Bay Company's boom in the fur trade

7. The destination of most of those who took the Oregon Trail was the
   A. Sacramento Valley
   B. Willamette Valley

      C.   Great Salt Lake
      D.   port cities of San Diego and San Francisco

8. James Polk's election to the presidency in 1844 was taken to be a popular endorsement for
      A.   extending slavery into the territories of the United States
      B.   war with Mexico
      C.   acquiring new territories
      D.   reopening the slave trade

9. Match the territory in the left column with its manner of attachment to the United States.
      A.   California   1. annexed by joint resolution of Congress
      B.   Oregon   2. claimed by treaty with Britain
      C.   Texas   3. acquired by conquest of Mexico
                           4. purchased from Spain
      A.   A-1, B-2, C-3
      B.   A-4, B-2, C-3
      C.   A-3, B-2, C-4
      D.   A-3, B-2, C-1

10. All of the following preceded America's war with Mexico EXCEPT
      A.   Zachary Taylor's forces occupied the territory just north of the Rio Grande
      B.   an emissary was sent to Mexico to try to purchase California
      C.   Texas was annexed to the United States
      D.   gold was discovered in California

11. Of those listed here, the earliest battle of the Mexican War was
      A.   Resaca de la Palma
      B.   Monterey
      C.   Vera Cruz
      D.   Cerro Gordo

12. Put in proper sequence, the United States acquired (A) Oregon, (B) Texas, (C) California
      A.   A then B then C
      B.   C then B then A
      C.   B then A then C
      D.   B then C then A

13. The Treaty of Guadalupe Hidalgo was negotiated by
      A.   Nicholas Trist
      B.   Winfield Scott
      C.   John Slidell
      D.   William Seward

14. The Treaty of Guadalupe Hidalgo provided for all of the following EXCEPT
      A.   Mexican recognition of the Rio Grande as its border with Texas
      B.   United States acquisition of both California and New Mexico

C. a $15 million payment from the United States to Mexico
D. prohibition of slavery in the territories Mexico ceded to the United States

15. If it had passed Congress, the Wilmot Proviso would have
    A. banned slavery from the territory ceded by Mexico
    B. reopened the territory north of 36° 30' to slavery
    C. left the question of slavery to be decided by vote of territorial legislatures
    D. provided for immediate admission of California as a free state

16. In the election of 1848 opposition to expansion of slavery into the territories was the position taken by
    A. Zachary Taylor
    B. Lewis Cass
    C. Martin Van Buren
    D. James Polk

17. In 1849, President Taylor outraged his southern supporters with his proposal to
    A. ban slavery from all U.S. territories
    B. admit California as a free state
    C. endorse the concept of popular sovereignty
    D. veto the Wilmot Proviso

18. The major concession made to the South in the Compromise of 1850 was the proposal regarding the
    A. return of fugitive slaves
    B. Texas-New Mexico boundary dispute
    C. slave trade in Washington, D.C.
    D. admission of California to statehood

19. The most upsetting proposal in the Compromise of 1850 to northerners was that it
    A. legalized slavery in Washington, D.C.
    B. gave the southern states control of the Senate
    C. guaranteed the protection of slave property in the territories
    D. compelled them to cooperate in the capture of runaway slaves.

20. Arrange these events in their proper time order: (A) David Wilmot proposes a proviso in Congress, (B) the Treaty of Guadalupe Hidalgo ends the Mexican War, (C) Congress passes the Compromise of 1850, (D) Zachary Taylor is elected president.
    A. A, B, C, D
    B. B, A, D, C
    C. C, D, B, A
    D. A, B, D, C

Essay Questions

1. Explain why Americans were susceptible to the expansionist impulses of manifest destiny in the 1840s.
2. State the causes of the Mexican War. Do you think President Polk provoked Mexico into an unnecessary war? Why or why not?
3. Describe the relationship between the Mexican War, the Treaty of Guadalupe Hidalgo, the Wilmot Proviso, and the great debate on slavery in the territories that led to the Compromise of 1850.
4. State the terms of the Compromise of 1850 and explain why many thought this was the final solution to the slavery issue in the United States.
5. Compare and contrast the views of Clay, Calhoun, Taylor, and Cass on the issue of slavery in the territories. Whose position do you find most persuasive? Why?

Critical Thinking Exercise

Cause and Effect

In previous chapters you completed exercises dealing with causal chains and with contributory causes to historical events. In this exercise you will consider both of these in relation to three events: Texas annexation to the United States, the Mexican War, and the Compromise of 1850.

Each of the following three groups of items is a causal chain leading to the stated effect. Arrange the items in the chain in correct chronological order by numbering them in the sequence in which they occurred.

1. Effect: Texas Annexation

    _____ Republic of Texas created

    _____ Texas Revolution begins

    _____ President Jackson recognizes the Republic of Texas

    _____ Battle of the Alamo

    _____ James K. Polk elected president

2. Effect: Mexican War

    _____ John Slidell's mission to Mexico City

    _____ Texas annexation

    _____ General Taylor's army skirmishes with Mexican troops on the Rio Grande

_____ Mexico breaks diplomatic relations with the United States

_____ General Taylor's army sent to South Texas

3. Effect: Compromise of 1850

_____ Treaty of Guadalupe Hidalgo

_____ Free Soil party organized

_____ Wilmot Proviso introduced to Congress

_____ California gold rush

_____ President Taylor dies

In the following exercise, describe how each of the listed items was a contributory cause of the effect indicated.

4. Effect: Texas Annexation

Election of 1844 _____

_____

British interest in Texas _____

_____

5. Effect: Mexican War

Annexation of Texas _____

_____

Manifest Destiny _____

_____

Mexican policies _____

_____

Election of 1844 _____

_____

President Polk's diplomacy _____

_____

Effect: Compromise of 1850

    Treaty of Guadalupe Hidalgo _____

_____

    death of President Taylor _____

_____

    popular sovereignty _____

_____

    Stephen A. Douglas _____

_____

12: Expansion and Slavery

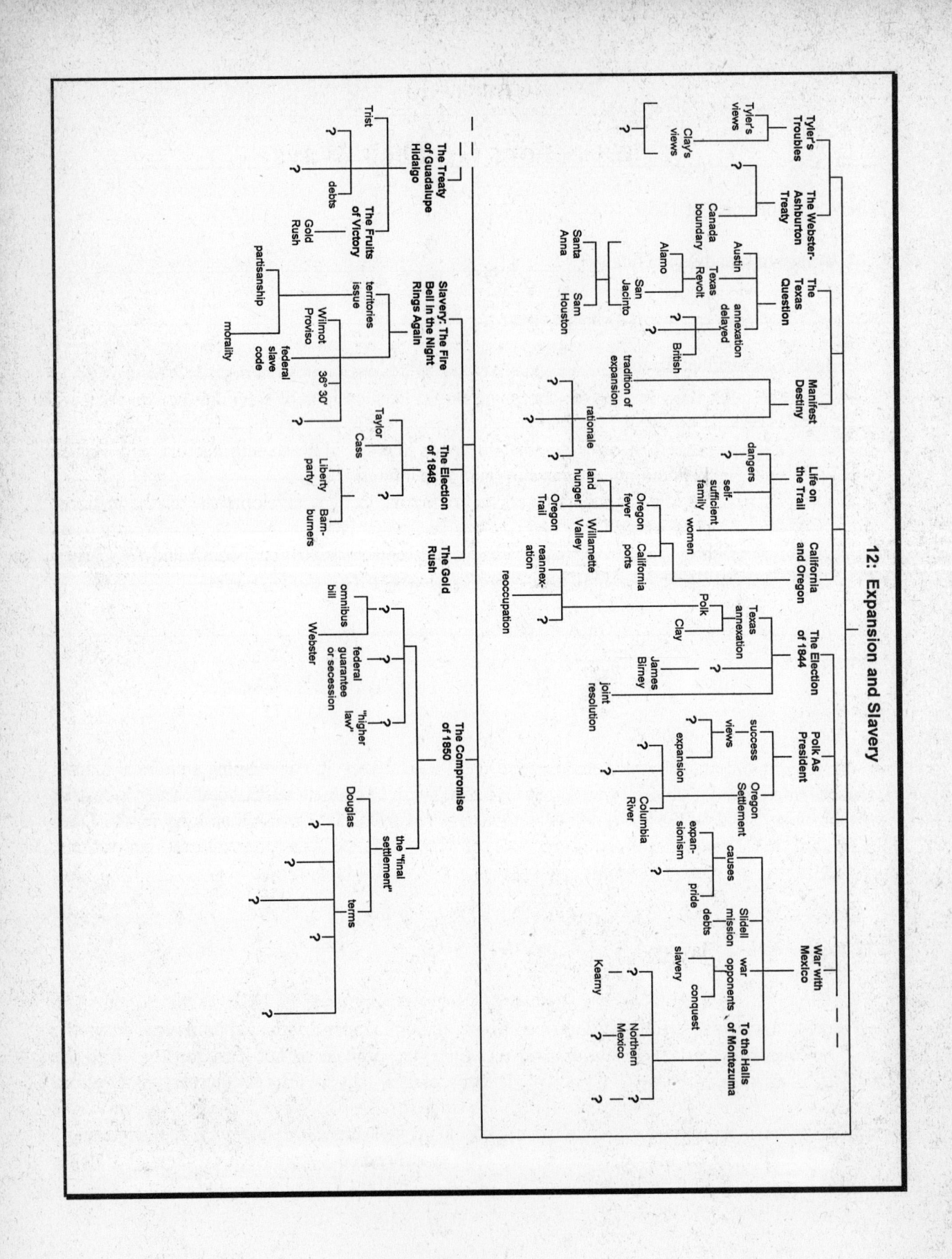

A hierarchical outline/tree diagram for the chapter, with the following branches:

- **The Webster-Ashburton Treaty**
  - Tyler's Troubles
    - Tyler's views
    - Clay's views
  - Canada boundary

- **The Texas Question**
  - Austin
  - Texas Revolt
    - Alamo
    - San Jacinto
      - Santa Anna
      - Sam Houston
  - annexation delayed
    - British

- **Manifest Destiny**
  - tradition of expansion
  - rationale

- **Life on the Trail**
  - dangers
  - self-sufficient family
  - women

- **California and Oregon**
  - Oregon Trail
    - land hunger
    - Willamette Valley
  - California ports
  - reannexation / reoccupation

- **The Election of 1844**
  - Texas annexation
    - Polk
    - Clay
    - James Birney
  - joint resolution

- **Polk As President**
  - success
  - views
    - expansion
  - Oregon Settlement
    - Columbia River
  - causes
    - expansionism
    - pride

- **War with Mexico**
  - Slidell mission
  - war opponents
    - debts
    - slavery
    - conquest
  - **To the Halls of Montezuma**
    - Kearny
    - Northern Mexico

- **The Fruits of Victory**
  - Trist
  - The Treaty of Guadalupe Hidalgo
    - debts
  - The Gold Rush
    - Gold Rush

- **Slavery: The Fire Bell in the Night Rings Again**
  - territories issue
    - Wilmot Proviso
    - 36°30'
    - federal slave code
  - partisanship
  - morality

- **The Election of 1848**
  - Taylor
  - Cass
  - Liberty party
  - Barn-burners

- **The Compromise of 1850**
  - omnibus bill
  - federal guarantee
  - "higher law"
  - or secession
  - Webster
  - Douglas
  - the "final settlement"
  - terms

180

Chapter 13

The Sections Go Their Ways

Learning Objectives

After reading Chapter 13 you should be able to:

1. Analyze the importance of slavery to the South's economy between 1820 and 1860.
2. Describe the sociological and psychological dimensions of slave life before the Civil War.
3. Describe the conditions of northern labor in the mid-nineteenth century and explain why workers did not organize in their own interests.
4. Summarize the significance of the railroads to the development of the national economy before the Civil War.
5. Explain how the economic differences between the North and South and the pattern of railroad construction fed sectional sentiment before the Civil War.

Overview

The South

By the middle of the nineteenth century the United States was developing a national market economy marked by interregional dependence and increased agricultural and industrial specialization. The South remained predominantly agricultural. Cotton was king in the Deep South, but the Upper South, with the use of fertilizers and other agricultural innovations, produced tobacco, corn, and wheat and a growing diversity of other crops.

The Economics of Slavery

As the cotton culture spread westward, slavery strengthened its hold on the South. The demand for slaves was greatest in the Deep South, and the Upper South sold its slaves "down the river" at ever higher prices. Slave trading was a profitable business, but it frequently led to the break up of slave families. As the price of slaves increased, only wealthy southerners could afford to buy them, so by 1860 only one-fourth of southern families owned slaves. Slavery was profitable, but it diverted southern capital away from investment in trade and manufacturing. Thus, the marketing of the southern cotton crop was handled by northern business firms. At bottom, slavery was a stagnant and inefficient labor system that wasted talent and energy.

Antebellum Plantation Life

A plantation resembled a small village. The sexual division of labor was less evident in the South than in the North, and southern women had immense responsibilities on the plantation. Both slave men and women worked as field hands, but slave children typically were given only small tasks until the age of ten. Slave families typically lived in crude one-room cabins.

The Sociology of Slavery

Unlike in other slave systems, the southern slave population grew by natural increase. Only about a half-million slaves had been imported by 1808 when the foreign slave trade ended, but there were 4 million blacks in the United States in 1860.

How slaves were treated depended on the master, although their economic value gave some protection to slaves, and white masters usually supplied adequate care to their slaves Still, slaves had a higher infant mortality rate and shorter life expectancy than whites. Slaves had no legal rights, but they found some relief from their oppression in their families and their religion. Within these institutions they were able to sustain a sense of their own worth and enjoy spiritual freedom.

Most whites thought slaves were inherently lazy. But this "laziness" was the slave's rational response to forced, uncompensated labor. Most whites also mistakenly believed that slaves were content with their situation. Paradoxically, whites also feared slave insurrection. Savage reprisal was the fate of slave rebels such as Denmark Vesey and Nat Turner, and white fears made the slave system increasingly oppressive.

Slaves were much harder to supervise and control in cities. So, because of slavery, the South remained rural and agricultural. Whites considered free blacks a dangerous example for slaves, and many states passed laws that required free blacks go emigrate. These laws were not strictly enforced because of the need for black labor, slave or free.

Psychological Effects of Slavery

Slavery was unjust and corroded the personalities of both slaves and whites. Slave revolts were infrequent, but runaways were common. Other slaves seemed resigned to their fate, or found less dramatic ways to protest the system. Slaves had strong families, their own culture, and a sense of community—all of which sustained them—but slavery discouraged their development of independent judgment and self-reliance.

Slavery also warped the whites. Whites developed contradictory stereotypes of slaves' nature. To whites, slaves were at the same time lazy and aggressive, nurturing and wanton. White men often took advantage of slave women, and the system generally encouraged them to be self-indulgent. Slavery also degraded manual labor in the eyes of poor whites. It also reinforced the tendency of male dominance in southern society and it caused otherwise decent people to be cruel.

Manufacturing in the South

There was some manufacturing in the antebellum South. The availability of cotton and waterpower made textile manufacturing profitable. But southern manufacturing was small in scale compared to the North; less than 15 percent of the nation's manufactured goods came from the South in 1860.

The Northern Industrial Juggernaut

Industry grew rapidly in the North. Steam power was critical to the expansion of the factory system and industry was remarkably receptive to technological change. In America, individual freedom encouraged resourcefulness and experimentation; business growth encouraged new techniques; and the shortage of skilled labor encouraged the substitution of machinery. America's industrial revolution also rested on a growing availability of a seemingly inexhaustible supply of natural resources. Americans were also losing their historical prejudice against corporations. Industrial growth increased the demand for labor, but the expanding western frontier drained off many eastern laborers and artisans who would not work for low wages in industry. Immigration and capital investment from Europe also helped stimulate industry and expand the national market.

Self-Generated Expansion

Industrial activity was interactive. Cotton production stimulated the textile industry which in turn stimulated the machine tool industry. The sewing machine revolutionized the shoe and clothing industries. Agricultural machinery stimulated many industries and expanded farm production.

A Nation of Immigrants

Industrial expansion created jobs that attracted thousands of immigrants to America. Resident "native" Americans tended to look down on these immigrants, and natives and immigrants alike were prejudiced toward blacks. By 1860 Irish immigrants, who seemed a more permanent and pliable work force, had largely replaced the young farm women who worked in New England textile mills.

How Wage Earners Lived

Immigrants and factory workers often lived in crowed slums in industrial cities where life was squalid and dangerous. Low wages meant wives and children of most factory workers also had to work to help the family survive. Nevertheless, most skilled workers improved their lot somewhat.

Most workers did not belong to unions. Early unions and workingmen's political parties were virtually destroyed by internal bickering and the depression of the late 1830s. Nevertheless, in the 1840s and 1850s many states passed laws that both limited the workday to ten hours and regulated child labor. In *Commonwealth* v. *Hunt* (1842), the Massachusetts courts established the legality of labor unions, and most other states followed this precedent. Still, before 1860 most labor unions were small and local. Laborers rarely thought of themselves as members of a permanent working class. Republican values, a high rate of social and geographic mobility, and the availability of female, child, and immigrant labor made labor organization difficult.

Progress and Poverty

Mid-nineteenth-century America was a land of opportunity with a relatively high standard of living. Yet, at the same time there was an underclass of poorly paid and unskilled workers, mostly immigrants. Toward these, middle-class Americans were indifferent or unaware. Society became more stratified and the distance between the top and bottom widened. Still, the ideology of egalitarian democracy endured.

Foreign Commerce

Foreign commerce grew dramatically in the 1840s and 1850s. The United States mostly exported raw materials (cotton was the most valuable export), and it usually imported more (mostly manufactured goods) than it exported. Britain was the best customer of the United States and its leading supplier. Regularly scheduled sailing packets concentrated trade in New York and other large cities. Fast, sleek, but expensive clipper ships enjoyed brief popularity at mid-century.

Steam Conquers the Atlantic

By the late 1840s, steamships had captured much of the Atlantic freight and passenger traffic. These British-built vessels, stronger and larger than wooden sailing ships, challenged America's shipbuilding industry. Competition, subsidies, and new technology reduced trans-Atlantic shipping rates. Bargain rates in steerage enabled tens of thousands of European immigrants to come to America.

Canals and Railroads

America's internal trade grew immensely and shifted directions. The Erie Canal heralded the origins of a significant east-west trade. Railroads did not at first compete with canal traffic; they were originally designed to handle only local trade. Engineering and technical problems and America's tough terrain inhibited the construction of long-distance lines. But, by 1860 four railroads stretched from the Atlantic coast to the Ohio Valley. Within the Northeast and Northwest building railroads went on at a feverish pace, but was much slower in the South.

Financing the Railroads

Slave labor built the South's railroads; immigrants built the North's. Private investors supplied most of the investment capital, particularly when their communities stood to profit from the railroad. Longer east-west rail lines usually required some public funding. Public aid came in the form of loans, investments, and tax exemptions. The federal government helped by granting federal lands to states to build railroads. Often, construction of the railroads was as profitable as their operation, and wheeler-dealing and corruption were common.

Railroads and the Economy

Farmers were profoundly affected by the railroads. Location of the lines helped determine what land could be profitably cultivated. Railroad companies created farms by selling portions of their federal land grants as farm sites. Prices for farm goods was high, but farm labor was scarce. Farm machinery appeared to ease the labor shortage. Steel plows and mechanical reapers reduced the labor and time required to plant and harvest.

Cities were also affected by the railroads. Chicago became the railroad center of the Midwest. Railroads also stimulated other kinds of economic activity. They influenced real estate values, spurred regional concentration of industry, increased the size of business units, and stimulated the growth of investment banking. Railroads also revolutionized business organization and management, and they sharply reduced freight and passenger rates. Finally, railroads revolutionized western agriculture; the center of wheat production moved westward.

Railroads and the Sectional Conflict

Although they helped boost the western farmer's income and standard of living, railroads also broke down his isolation and self-sufficiency. This commercialization of agriculture meant that western farmers became more dependent on middlemen to market their crop. Overproduction also became a problem, and it became increasingly more costly to start and operate a farm.

The linking of the East and West had fateful effects in politics. The increasing movement of goods and people by railroads and canals stimulated nationalism in the Northeast and Northwest. With the Northwest no longer dependent on the Mississippi River trade route, its citizens could now oppose slavery and its westward expansion. The anticommercial attitudes of southern leaders, together with its scattered population, absence of large cities, and stubborn reliance on the Mississippi River prevented the South from keeping pace with the northern railroad construction.

The Economy on the Eve of the Civil War

Between 1845 and 1860 every economic indicator expressed the remarkable growth of the American economy. This growth caused some problems. The Panic of 1857 was a serious, though short-lived collapse that was especially hard on the Northwest. The South, however, was affected very little by the Panic, and this encouraged many southerners to believe they had a superior economic system and might be better off outside the Union.

People, Places, and Things

Define the following:

antebellum _____

_____

plantation _____

_____

slave stereotypes _____

_____

sailing packet _____

_____

clipper ship _____

_____

Describe the following:

Commonwealth v. *Hunt* _____

_____

Baltimore and Ohio Railroad _____

_____

Panic of 1857 _____

_____

Identify the following:

"poor white trash" _____

_____

Denmark Vesey _____

_____

Nat Turner _____

_____

John Deere _____

_____

Cyrus McCormick _____

_____

Self-Test

Multiple-Choice Questions

1. By the middle of the nineteenth century, the nation's economy was marked by all of the following EXCEPT
   A. increasing interregional dependence
   B. regional specialization of production
   C. several transportation improvements
   D. the decline of slavery

2. As the cotton culture spread westward in the early nineteenth century,
   A. planters in the Deep South diversified their crops
   B. the price of slaves declined
   C. the demand for slaves increased
   D. slave ownership became less profitable

3. By 1860 about _____ percent of southern families owned slaves.
   A. 10
   B. 25
   C. 50
   D. 65

4. Antebellum slaves had all the following EXCEPT
   A. many basic legal rights
   B. a higher infant mortality rate than whites
   C. a shorter life span than whites
   D. adequate food, housing, and clothing

5. Generally, southern whites did NOT believe that slaves were
   A. innately lazy
   B. prone to rebellion
   C. content with their enslavement
   D. incapable of hard work

6. The LEAST frequent means used by slaves to protest their condition was
   A. revolt
   B. escape
   C. feigned laziness
   D. subterfuge

7. In the antebellum period, slaves were NOT able to develop
   A. their own slave culture
   B. a strong sense of community
   C. individual self-reliance
   D. a sense of their own self-worth

8. Mid-nineteenth-century American industry lacked
   A. technological inventiveness
   B. a stable labor force
   C. availability of ample raw materials
   D. organizational and managerial skill

9. Most immigrants to mid-nineteenth-century America were attracted by the promise of
   A. religious freedom
   B. political freedom
   C. social respect
   D. economic opportunity

10. In *Commonwealth* v. *Hunt* the courts legalized
    A. child labor
    B. corporations
    C. slave marriages
    D. labor unions

11. In mid-nineteenth-century America
    A. class distinctions were narrowing
    B. faith in the idea of egalitarian democracy was fading
    C. Americans enjoyed a relatively high standard of living
    D. geographical population mobility was declining

12. In its foreign commerce the United States usually _____ raw materials and _____ manufactured goods; and it usually _____ more than it _____.
    A. exported, imported; exported, imported
    B. imported, exported; imported, exported
    C. exported, imported; imported, exported
    D. imported, exported; exported, imported

13. America's dominance in the shipbuilding industry was most severely challenged by the development of ocean-going
    A. sailing packets
    B. clipper ships
    C. commerce raiders
    D. steamships

14. Railroad construction by 1860 most closely tied together the economies of the
    A. Northeast and Northwest
    B. Northeast and South
    C. Northwest and South
    D. Northwest and Far West

15. Most of the capital available for railroad construction before the Civil War was supplied by
    A. local community loans
    B. private investors
    C. state tax exemptions
    D. federal land grants

16. All of the following were true of mid-nineteenth-century American farms EXCEPT
    A. farm labor was scarce
    B. the standard of living was declining
    C. reliance on the railroad was increasing
    D. reliance on machinery was increasing

17. _____ became the railroad center of the Midwest by 1860.
    A. Cincinnati
    B. Louisville
    C. Chicago
    D. St. Louis

18. Railroads did NOT stimulate
    A. the growth of business corporations
    B. decentralization of industrial production
    C. investment banking
    D. adoption of new forms of business management

19. The coming of the railroad and machinery to western farmers did NOT increase their
    A. self-sufficiency
    B. reliance on middlemen

C. operating costs
D. productivity

20. The Panic of 1857 was of relatively little consequence to the economy of the ___C___.
    A. Northwest
    B. Northeast
    C. South
    D. New England states

Essay Questions

1. Explain why, in economic terms, the South could not abandon its system of slave labor between 1820 and 1860.
2. Assume the role of an antebellum slave. Describe a sequence of "typical" experiences in your life and relate your thoughts and feelings about these experiences.
3. Assume the role of a northern wage laborer in the 1840s. Describe a sequence of "typical" experiences in your life and relate your thoughts and feelings about these experiences.
4. List the contributions the railroads made to the growth of the national economy in the mid-nineteenth century.
5. Analyze the role that agriculture, industry, commerce, and transportation played in the growth of sectional consciousness between 1830 and 1860.

Critical Thinking Exercise

Facts, Inferences, and Judgments

As you have done in previous exercises of this type, search the following narrative for statements of fact, inference, and judgment. Circle the appropriate letter on the answer grid for each numbered statement.

---

(1) The injustice of slavery needs no proof.... (2) By "the making of a human being an animal without hope," the system bore heavily on all slaves' sense of their own worth. (3) Some found the condition absolutely unbearable....

(4) Denmark Vesey of South Carolina, even after buying his freedom, could not stomach the subservience demanded of slaves by the system. (5) When he saw Charleston slaves step into the gutter to make way for whites, he taunted them: "You deserve to remain slaves!" ... (6) So vehemently did he argue that some of his followers claimed they feared Vesey more than their masters, even more than God.... (7) For Denmark Vesey, death was probably preferable to living with such rage as his soul contained.

(8) Most slaves appeared, if not contented, at least resigned to their fate. (9) Many seemed even to accept the whites' evaluation of their inherent abilities and place in society. (10) Of course in most instances it is impossible to know whether or not this apparent

subservience was feigned in order to avoid trouble. . . .

(11) Professor Fox-Genovese has shown how slaveholders developed contradictory stereotypes of slave nature. (12) They described black men either as "Sambos" (lazy and subservient) or "Bucks" (superpotent and aggressive), females either as "Mammys" (nurturing and faithful) or "Jezebels" (wanton and seductive). . . .

(13) The harm done to the slaves by such mental distortions is obvious. (14) More obscure is the effect on the masters: Self indulgence is perhaps only contemptible; self-delusion is pitiable and ultimately destructive.

(15) Probably the large majority of owners respected the most fundamental personal rights of their slaves. (16) Indeed, so far as sexual behavior is concerned, there are countless known cases of lasting relationships based on love and mutual respect between owners and what law and the community defined as their property [that is, their slaves].

1. F I J	5. F I J	9. F I J	13. F I J
2. F I J	6. F I J	10. F I J	14. F I J
3. F I J	7. F I J	11. F I J	15. F I J
4. F I J	8. F I J	12. F I J	16. F I J

13: The Sections Go Their Ways

The South

The Economics of Slavery
- Upper South
  - ? Lower South
  - ? scientific agriculture
- ? domestic slave trade
- ? slave labor
- ? investment
- inefficient

Antebellum Plantation Life
- self-sufficiency
- ? value
- ? mortality
- ? family
- slave community

The Sociology of Slavery
- treatment
- white perceptions
- free blacks

Psychological Effects of Slavery
- personal effects
- ? resistance
  - escape covert
- on whites
  - ? degrade
  - self-indulgence
  - labor

Manufacturing in the South
- textiles
- ? labor
- ? investment
- machine tools
- capital

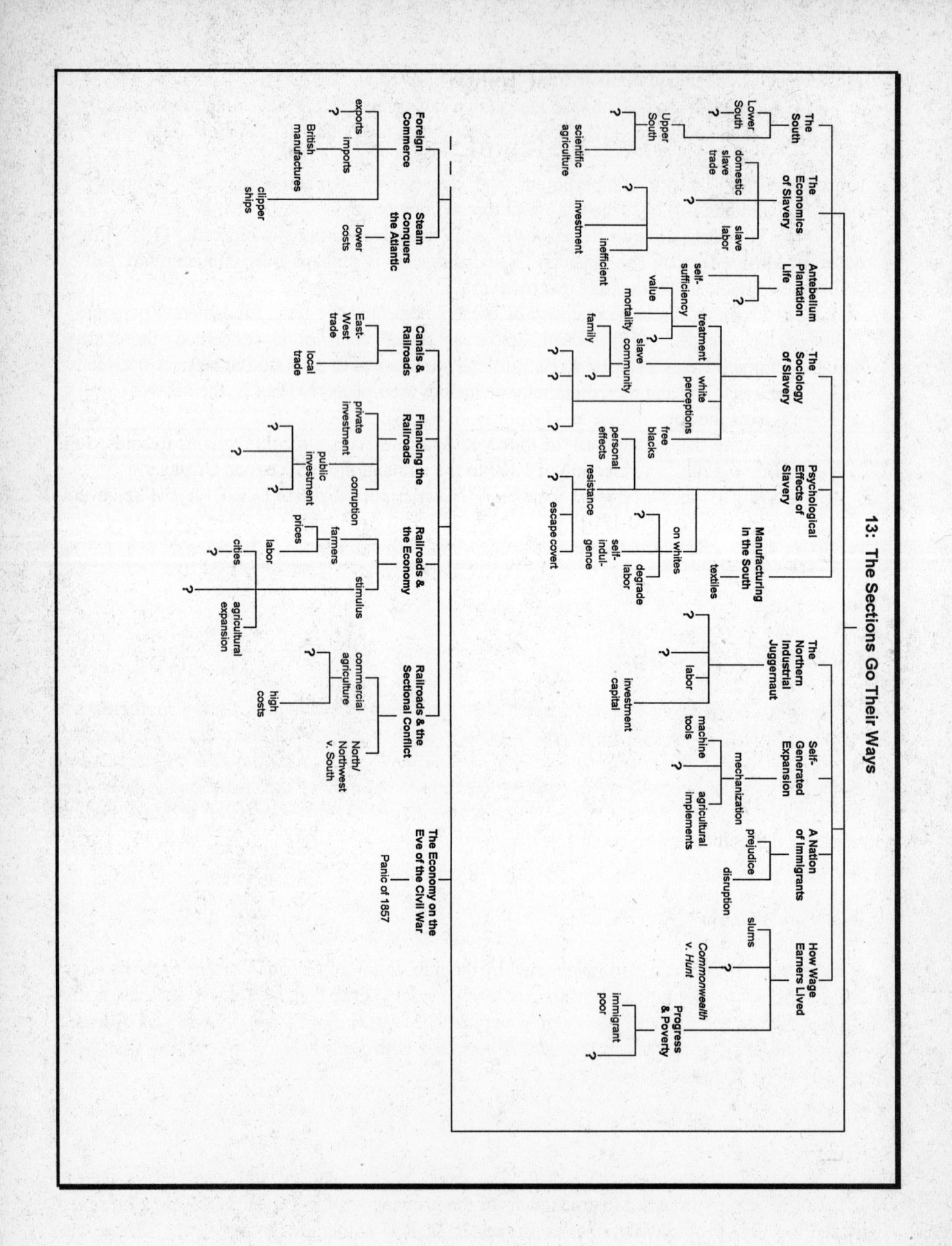

The Northern Industrial Juggernaut

Self-Generated Expansion
- mechanization
- ? agricultural implements

A Nation of Immigrants
- prejudice
- disruption

How Wage Earners Lived
- slums
- ? *Commonwealth v. Hunt*

Progress & Poverty
- immigrant poor
- ?

Foreign Commerce
- ? exports
- imports
  - British manufactures

Steam Conquers the Atlantic
- lower costs
- clipper ships

Canals & Railroads
- East-West trade
- local trade

Financing the Railroads
- ? private investment
- ? public investment
- corruption

Railroads & the Economy
- stimulus
  - prices
  - farmers
  - labor
  - ? cities
  - agricultural expansion

Railroads & the Sectional Conflict
- ? commercial agriculture
- high costs
- North/Northwest v. South

The Economy on the Eve of the Civil War
- Panic of 1857

192

Chapter 14

The Coming of the Civil War

Learning Objectives

After reading Chapter 14 you should be able to:

1. Explain why the Compromise of 1850 failed to end the debate on slavery.
2. Describe the intent, provisions, and impact of the Kansas-Nebraska Act.
3. Assess the role of Kansas Territory in the crises of the 1850s.
4. Evaluate the contribution of the Dred Scott decision, Lincoln-Douglas debates, John Brown's raid, and election of 1860 to the coming of the Secession Crisis.
5. Describe the centrality of Stephen A. Douglas and Abraham Lincoln to the key events of the period 1850-1861.

Overview

The Slave Power Comes North

The 1850 Fugitive Slave Act panicked northern blacks and encouraged more southerners to try to recover escaped slaves. Abolitionists often interfered with the enforcement of the law, and their efforts worsened sectional feelings. Northerners were outraged by the sight of blacks being carried off to slavery, and southerners resented the northerner's refusal to obey the law. The Supreme Court upheld the constitutionality of the Fugitive Slave Act, but the law became increasingly difficult to enforce in the North.

"Uncle Tom's Cabin"

Sectional tension was also heightened by the publication of Harriet Beecher Stowe's novel, *Uncle Tom's Cabin.* Like other northerners, Stowe's conscience had been stirred by the Fugitive Slave Act. While Stowe new little about slavery and her depiction of plantation life was distorted, her story had sympathetic characters and it was told with sensitivity. She was the first white American writer to look at slaves as people.

"Young America"

Foreign affairs offered a distraction from the growing sectional hostility. Sympathies were extended to European revolutionaries in revolt against autocratic government. Some also dreamed of territorial acquisitions in Mexico, Central America, and the Caribbean. The need for better communication with California resulted in the Clayton-Bulwer Treaty that gave the United States and Britain joint control of any canal built across Central America. American diplomats who signed the Ostend Manifesto proposed the acquisition of Cuba by force if necessary, but when northerners charged that it was a plot to expand slavery, the idea was dropped. The United States also signed a trade agreement and opened diplomatic relations with Japan in this period.

The Little Giant

Senator Stephen A. Douglas saw the needs of the nation in a broad perspective. He advocated territorial expansion and popular sovereignty. He opposed slavery, but did not find it morally repugnant. Generally, he thought it was unwise and unnecessary for the nation to expend its energy on the slavery issue. In the 1852 presidential campaign both parties endorsed the Comprise of 1850, but the Whig party was disintegrating and proslavery southerners were coming to dominate both the Democratic party and Congress.

The Kansas-Nebraska Act

In 1854, Douglas introduced a bill to organize the Nebraska Territory. The area had a growing population and Douglas hoped to speed construction of a transcontinental railroad through the territory. Southerners balked because they wanted the railroad further south and they feared Nebraska would become a free state. Under southern pressure, Douglas amended his bill to open the Kansas-Nebraska Territory to the possibility of slavery by popular sovereignty. Many northerners were outraged at this repeal of the Missouri Compromise that had banned slavery north of 36° 30'. Nevertheless, with solid southern support, the bill passed and the nation took a giant step toward disunion.

Know-Nothings and Republicans

The Kansas-Nebraska Act compelled former Whigs and antislavery northern Democrats to join new parties. The Know-Nothing party was founded by nativists who blamed the recent flood of Catholic immigrants for causing social problems. The party enjoyed support in both the North and South because it was flexible on the slavery issue. More significant in the long run was the founding of the Republican party, a party dedicated to opposing the expansion of slavery into the territories. It was a sectional party that appealed to the growing antislavery sentiment among northerners.

"Bleeding Kansas"

Kansas Territory became a testing ground over slavery and it eventually exposed a fatal flaw in the idea of popular sovereignty. The Kansas-Nebraska Act had been ambiguous about when a vote on slavery in the territory would be held and who would be allowed to vote. Both sections sought to influence the situation in Kansas: New England sent organized groups of antislavery settlers to Kansas, and proslavery Missourians crossed the border to vote in key

Kansas elections. The result was a virtual civil war in Kansas. The Pierce administration refused to insist on order and honesty; instead, it backed the proslavery element in Kansas.

Making a Senator a Martyr

Charles Sumner, an abolitionist senator from Massachusetts, relentlessly demeaned slavery and southerners alike. His insistence on the admission of Kansas as a free state and his personal attack on a southern senator resulted in his being assaulted by a South Carolina congressman, Preston Brooks. The incident was viewed by northerners as an illustration of the brutalizing effects of slavery on southern whites.

Buchanan Tries His Hand

In the 1856 election the Democratic candidate, James Buchanan, won by portraying the Republicans as a sectional party that threatened the Union. Republicans labeled Buchanan a "Doughface." They believed he lacked the force of character to stand up against southern extremists.

The Court's Turn

The Dred Scott decision drove another wedge between North and South. Scott was a Missouri slave whose master had taken him into Illinois and Wisconsin Territory, then returned to Missouri. Scott sued for his freedom on the basis of his temporary residence on free soil. The real issue was the question of Congress' authority to ban slavery from the territories. In 1857, the Supreme Court ruled that blacks were not citizens, so Scott could not sue in federal court. Further, the Court ruled that the Missouri Compromise (which had banned slavery from Wisconsin Territory) was unconstitutional because it violated the slaveowners' Fifth Amendment guarantee of due process. The decision also challenged the concept of popular sovereignty, undercut the foundation of the Republican party, and threatened to make slavery a national institution.

The Lecompton Constitution

President Buchanan tried to get Congress to accept Kansas' proslavery Lecompton constitution and admit Kansas as a slave state. But Douglas, concerned for his reelection to the Senate and the credibility of popular sovereignty, opposed the fraudulently drawn constitution. This clash between Buchanan and Douglas shattered the Democratic party. Ultimately, the Lecompton constitution was rejected both by Congress and a majority of Kansas voters.

The Emergence of Lincoln

To many, Douglas seemed the best hope to preserve the dividing Union. Republicans nominated Abraham Lincoln to oppose Douglas' bid for reelection to the Senate in 1858. Lincoln had served a single term in the House during the Mexican War, and he was admired in Illinois for his wit and integrity. He was not an abolitionist and he did not condemn southern slaveowners, but he condemned slavery as morally wrong. Although he had no immediate solution to the slavery problem, Lincoln insisted that the nation could not much longer remain divided over slavery.

The Lincoln-Douglas Debates

Although Lincoln and Douglas had contrasting styles, their campaign debates were pitched at a high intellectual level though they tended to exaggerate the differences between them. Both men opposed the expansion of slavery, and both believed blacks were inferior to whites, but neither was an abolitionist.

Nevertheless, Douglas tried to portray Lincoln as an abolitionist and racial equalitarian, and he painted himself as the champion of democracy. Lincoln countered by pointing to his own opposition to black suffrage and black citizenship, and his opposition to repealing the Fugitive Slave Act. Lincoln tried to picture Douglas as proslavery and an unconscionable defender of the Dred Scott decision. Douglas countered by arguing in the Freeport Doctrine that slavery could still be "banned" in a territory by passing local laws that were hostile to slavery. The Doctrine probably won Douglas reelection, but it cost him southern support when he ran for president in 1860. The debates revitalized Lincoln's political career.

Elsewhere in 1858, the Republicans fared well. Still, a southern-dominated Congress refused to enact any of the Republican's probusiness proposals. Southerners were growing increasingly uneasy in their relationship with the North, and radical southern "fire-eaters" demanded a federal slave code, and talked of annexing Cuba and reopening the African slave trade.

John Brown's Raid

John Brown, a mentally imbalanced abolitionist who had led a massacre of proslavery settlers in Kansas in 1856, organized a raid on the federal arsenal in Harpers Ferry, Virginia, in 1859. He intended to foment a slave uprising and create a black republic. Southerners were outraged. Brown was captured and executed for treason. Republicans denounced Brown's use of violence, but he conducted himself with such dignity during his trial that he was martyred by many in the North. But to southerners, John Brown was a symbol of northern ruthlessness.

The Election of 1860

Radicals in the North and South were heedlessly provoking one another, but extremists were more evident in the South. Yet, southerners sincerely felt they were merely defending themselves against the hostility and growing power of the North. Secession was openly talked about as a way to relieve the sectional tensions. Southern Democrats refused to nominate Douglas as the party's presidential candidate in 1860, and the party split in two. Later, Northern Democrats nominated Douglas on a platform upholding the Freeport Doctrine, and Southern Democrats nominated Vice-President John Breckenridge and insisted on enforcement of the Dred Scott decision.

The Republicans, drawn by his moderation, debating skills, and homespun personality, nominated Lincoln. Their platform unequivocally opposed slavery in the territories and advocated a high tariff, a homestead law, and the construction of a transcontinental railroad. With Lincoln as their nominee, Republicans hoped to capture the key states just north of the Ohio River. Remnants of the Know-Nothing (American) and Whig parties formed a Constitutional Union party, nominated John Bell, and endorsed the Constitution. Lincoln won the election with only a plurality of the popular vote, but he swept the North and West and amassed a comfortable electoral majority.

The Secession Crisis

When news of Lincoln's election was confirmed, South Carolina seceded. By February, 1861, six other Deep South states had seceded and founded the Confederate States of America.

Secession came even though Lincoln posed no immediate threat to slavery in the South, the Democrats still controlled Congress, and the Supreme Court was decidedly prosouthern. Southern states seceded in part to liberate the southern economy from northern dominance, but it was also a move to defend slavery and resist dishonorable submission to northern power. States' rights and strict constitutionalism provided the rationale for secession, but these economic and emotional concerns were more basic.

Many northerners, including Lincoln, viewed secession as a bluff. Also, many southerners refused to believe northerners would resist secession with force. President Buchanan was paralyzed by his own view that secession was illegal, but that there was no legal way for the federal government to prevent it. Congressional moderates debated then, at Lincoln's insistence, rejected the Crittenden Compromise that would have guaranteed slavery south of 36° 30' and constitutionally prohibited any future tampering with slavery in the slave states. In the South, Jefferson Davis was elected president of the Confederacy, and he set about trying to establish a new nation.

People, Places, and Things

Define the following:

"Young America" _the spirit of America growing - democracy will triumph_

popular sovereignty _up to settlers through territorial legislature to determine their own institutions (slavery)_

"Bleeding Kansas" _Everyone fighting over Kansas becoming a slave state or not_

"Doughface" _James Buchanan President of U.S._

secession _Southern States left U.S to form on Confederacy_

Describe the following:

Fugitive Slave Act _No. had to comply slaves could be seized anywhere and sent back to South_

Uncle Tom's Cabin _Book on Slavery - portrayed as people_

Clayton-Bulwer Treaty _gave U.S. + Britan joint control of any canal built across Central America_

Ostend Manifesto _acquisition of Cuba by force if necessary_

Kansas-Nebraska Act _repealed Missouri Compromise - (No Slavery north of 36° 30')_

Dred Scott decision _Since blacks could not be citizens had no right to sue in Fed. Court - Taney_

Lecompton Constitution _Pro-Slavery - rejected by Free-Soilers - wanted by Buchanan_

Lincoln-Douglas debates _1858 debates - Douglas had Flair Lincoln was "homespun"_

Freeport Doctrine _Slavery could banned in a Territory by passage of local laws_

Harpers Ferry raid _raid on fed. arsenal in Harpers Ferry, Va._

Crittenden Compromise _Slavery would exist in all territories south of 36°30'._

Identify the following:

Harriet Beecher Stowe _Uncle Tom's Cabin_

Stephen A. Douglas _Senator from Il' ran against Lincoln_

Franklin Pierce _Pres. of U.S. played both ends against middle - Take Cuba by force - Ostend Manifesto_

Know-Nothing party _American Party - I don't Know - Nativists - disliked ~~South~~ Blacks but opposed the Kansas-Nebraska Act_

Republican party _Former Free Soilers, Conscience Whigs + Anti-Neb. Democrats - For Freedom - opportunity + Free white labor_

New England Immigrant Aid Society _transported anti-slavery settlers to Kansas_

"border ruffians" _5000 people from outside of Kansas came in to vote for slavery_

John Brown _responsible for Harpers Ferry - wanted blacks to uprise_

Charles Sumner _Senator from Mass. reformer got beat up by So. Carolina Congressman Preston S. Brooks_

John C. Fremont _Republican Nominee "Pathfinder" Mexican War "Free soil, Free Speech & Fremont" No Pol. Experience_

James Buchanan _Dough-Face Pres. of U.S. after Pierce lacked force of character_

Abraham Lincoln _Senator from IL. - moderation, debating skills, home spun_

John Breckenridge _So. Dems elect for Pres_

John Bell _re m'ents Know-Nothing & Whigs = Constitutional Union Party from Tenn - border states went this way_

Jefferson Davis _Pres. of Confederates_

Self-Test

Multiple-Choice Questions

1. In the early 1850s, enforcement of the _____ gave large numbers of northerners an eyewitness view of the heartlessness of slavery.
   - (A.) Fugitive Slave Act
   - B. Kansas-Nebraska Act
   - C. Dred Scott decision
   - D. Freeport Doctrine

2. Harriet Beecher Stowe's *Uncle Tom's Cabin* aroused northern outrage over the implications of the
   - A. Lecompton Constitution
   - (B) Fugitive Slave Act
   - C. Kansas-Nebraska Act
   - D. Dred Scott decision

3. American acquisition of Cuba was advocated in the
   A. Compromise of 1850
   B. Gadsden Purchase
   C. Ostend Manifesto
   D. Clayton-Bulwer Treaty

4. In the 1850s, Senator Stephen Douglas became the national spokesman for
   A. popular sovereignty
   B. banning slavery from American territories
   C. a federal slave code
   D. abolitionism

5. Northerners thought they saw evidence of a slave power conspiracy designed to give southerners control of national policy in all these events EXCEPT the
   A. Ostend Manifesto
   B. Kansas-Nebraska Act
   C. Freeport Doctrine
   D. Dred Scott decision

6. To decide the fate of slavery in the territories, Stephen Douglas' Kansas-Nebraska bill applied the same concept that had been used in the
   A. Northwest Ordinance
   B. Wilmot Proviso
   C. Missouri Compromise
   D. Compromise of 1850

7. The greatest beneficiary of the northern outrage over passage of the Kansas-Nebraska Act was the _____ party.
   A. Democratic
   B. Whig
   C. Republican
   D. Know-Nothing

8. The concept of popular sovereignty caused problems when it was applied in Kansas because it
   A. was illegal
   B. was ambiguous
   C. carried a moral condemnation of slavery
   D. made abolition a capital offense

9. Charles Sumner was a Senate spokesman for
   A. popular sovereignty
   B. abolitionism
   C. secession
   D. nativism

10. It was NOT true that President Buchanan
    A. was a "Doughface"
    B. believed secession was legal
    C. supported the Lecompton Constitution
    D. supported the Dred Scott decision

11. Which one of the following was NOT associated with the proslavery element in Kansas Territory?
    A. the sack of Lawrence
    B. "border ruffians"
    C. Lecompton Constitution
    D. John Brown

12. In the Dred Scott decision the Supreme Court did NOT rule that
    A. Dred Scott was legally held in slavery
    B. Dred Scott was not a citizen of the United States
    C. the Missouri Compromise was unconstitutional
    D. slavery in the territories must be decided by popular sovereignty

13. The Lecompton Constitution was approved by
    A. President Buchanan
    B. Stephen Douglas
    C. a majority of the eligible voters in Kansas
    D. Republicans

14. When he ran for the U.S. Senate from Illinois in 1858, Lincoln was generally considered _____ on the slavery issue.
    A. an abolitionist
    B. indifferent
    C. naive
    D. a moderate

15. In their 1858 debates, Lincoln and Douglas were in agreement as to the
    A. status of slavery in the territories
    B. implication of the Dred Scott decision
    C. probable inferiority of blacks
    D. morality of slavery

16. When he raided Harpers Ferry, John Brown apparently hoped to
    A. frighten the North and South into negotiating a compromise on slavery
    B. provoke a slave insurrection
    C. discredit northern abolitionists
    D. help make Kansas a free state

17. Match the 1860 presidential candidate with his position on the issue of slavery in the territories
    - A. Lincoln
    - B. Douglas
    - C. Breckenridge

    1. federal slave code
    2. ban slavery
    3. popular sovereignty
    4. have Congress divide territories; half slave and half free

    A. A-1, B-2, C-3
    B. A-2, B-1, C-3
    C. A-3, B-1, C-2
    D. A-2, B-3, C-1 ✓

18. Which one of the following was NOT a feature of the election of 1860?
    A. the nation now had a president who had virtually no support in the South
    B. the Republican party divided over the the issue of slavery in the territories ✓
    C. the Democratic party divided into hostile northern and southern wings
    D. the winner won less than a majority of the popular vote

19. The proposed Crittenden Comprise would have
    A. banned slavery in all U.S. territories
    B. amended the Constitution to protect slavery
    C. repealed the Fugitive Slave Act
    D. repealed the Missouri Compromise ✓

20. Arrange these events in their proper time order: (A) Dred Scott decision, (B) Lincoln-Douglas debates, (C) Kansas-Nebraska Act, (D) Harpers Ferry raid.
    A. A, C, B, D
    B. B, D, C, A
    C. C, A, B, D ✓
    D. D, B, A, C

Essay Questions

1. Explain why it might be said that the South's insistence on the strict enforcement of the Fugitive Slave Act may have been a fatal error.
2. Explain why "the nation took the greatest single step in its march toward the abyss of secession and civil war" when Congress passed the Kansas-Nebraska Act.
3. Explain why Kansas Territory came to be the focus of sectional hostilities in the mid-1850s.
4. Evaluate the importance of the Dred Scott decision, Lincoln-Douglas debates, Harper's Ferry raid, and the Election of 1860 to the coming of secession and civil war. Which of these events do you think was the *most* significant? Why?
5. Choose either Stephen Douglas or Abraham Lincoln. Then make an argument that he was the nation's single most important political leader between 1852 and 1861.

Critical Thinking Exercise

Cause and Effect

Understanding the coming of the Civil War depends on your being able to see the chain of causal relationships that preceded it. In the following exercise, a series of *effects* is sequentially listed in Column B. Column A is a list of *causes*. You must match the appropriate cause in Column A with the effect it produced in Column B. Items in Column A may be used more than once.

Column A

a. Catholic immigration reaches high levels
b. Fugitive Slave Act strictly enforced
c. John Brown's Raid
d. popular sovereignty election generates conflict
e. Lincoln wins the 1860 election
f. northerners charge a plot to expand slavery
g. Republicans refuse to compromise on slavery in the territories
h. northern outrage at the Kansas-Nebraska Act
i. Missouri Compromise repealed
j. Dred Scott decision
k. Freeport Doctrine pronounced
l. interest develops in a transcontinental railroad from Chicago to San Francisco

Column B

__B__ 1. northerners get first taste of "real" slavery
__B__ 2. Harriet Beecher Stowe writes *Uncle Tom's Cabin*
__F__ 3. the Ostend Manifesto is repudiated
__L__ 4. Kansas-Nebraska Bill introduced
__i__ 5. northerners outraged at slavery expansion
__a__ 6. founding of the Know-Nothing party
__h__ 7. founding of the Republican party
__D__ 8. civil war in Kansas
__j__ 9. slavery made legal in all territories
__K__ 10. Senator Douglas loses southern support
__C__ 11. Southern fears of abolitionist threat
__e__ 12. South Carolina secedes
__G__ 13. the Crittenden Compromise proposals are rejected

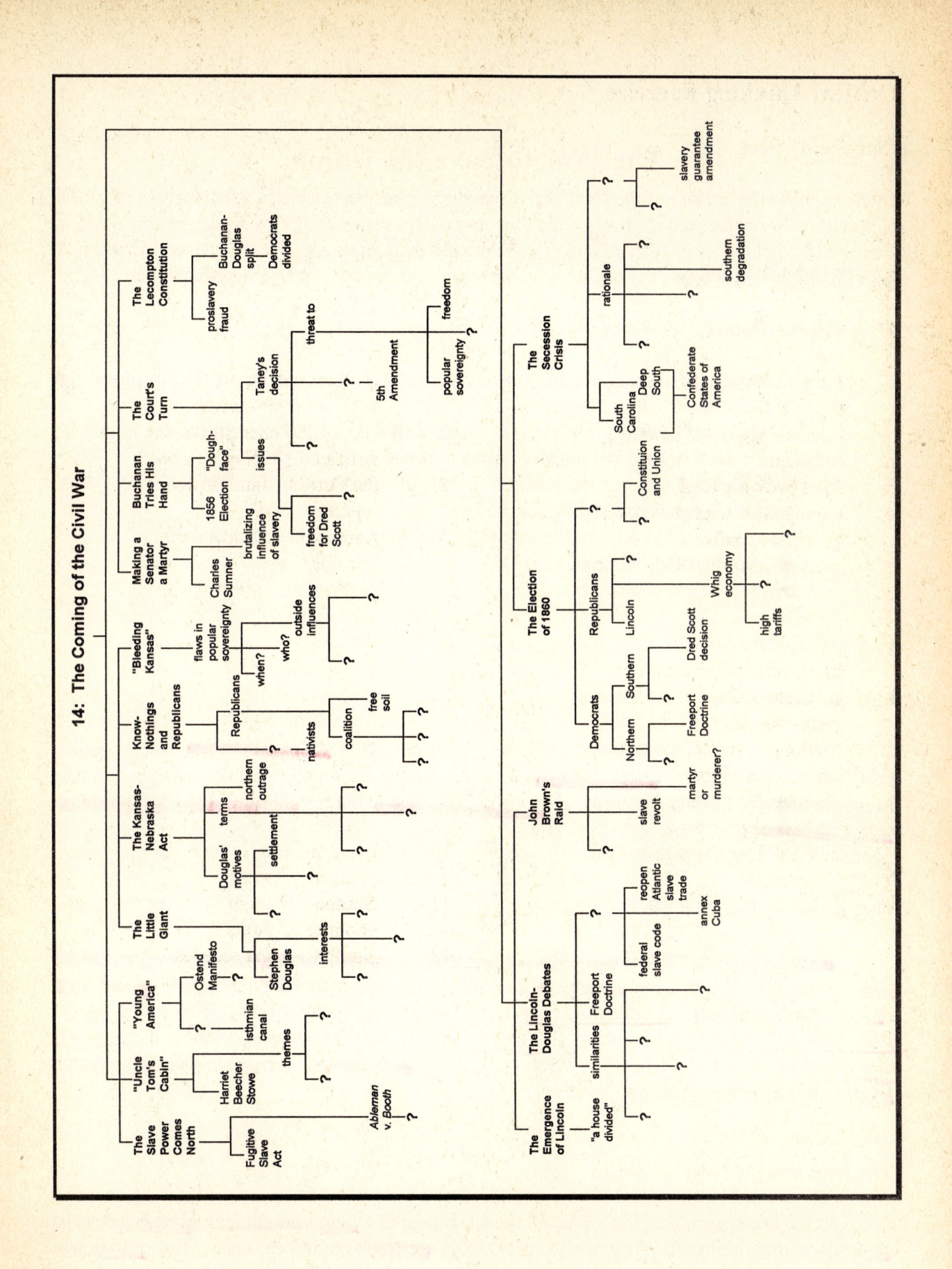

14: The Coming of the Civil War

- The Slave Power Comes North
  - Fugitive Slave Act
    - *Ableman v. Booth*
- "Uncle Tom's Cabin"
  - Harriet Beecher Stowe
  - themes
    - ?
    - ?
- "Young America"
  - Ostend Manifesto
    - ?
  - isthmian canal
- The Little Giant
  - Stephen Douglas
    - interests
      - ?
- The Kansas-Nebraska Act
  - Douglas' motives
    - terms — northern outrage
    - settlement
      - ?
    - ?
- Know-Nothings and Republicans
  - Republicans
    - ?
    - nativists
    - coalition
      - free soil
        - ?
        - ?
- "Bleeding Kansas"
  - flaws in popular sovereignty
    - when?
    - who? — outside influences
      - ?
      - ?
- Making a Senator a Martyr
  - Charles Sumner
    - brutalizing influence of slavery
    - freedom for Dred Scott
- Buchanan Tries His Hand
  - 1856 Election
    - "Dough-face"
  - issues
    - ?
- The Court's Turn
  - Taney's decision
    - threat to — 5th Amendment
      - freedom
      - popular sovereignty
        - ?
    - ?
- The Lecompton Constitution
  - proslavery fraud
  - Buchanan-Douglas split
  - Democrats divided

- The Emergence of Lincoln
  - "a house divided"
    - ?
- The Lincoln-Douglas Debates
  - similarities
    - ?
    - Freeport Doctrine
      - federal slave code
        - reopen Atlantic slave trade
        - annex Cuba
      - ?
- John Brown's Raid
  - slave revolt
    - ?
  - martyr or murderer?
- The Election of 1860
  - Democrats
    - Northern — Freeport Doctrine
      - ?
    - Southern — Dred Scott decision
      - ?
  - Republicans
    - Lincoln
    - Whig economy
      - high tariffs
      - ?
  - Constitution and Union
    - ?
- The Secession Crisis
  - South Carolina
  - Deep South
    - Confederate States of America
  - rationale
    - ?
    - ? — southern degradation
    - ? — slavery guarantee amendment

205

Chapter 15

The War to Save the Union

Learning Objectives

After reading Chapter 15 you should be able to:

1. Compare and contrast the relative advantages and disadvantages of the North and the South as the Civil War began.
2. Evaluate the Civil War's impact on the homefront in both the North and the South.
3. Trace the course of key military events between 1861 and 1865.
4. Compare and contrast the leadership skills of Abraham Lincoln and Jefferson Davis, and of Ulysses Grant and Robert E. Lee.
5. Assess the significance of the Emancipation Proclamation as an instrument of war and as a source of social revolution.

Overview

Cabinet Making

President Lincoln assembled a balanced Cabinet headed by William Seward, who hoped to conciliate the South, and Salmon Chase, who was a spokesman for abolitionists. In his first inaugural address, Lincoln declared that secession was illegal, but that his administration posed no threat to slavery.

Fort Sumter: The First Shot

When Lincoln tried to resupply Fort Sumter in Charleston harbor, Confederates fired on the fort. Lincoln then called for volunteers to suppress the southern rebellion which caused four border states to secede. Southerners considered Lincoln's call an act of aggression that denied them their right to self-determination. In Lincoln's view, secession was undemocratic because it challenged the results of a freely held election. In 1861, northerners were committed to saving the Union, not to freeing the slaves.

The Blue and the Gray

As the war began, the North enjoyed the advantage of a larger population, greater industrial capacity, a better railroad system, and control of the merchant marine and navy. But southerners believed northerners would not support the war because northern business interests were closely tied to the South. Southerners also expected economic and military aid from Europe. They also rightly believed that they had superior military leadership and the advantage of defensive warfare.

Both sides faced great difficulties. In the North, recruiting was left to the states and most enlistees knew little of soldiering. But Lincoln claimed emergency powers for his presidency and provided bold leadership. The South had greater problems. It was handicapped by the states' rights philosophy that hindered a unified Confederate war effort. Unlike Lincoln who had an ability to think problems through and act unflinchingly, Jefferson Davis, a mediocre military thinker, meddled in details and would not delegate authority.

The Test of Battle: Bull Run

The first military engagement between the inexperienced armies came near Manassas Junction, Virginia. Confederate troops routed Union forces, but the battle's significance was psychological; southern morale soared while northerners set about making more realistic preparations for a long war. Lincoln's basic strategy called for a naval blockade of the Confederate coast, control of the Mississippi River, and the invasion of Virginia. He appointed General George McClellan to command Union forces. McClellan had experience and was a talented administrator. To restore northern confidence, he began organizing, training, and supplying his army.

Paying for the War

The Union government's demand for war supplies accelerated the tendency toward industrialization. To pay for the war, the North used income and excise taxes, and a direct tax on states, but loans and currency inflation were the key sources of revenue.

Politics as Usual

With southern Democrats in secession, Republicans dominated Congress. That party's radical faction grew stronger under the leadership of Charles Sumner and Thaddeus Stevens, both of whom insisted on abolition and political and civil rights for blacks. Northern Peace Democrats led by Charles Vallandigham demanded a negotiated peace. Lincoln periodically used martial law and suspended the writ of habeas corpus to control antiwar dissent.

Behind Confederate Lines

Jefferson Davis' strategy was to defend the South and, with time, wear down the Union's will to fight. Confederates were the first to draft men into military service, but wealthy planters easily escaped the draft. The South did not develop a two-party system, but Davis and southern governors were constantly at odds over policy. Like the North, the Confederacy turned to income and excise taxes, borrowing, and currency inflation to pay for the war. Confederates also mortgaged the cotton crop to raise revenue. They also hoped to use King Cotton to compel Britain to come to their aid, but the British had a surplus of cotton when the war began and they found alternative sources of the fiber. In addition, crop failures forced Britain to import northern wheat, thus tying their economy more closely to the North than to the South.

Still, the relationship between the Union and Britain was troubled. The *Trent* affair nearly provoked war, and Lincoln's government threatened war if the British government allowed British-built iron-clad rams to be delivered to the Confederacy. The possibility of British intervention on behalf of the Confederacy faded as the North gained battlefield superiority.

No Central gov.

War in the West

In early 1862, General Grant captured strategic forts in western Tennessee and invaded northern Mississippi. The carnage was appalling at the bloody battle of Shiloh, shaking the confidence of both armies. Modern technology had produced weapons of unprecedented accuracy and destructive power. Both sides now recognized how grim the war would be.

McClellan, the Reluctant Warrior

McClellan's plan was to invade Richmond through the peninsula formed by the York and James rivers in Virginia. But he had no intellectual grasp of the demands of modern warfare. McClellan thought it uncivilized to think of crushing the South. He was an unsurpassed military administrator and planner, but he did not like to fight and risk damage to his excellently prepared army.

Thus, McClellan's Peninsula Campaign was conducted with too much caution. Confederate commander Robert E. Lee was an excellent tactician, and, unlike McClellan, was bold and masterful on the battlefield. His plan for the Seven Days battle for Richmond placed McClellan on the defensive. Again, the loss of life was appalling.

Lee Counterattacks: Antietam

McClellan's successor, General Henry Halleck, called off the Peninsula Campaign. As Union troops withdrew, Lee seized the initiative, won the second battle of Bull Run, and invaded Maryland. He hoped that a dramatic blow on Union soil would unnerve the northern public who would then demand a negotiated peace. But he was effectively countered at Antietam and withdrew his badly mauled army back into Virginia.

The Emancipation Proclamation

When the war began, Lincoln feared any move against slavery would alienate the border states. But he came under increasingly heavy pressure to emancipate the slaves as a way to crush the Confederacy by encouraging slaves to revolt. Radical Republicans in Congress had already abolished slavery in Washington, D.C., and the territories, and the Confiscation Act freed all slaves owned by southern rebels. Lincoln was personally sympathetic to the idea of freeing the slaves, but he preferred compensated emancipation by state law and colonization of those freed. He was concerned that emancipation would divide the North and injure the war effort. But by mid-1862, Lincoln was convinced for military reasons that emancipation should become a northern war aim. Following the Battle of Antietam, he issued the Emancipation Proclamation that freed all slaves in areas still in rebellion. It did not free slaves in the border states or in former Confederate territories then occupied by Union forces. He justified emancipation as a way to weaken the Confederacy.

Southerners saw the Emancipation Proclamation as an incitement to slave rebellion while some northerners did not think it went far enough to end slavery. It immediately aggravated racial prejudice in the North because many whites feared a massive migration of former slaves into northern communities. Consequently, as slaves were freed under the proclamation, the government adopted a containment policy to keep them in the South.

Negrophobia and the Draft Riots

The Union's 1863 Conscription Act was patently discriminatory against the poor. It provoked rioting in New York City where poor Irish Catholic workers resented blacks with whom they competed for jobs. This resentment and violent rioting reflected the public's awareness that emancipation had produced a revolutionary change in American society. Nevertheless, most whites remained racists.

The Emancipated People

To blacks, the Emancipation Proclamation was a promise of future improvement and they expressed their appreciation to President Lincoln. In the South, as Union armies approached, slaves abandoned the plantations and flocked to the Union lines.

Black Soldiers

When the war began, blacks were not enlisted for military service. But by 1862 manpower needs altered white thinking, and the Emancipation Proclamation authorized black enlistment. Ending slavery had now clearly become a northern war goal. Black soldiers were segregated and commanded by white officers, but they proved themselves in battle. Southerners had a special hatred for the Union's black troops.

Antietam to Gettysburg

In the winter of 1862-1863, further Union attempts to capture Richmond were turned back at Fredricksburg and Chancellorsville. Lee again decided to risk a move into Union soil at Gettysburg, Pennsylvania. But three days of bloody battle failed and he again pulled back into Virginia.

Lincoln Finds His General: Vicksburg

In the same week as Gettysburg, Grant laid siege to Vicksburg, a Confederate stronghold on the Mississippi River. His capture of Vicksburg effectively severed the trans-Mississippi region from the rest of the Confederacy. The success of his brilliant campaign caused Lincoln to place Grant in charge of all trans-Appalachian armies. In a short time his forces captured the rail center of Chattanooga and cleared the way for an invasion of Georgia. Lincoln then gave Grant supreme command of all Union forces.

Economic and Social Effects, North and South

Shortages produced by the blockade and the printing of paper currency led to drastic inflation in the Confederacy. The South also faced a deteriorating railroad network and shortages in labor, capital, and technology. States' rights sentiment prevented the Confederacy from making effective use of its scarce resources.

By contrast, the northern economy flourished. Government purchases stimulated railroad operations and manufacturing, and agricultural prices were high. The Republican Congress passed legislation to encourage western settlement, build colleges, raise tariffs, construct a transcontinental railroad, and provide a uniform currency. These all stimulated the economy, but there were problems. Prices soared and there was a chronic shortage of labor and numerous strikes. Inflation and shortages fostered the speculative spirit and a selfish materialism. Illegal but highly profitable trade with the southern enemy was common.

The war hastened industrialization and created a more complex and efficient economy. It also trained people to organize and plan on a large scale, stimulated the growth of large corporations, and created a better banking system.

Women in Wartime

In both the North and the South, women took over management of farms and plantations and enlisted in the army medical corps. Northern women also took jobs in industry and government agencies.

Grant in the Wilderness

Grant's strategy was to have his Army of the Potomac capture Richmond while Sherman captured Atlanta; then the two armies would close a pincer movement on Lee's army in Virginia. Grant's forces fought a series of frustrating and extremely costly flanking movements around Richmond. Grant knew he could eventually win by grinding down Lee's depleted forces with his own superior numbers and resources.

Sherman in Georgia

Huge casualty figures and the absence of a decisive victory made the northern public pessimistic. It appeared that Lincoln may not be able to win reelection in 1864. But on the eve of the election, General Sherman's army captured Atlanta, then began its march to the sea. Sherman's aim was to destroy southern resources and break the Confederate's will to fight. Lincoln was reelected and the South's will began to falter. Sherman reached Savannah, then turned north to close the vise on Lee.

To Appomattox Court House

In his second inaugural, Lincoln extended a conciliatory hand to the South. He asked for northern tolerance and mercy for a just and lasting peace. Grant captured Richmond in April 1865 and received Lee's surrender at Appomattox Court House.

Costs and Prospects

The Civil War cost the nation more than 600,000 lives and untold millions of dollars in lost property. It instilled hatred and bitterness that lasted for generations. It nurtured corruption, gross materialism, and selfishness. These more sordid effects of the war overshadow the numerous examples of wartime charity, self-sacrifice, and devotion to duty. Still, the war ended slavery, cemented the nation, and utterly discredited secession. The northern victory heartened the friends of republican government and democracy everywhere. The war created a better-integrated society and a more technologically advanced and productive economic system. It also left to the postwar generation a number of difficult problems.

People, Places, and Things

Define the following:

self-determination *So. blamed Lincoln for 1st shot - Not letting them do as they pleased*

greenbacks *money - Paper Feds*

writ of habeas corpus *Suspension of some freedoms to control dissenters* martial law <u>Lincoln had dissenters arrested & held without trial</u>

conscription <u>permitted hiring ^(substitutes) others for war</u>

Describe the following:

Trent affair <u>U.S stopped Brit ship (trent) & took ^(arrested) 2 confederate envoys enroute to London - Lincoln let them loose</u>

Emancipation Proclamation <u>Freed ~~all~~ slaves in states in rebellion</u>

Homestead Act <u>1862 gave 160 acres to settler to farm land for 5 yrs.</u>

Morrill Land Grant Act <u>30,000 acres in support of state agricultural colleges</u>

Pacific Railway Act <u>subsidies in land & money for construction of trancontinetal railroad</u>

National Banking Act <u>gave country uniform currency</u>

New York draft riots <u>worker felt law unfair - rich could pay $300 to stay out of war - didn't want to fight ^(blacks) for free</u>

Sherman's march to the sea <u>to terrorize the south as proof the North would prevail.</u>

Identify the following:

William Seward Sec of State - hoped to conciliate the South

Abraham Lincoln Strong

Jefferson Davis Weak

Stonewall Jackson Cruel Gen. for South

George McClellan General of North

Charles Sumner Now radical ↓

Thaddeus Stevens Pennsylvania Congressman radical with Sumner - granting full Political + civil rights to blacks

Copperheads Peace Democrats - opposed war

Clement Vallandigham Peace Democrate - Ohio - domestic foe against war + abolition - Sent to Canada

George G. Meade Union - General commanded army

Ulysses S. Grant Gen for U.S. captured parts of Eastern Tenn and invaded Northern Miss. - Fired once later took over after Vicksburg.

William T. Sherman _____
_____

Locate the following places: Write in both the place name and its map location number.

1. Where the "first shot" of the Civil War was fired.

   _____ _____

2. The four states that seceded and joined with the original seven in the Confederacy in 1861.

   _____ _____

   _____ _____

   _____ _____

   _____ _____

3. Site of the first pitched battle of the Civil War.

   _____ _____

4. Counties of a Confederate state that "seceded" from that state and joined the Union.

   _____ _____

5. The two major battles of the Civil War that were fought on Union soil.

   _____ _____

   _____ _____

6. The last major Confederate stronghold on the Mississippi River. It fell to Grant's siege in 1863.

   _____ _____

7. The Confederate capital during the Civil War.

   _____ _____

8. The southern rail center where a Union victory helped Lincoln win reelection in 1864.

   _____ _____

9. The state traversed by General Sherman's army in its march to the sea.

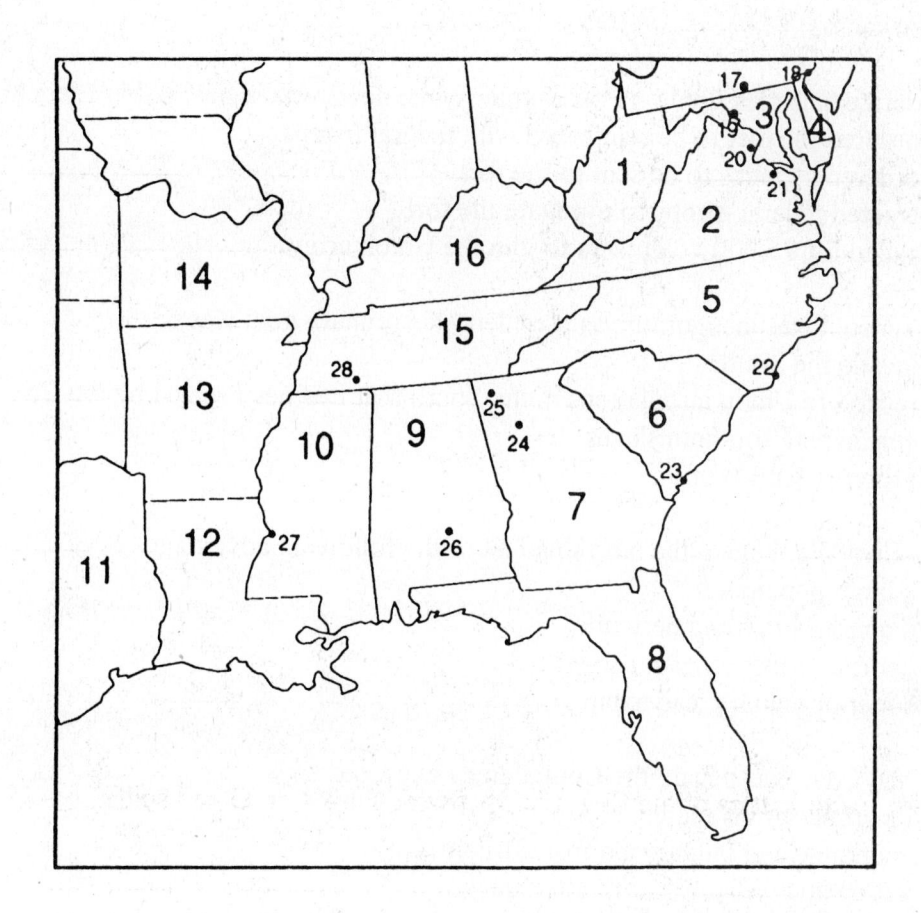

   _____ _____

Self-Test

Multiple-Choice Questions

1. Which one of the following states did NOT secede from the Union after the firing on Fort Sumter?
   A. Kentucky
   B. Tennessee
   C. Virginia
   D. Arkansas

2. Confederate batteries fired on Fort Sumter when news was received that Lincoln
   A. ordered the fort to be reinforced with federal troops
   B. ordered supplies to be sent to the fort
   C. wanted federal troops to evacuate the fort
   D. called for 75,000 volunteers to join the Union army

3. When Lincoln was inaugurated as president, his primary goal was to
   A. invade the South
   B. recapture Union installations in the South that had been seized by the Confederates
   C. emancipate southern slaves
   D. preserve the Union

4. As the Civil War began, the North had all of the following advantages EXCEPT
   A. a large population
   B. a complex railroad network
   C. enormous industrial capabilities
   D. superior military leadership

5. When the Civil War began, the Confederacy expected
   A. its armies to invade the North
   B. economic and military aid from Britain
   C. a long and difficult war of attrition
   D. that to win, they would have to abandon their states' rights philosophy

6. The Union's strategy for the Civil War was to do all the following EXCEPT
   A. blockade the Confederate coastline
   B. pressure the Confederates to negotiate a compromise peace
   C. divide the Confederacy by gaining control of the Mississippi River
   D. capture Richmond

7. The Union government did NOT help finance the Civil War by using
   A. income taxes
   B. excise taxes
   C. borrowing
   D. direct taxes on states

8. The outspoken leader of the antiwar Peace Democrats in the North during the Civil War was
   A. Charles Sumner
   B. Clement Vallandigham
   C. Thaddeus Stevens
   D. Samuel Chase

9. During the Civil War the Confederate cause was hampered by all of the following EXCEPT
   A. having to fight a defensive war
   B. currency inflation
   C. its own states' rights philosophy
   D. shortages of supplies and equipment

10. England and the Union were nearly provoked into war by
    A. the incompetence of Charles Francis Adams, the American ambassador to England
    B. England's refusal to buy American cotton
    C. the Union's seizure of Confederate diplomats aboard a British ship
    D. British commerce raider attacks on northern shipping

11. During the first year of the Civil War the Union's most important success came
    A. in northwestern Tennessee
    B. at the Battle of Bull Run
    C. in northern Virginia
    D. at Antietam

12. President Lincoln eventually concluded that General George McClellan was
    A. too cautious
    B. a poor administrator
    C. incapable of disciplining his troops
    D. careless

13. President Lincoln was originally cautious about emancipating the slaves because he claimed that it would do all of the following EXCEPT
    A. divide public opinion in the North
    B. alienate the Union's border states
    C. encourage the slaves to revolt
    D. infuriate Radical Republicans in Congress

14. Lincoln justified the Emancipation Proclamation on grounds of
    A. moral imperatives
    B. natural rights
    C. economic advantage
    D. military necessity

15. The Emancipation Proclamation promised freedom to slaves
    A. in the Union border states
    B. in Confederate-held states and territories

C. in Union territories
D. if they agreed to stay in the South

16. The New York City draft riots were primarily a protest against
    A. the Emancipation Proclamation
    B. conscription
    C. Lincoln's suspension of the writ of habeas corpus
    D. the temporary declaration of martial law in the city

17. After the Emancipation Proclamation, when blacks enlisted in the Union army they were
    A. segregated into black units
    B. allowed to elect their own commanders
    C. generally poor combat soldiers
    D. not allowed to engage in combat

18. During the Civil War, Congress passed legislation to do all of the following EXCEPT
    A. provide free homesteads to settlers
    B. build a transcontinental railroad
    C. supply a uniform currency
    D. lower tariff rates

19. The proper sequence of these battles is: (A) Gettysburg, (B) Shiloh, (C) First Bull Run, (D) Antietam.
    A. B, C, D, A
    B. D, A, B, C
    C. A, B, C, D
    D. C, B, D, A

20. During the Civil War, the Confederacy won all the following battles EXCEPT
    A. Vicksburg
    B. Fredricksburg
    C. Chancellorsville
    D. Second Bull Run

Essay Questions

1. Based on a consideration of their perceived advantages, explain why both sides felt confident of victory as the Civil War began.
2. Describe the economic and social changes in both the North and the South that accompanied the Civil War.
3. Select what you think were the five most important battles of the Civil War. Explain why you chose these battles; then tell how each battle contributed to the outcome of the Civil War.

4. Describe the personal and leadership qualities that made Lincoln a better wartime president than Jefferson Davis. Also, explain what command skills Grant utilized to overcome Lee's recognized tactical expertise.
5. Evaluate the contribution the Emancipation Proclamation made to the war effort, and list ways it altered the social and economic systems of both the North and the South.

Critical Thinking Exercise

Compare and Contrast

You have seen several times how historians compare and contrast information to gain a better understanding of two or more elements of historical study. The Civil War, pitting North against South, is a natural for comparing and contrasting. In the following exercise match each of the numbered statement to the key below.

N - if the statement is true of the *North only*
S - if the statement is true of the *South only*
B - if the statement is true of *both* the North and the South
X - if the statement is true of *neither* the North nor the South

_____ 1. Counting both blacks and whites, it had a population of over 20 million people in 1861.

_____ 2. It had control of the merchant marine and navy.

_____ 3. It expected Great Britain would provide it with crucial military and economic aid.

_____ 4. It had the advantage of fighting a defensive war.

_____ 5. It experienced no significant division or antiwar sentiment within its population.

_____ 6. At first it benefited from superior military leadership.

_____ 7. It won a decisive victory at Antietam.

_____ 8. It suffered the divisive handicap of the states' rights philosophy.

_____ 9. Its president devoted too much time to details and failed to delegate authority well.

_____ 10. Its president's strength lay in his ability to think problems through and act unflinchingly.

_____ 11. Its navy clamped a blockade on all enemy ports.

_____ 12. It managed to wage war without spending the nation into significant indebtedness.

_____ 13. Its Congress passed an income tax law and new excise taxes.

_____ 14. Its Congress assessed a direct tax on the states.

_____ 15. Its government authorized loans to help finance the war.

_____ 16. Some of its financial obligations were met by printing paper money.

_____ 17. It relied primarily on a strong defense to wear down the enemy's will to fight.

_____ 18. It suffered from shortages of labor.

_____ 19. It experienced shortages and printed great amounts of paper currency.

_____ 20. Its railroads operated close to capacity and with increasing efficiency.

_____ 21. As the war dragged on the continuing inflation eroded purchasing power.

_____ 22. The war stimulated production and the growth of large corporations.

_____ 23. Its women took over the management of farms when their men went off to war.

_____ 24. Its commanding general grasped the fundamental truth that the best tactic was to wage total war.

_____ 25. Its supply of volunteer enlistments was sufficient to prevent having to draft men into military service.

15: The War to Save the Union

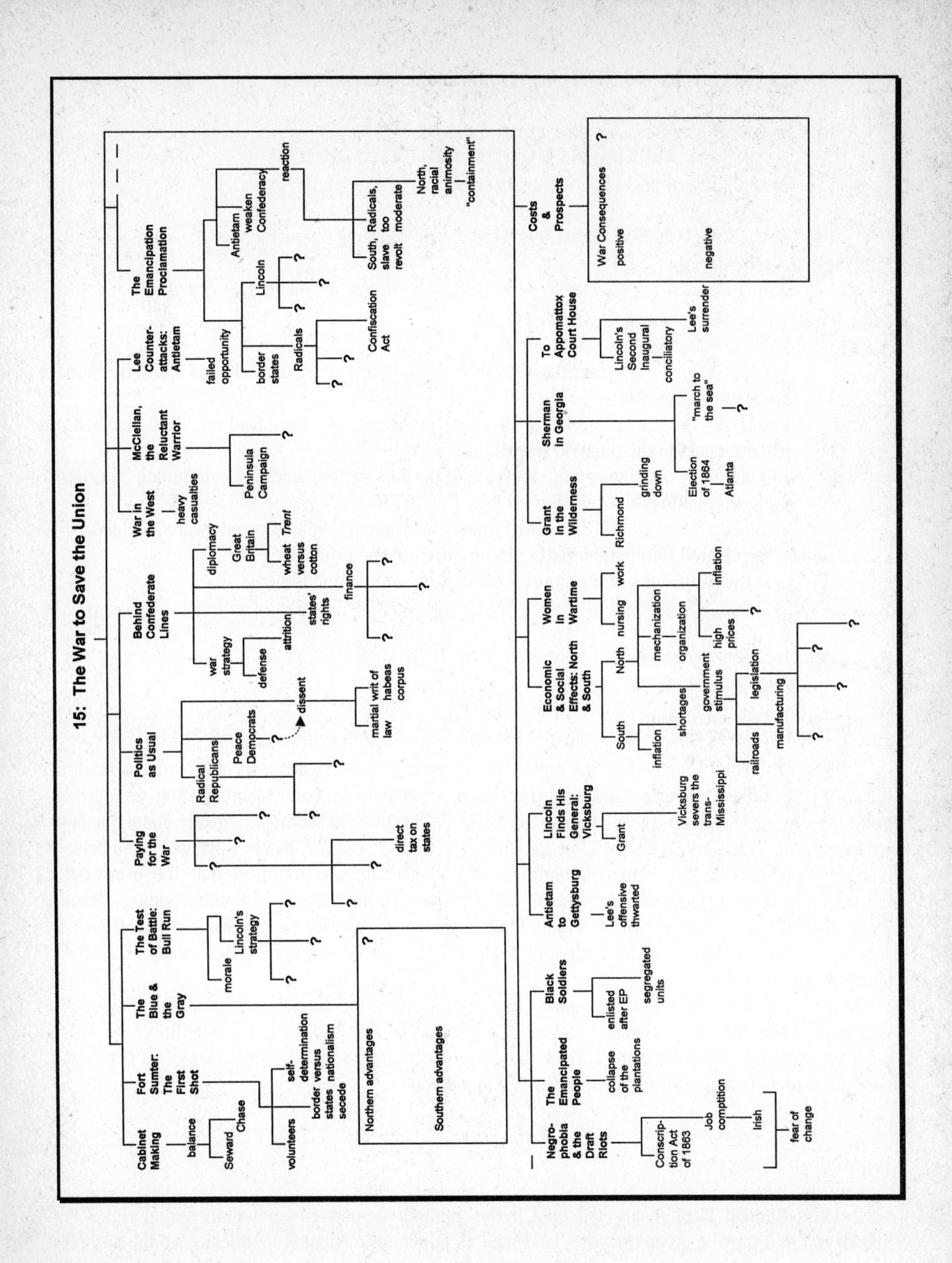

- **Cabinet Making**
  - balance
  - Seward
  - Chase
- **Fort Sumter: The First Shot**
  - volunteers
  - self-determination versus states nationalism
  - border states secede
  - Northern advantages — ?
  - Southern advantages — ?
- **The Blue & the Gray**
  - morale
- **The Test of Battle: Bull Run**
  - Lincoln's strategy — ?
  - ?
- **Paying for the War**
  - ?
  - ?
  - direct tax on states
- **Politics as Usual**
  - Radical Republicans
  - Peace Democrats — ? (dissent)
  - martial law / writ of habeas corpus
- **Behind Confederate Lines**
  - war strategy
  - defense
  - attrition
  - states' rights
  - finance — ?
  - ?
  - diplomacy
    - Great Britain
    - wheat versus cotton
    - *Trent*
- **War in the West**
  - heavy casualties
- **McClellan, the Reluctant Warrior**
  - Peninsula Campaign — ?
- **Lee Counterattacks: Antietam**
  - failed opportunity
  - border states
  - Radicals
  - Confiscation Act — ?
  - ?
- **The Emancipation Proclamation**
  - Antietam weaken Confederacy
  - reaction
  - Lincoln — ?
  - ?
  - South, slave revolt
  - Radicals, too moderate
  - North, racial animosity
  - "containment"
- **Costs & Prospects**
  - **War Consequences**
    - positive
    - negative
    - ?

- **Negrophobia & the Draft Riots**
  - Conscription Act of 1863
    - Job competition
    - Irish
    - fear of change
- **The Emancipated People**
  - collapse of the plantations
  - enlisted after EP
- **Black Soldiers**
  - segregated units
- **Antietam to Gettysburg**
  - Lee's offensive thwarted
- **Lincoln Finds His General: Vicksburg**
  - Grant
  - Vicksburg severs the trans-Mississippi
- **Economic & Social Effects: North & South**
  - North
    - nursing work
    - mechanization
    - organization
    - high prices
    - inflation — ?
  - South
    - inflation
    - shortages
    - government stimulus
    - railroads
    - manufacturing
    - legislation — ?, ?
- **Women in Wartime**
- **Grant in the Wilderness**
  - Richmond
  - grinding down
  - Election of 1864
  - Atlanta
- **Sherman in Georgia**
  - "march to the sea" — ?
- **To Appomattox Court House**
  - Lincoln's Second Inaugural conciliatory
  - Lee's surrender

221

Chapter 16

Reconstruction and the South

Learning Objectives

After reading Chapter 16 you should be able to:

1. Compare and contrast the provisions of both Presidential and Congressional Reconstruction plans.
2. Describe the problems and accomplishments of the Radical Reconstruction governments in the postwar South.
3. Explain why sharecropping and the crop-lien system came to dominate southern agriculture after the Civil War.
4. Explain why Radical Reconstruction governments faltered and were replaced by conservative Democratic party governments in the South by 1877.
5. List the provisions of the Fourteenth and Fifteenth Amendments.

Overview

Presidential Reconstruction

When the Civil War ended, the nation faced the complex legal question of how to readmit the former Confederate states back into the Union. President Lincoln's lenient 1862 ten percent plan merely required southern states to adopt a republican form of government, accept emancipation, and provide for black education. It did not require black suffrage. Radicals in Congress objected to the plan's moderation and to Lincoln's assumption that the president's pardoning power mandated his control of Reconstruction policy. Lincoln pocket vetoed Congress' Wade-Davis bill which would have required a majority (not merely ten percent) of southern voters to take a loyalty oath, and would have required southern states to repudiate their Confederate debt.

President Johnson was a spokesman for small farmers, but he held contempt for blacks and was a stubborn defender of states' rights. He granted amnesty to all but a handful of southern planters and former Confederate officials, and by December 1865 southern states had organized new governments and ratified the Thirteenth Amendment.

Republican Radicals

Ultra-Radical Republicans led by Charles Sumner demanded immediate equal rights for blacks and that they be given the vote, land, and an education. Most Republicans would settle for less. Congress objected to Johnson's Reconstruction proposal because it would increase southern

(Democratic party) representation in Congress; it allowed former Confederate leaders to hold public office; and it allowed southerners to adopt restrictive Black Codes to exploit and control blacks. Johnson alienated Congress by vetoing a new Freedmen's Bureau bill and a Civil Rights Act that were designed to aid and protect freedmen. Congress overrode his veto and took control of Reconstruction. Johnson's combative personality played into the hands of the Radicals even though few northerners believed in racial equality or in providing special protection for the rights of the freedmen.

The Fourteenth Amendment

The Fourteenth Amendment increased the power of the federal government over the states. The amendment made blacks citizens and protected all citizens against state violations of their right to due process and equal protection of the law. It temporarily disfranchised some former Confederates, repudiated the Confederate debt, and encouraged southern states to give blacks the right to vote. In his 1866 "swing around the circle" campaign, President Johnson denounced the amendment and encouraged southern states not to ratify it. But most northerners were determined that blacks have at least formal legal equality and they elected Radical Republicans in numbers sufficient to give them control of Congress.

The Reconstruction Acts

Southern recalcitrance and abuse of black rights led to several Reconstruction Acts in 1867. The South was divided into five military districts. In these districts, commanding officers were empowered to protect civil rights, maintain order, and supervise the organization of new state governments. These governments would ratify the Fourteenth Amendment and guarantee blacks the right to vote.

Congress Takes Charge

The North's effort to impose its will on the South was provoked by the suffering and frustration of the war years, postwar southern recalcitrance, Johnson's stubbornness, and the threat of a Democratic party resurgence. In the course of Reconstruction, Republicans attempted a grand revision of the federal government that was designed to increase the authority of Congress. It culminated in an attempt to impeach President Johnson. The Senate failed to convict him of impeachment charges by a single vote. The trial weakened the presidency, but its outcome preserved the checks-and-balance system.

The Fifteenth Amendment

The Reconstruction Acts and the Fourteenth Amendment enfranchised blacks who immediately used their votes to help Ulysses S. Grant win the 1868 presidential election. Hoping to cement black suffrage rights, Congress proposed the Fifteenth Amendment that forbid all states to deny the vote on account of race, color, or previous servitude (but not sex). The amendment was motivated in part by considerations of partisan advantage, but it also reflected the North's discomfort with a double standard on voting rights, appreciation for black soldiers' service during the war, and hope that it would end the strife of Reconstruction. The amendment contained loopholes and was later subverted by southern states, but a more strongly worded amendment could not have been ratified at the time.

"Black Republican" Reconstruction: Scalawags and Carpetbaggers

Former slaves voted Republican, but there were few black office holders. The real rulers of the "black Republican" governments in the South were mostly white Republicans and former southern Whigs—"scalawags," and, less frequently, idealistic and ambitions northern "carpetbaggers." Most of the few blacks who held office were better educated and more prosperous than most southern blacks, and a disproportionate number of them were muiattos and had been free blacks before the war. Like governments in all sections at all levels at the time, Reconstruction state governments were guilty of waste and corruption and a callous disregard of the public interest. Also, Radical southern governments accomplished much: With higher taxes they financed railroad construction and expanded social services like free public education. Blacks eagerly grasped the opportunity to learn how to read and write, even though schools were segregated.

The Ravaged Land

The Civil War ravaged southern property, and emancipation created confusion. Most former slaves wanted their own land, and Thaddeus Stevens tried to design a way to seize former plantations and divide the land among freedmen. But most Americans had too much respect for private property to support his confiscation policy. Southern whites expected blacks would not work as free men, and the abolition of slavery did diminish cotton production. The decline in productivity was not due to the inability of freedmen to work independently but to their refusal to work *like slaves*. They quite reasonably devoted more time to their family and to leisure and refused to send their wives and children to the fields. In freedom, black families became more like white families.

Sharecropping and the Crop-Lien System

Paying ex-slaves wages to work in the fields was unsuccessful because money was scarce and blacks disliked working for wages. They wanted independence. So planters broke up their estates into small units and "rented" land and supplies to black families who supplied the labor to work the land. The two then shared the crop at the end of the harvest—sharecropping. The scarcity of capital produced the crop-lien system where local merchants made loans against the collateral of the fall cotton harvest. It made both landowners and sharecroppers dependent on credit obtained only at high rates of interest.

Southern manufacturing made some gains during Reconstruction. The cigarette, coal and iron, and textile industries all increased productivity. Overall, however, the South's share of manufacturing declined during Reconstruction.

The White Backlash

The key to the survival of Radical southern governments was the ability of wealthy merchants and planters to mobilize the black vote. But racist vigilante groups like the Ku Klux Klan gradually drove blacks out of politics by using force and intimidation. Congress responded to the KKK by placing southern elections under federal jurisdiction. But the Klan's actions cowed many blacks and weakened the will of southern white Republicans.

Northern and southern whites edged toward a new solidarity based on white supremacy. With freedmen protected against reenslavement, northern commitment to Radical Reconstruction was waning, as was their interest in racial equality. Also, northern industrialists, who were coming to see the importance of a well-disciplined labor force, became more sympathetic to the southern insistence on more control over their own labor force—blacks.

Grant As President

Interest in Reconstruction also flagged because other matters diverted the attention of northerners: industrial development, railroad construction, western settlement, and tariff and currency policy all demanded attention. The Republican party was also damaged by the incompetence, graft, and corruption that permeated the Grant administration. In 1872, a reform element organized the Liberal Republican party and nominated Horace Greeley for president. They advocated low tariffs, sound money, and termination of special attention to the rights of blacks. Grant was reelected, but the Democrats regained control of the House of Representatives in 1874.

The Disputed Election of 1876

In 1876, both the Republicans and the Democrats nominated presidential candidates who were unblemished by corruption. The election results were confused when electoral college votes in three southern states were disputed. Congress created a special electoral commission to assign the disputed votes. The commission gave all the disputed votes to the Republican candidate, Rutherford B. Hayes. Outraged Democrats threatened to disrupt his inauguration.

The Compromise of 1877

But compromise-minded southern Democrats indicated they were willing to accept Hayes if he would end Reconstruction. After his inauguration, Hayes withdrew all occupying federal troops from the South and appointed a former Confederate official to his cabinet. This Compromise of 1877 marked the abandonment of force and principle in relations between the sections, and the return of expediency and concession. But this new sectional harmony came at the expense of former slaves, now condemned to lives of poverty, indignity, and near hopelessness.

People, Places, and Things

Define the following:

pocket veto _____

_____

amnesty _____

_____

impeachment _____

_____

sharecropping _____

_____

crop-lien system _____

_____

Describe the following:

ten percent plan _____

_____

Wade-Davis bill _____

_____

Thirteenth Amendment _____

_____

Black Codes _____

_____

Freedmen's Bureau _____

_____

Civil Rights Act _____

_____

"swing around the circle" _____

_____

Fourteenth Amendment _____

_____

Reconstruction Acts _____

_____

Tenure of Office Act _____

_____

Fifteenth Amendment _____

_____

Force Acts _____

_____

Compromise of 1877 _____

_____

Identify the following:

Thaddeus Stevens _____

_____

Charles Sumner _____

_____

Andrew Johnson _____

_____

Radical Republicans _____

_____

scalawags _____

_____

carpetbaggers _____

_____

Ku Klux Klan _____

_____

Ulysses S. Grant _____

_____

Liberal Republicans _____

_____

Horace Greeley _____

_____

Rutherford B. Hayes _____

_____

Electoral Commission _____

_____

Self-Test

Multiple-Choice Questions

1. On the complex question of bringing the defeated Confederate states back into the Union,
   A. southerners believed that they had legally seceded and would have to be formally readmitted back into the Union
   B. Radical Republicans believed that secession was illegal and that former Confederate states needed no formal readmission to the Union

- C. President Lincoln believed secession was illegal, but that southern states still needed to be formally readmitted to the Union
- D. Charles Sumner believed that the Confederate states had ceased to exist as states and must be treated as conquered territory

2. President Lincoln's ten percent plan for Reconstruction did NOT require southern states to
   - A. adopt a republican form of government
   - B. accept the fact of slavery's abolition
   - C. provide schooling for former slaves
   - D. guarantee blacks the right to vote

3. Congress' Wade-Davis bill required southern states to
   - A. guarantee black equality
   - B. guarantee universal manhood suffrage
   - C. repudiate the Confederate debt
   - D. gradually abolish slavery

4. Andrew Johnson was made President Lincoln's running mate in 1864 primarily for the political benefits that would result from his
   - A. being a Radical Republican leader
   - B. patient and compromising manner
   - C. being a Democrat from a border slave state
   - D. having been a southern slaveowner

5. President Johnson's Reconstruction proposal would NOT have
   - A. allowed former Confederates to hold public office
   - B. increased the number of southerners in Congress
   - C. required full civil and political equality for blacks
   - D. allowed southern states to use special legal codes to control former slaves

6. President Andrew Johnson did NOT veto the
   - A. Civil Rights Act
   - B. Freedmen's Bureau bill
   - C. Wade-Davis bill
   - D. Reconstruction Act

7. The Fourteenth Amendment guaranteed
   - A. U.S. citizenship to former slaves
   - B. land ownership for former slaves
   - C. freedom to slaves
   - D. former slaves the right to vote

8. The Fourteenth Amendment did NOT
   - A. require former Confederate states to pay their war debts
   - B. prohibit former Confederate officials from voting
   - C. guarantee former slaves due process of law
   - D. guarantee all citizens equal protection of the law

9. The Fourteenth Amendment
   A. specifically outlawed racial segregation
   B. specifically prevented any state from denying blacks the right to vote
   C. significantly altered the power relationship between the federal government and the state governments
   D. established legal Black Codes to protect freedmen's rights

10. The South was divided into five military districts under the provisions of the
    A. Tenure of Office Act
    B. Civil Rights Act
    C. Reconstruction Act
    D. Confiscation Act

11. Congress' decision to bring impeachment charges against President Johnson was most immediately provoked by his
    A. highly partisan "swing around the circle" in 1866
    B. readmission of former Confederate states
    C. dismissal of Secretary of War Edwin M. Stanton
    D. advice to southern states not to ratify the Fourteenth Amendment

12. The Fifteenth Amendment was an attempt to gain _____ for former slaves.
    A. land ownership
    B. the right to vote
    C. an education
    D. citizenship

13. The _____ were LEAST likely to hold powerful positions in Radical Reconstruction governments in the South
    A. scalawags
    B. carpetbaggers
    C. freedmen
    D. Republicans

14. Radical Reconstruction governments in the South did NOT
    A. clean up government corruption
    B. raise taxes
    C. initiate public schooling
    D. finance railroad construction

15. After the Civil War,
    A. the South's general economic condition declined
    B. the planter elite no longer controlled land ownership
    C. the sharecropping system of labor management declined
    D. most former slaves became small landowners

16. All of the following are true of the southern economy during Reconstruction EXCEPT
    A. former slaves disliked working for wages
    B. money was scarce
    C. cotton production declined
    D. the South's share of national manufacturing increased

17. The Liberal Republican party in 1872 did NOT demand
    A. lower tariffs
    B. sound money
    C. civil liberties for blacks
    D. honest government

18. The disputed votes in the 1876 presidential election were assigned to candidates by
    A. the Joint Committee on Reconstruction
    B. a special Electoral Commission
    C. the Supreme Court
    D. the Electoral College

19. After his inauguration in 1877, President Hayes
    A. demanded that all southern states ratify the Fifteenth Amendment
    B. became the first Democrat in the presidency since 1856
    C. withdrew all federal occupying troops from the South
    D. pardoned former president Grant for his involvement in political corruption

20. Arrange the following events in their proper time order: (A) Wade-Davis bill, (B) Reconstruction Act (C) Fifteenth Amendment, (D) Compromise of 1877.
    A. A, B, D, C
    B. A, B, C, D
    C. C, D, B, A
    D. B, A, C, D

Essay Questions

1. Compare and contrast the provisions of the ten percent plan, Wade-Davis bill, Johnson's Amnesty plan, and the Radical Republicans plan for Reconstruction. Explain why the Radicals' plan came to be the one adopted.
2. Define the problems faced by Radical Reconstruction governments in the postwar South. List the major accomplishments of these governments.
3. Define "sharecropping" and the "crop-lien system" and explain why these came to dominate the landowner-merchant-labor relationship in the post-Civil War southern economy.
4. Explain why Radical Reconstruction failed to accomplish all it set out to do.
5. State the provisions of the Fourteenth and Fifteenth amendments and describe the historical context in which they were proposed and ratified.

Critical Thinking Exercise

Facts, Inferences, and Judgments

As you have done in previous exercises of this type, search the following excerpt from the textbook for statements of fact, inference, and judgment. For each of the numbered statements in the excerpt circle F for fact, I for inference, or J for judgment on the answer grid that follows the excerpt.

---

(1) The real rulers of the "black Republican" governments were white: the "scalawags" ... and the "carpetbaggers.... (2) The scalawags were by far the more numerous. (3) A few were prewar politicians or well-to-do planters.... (4) But most were people who had supported the Whig party before the secession crisis....

(5) That blacks should fail to dominate southern governments is certainly understandable. (6) They lacked experience in politics and were mostly poor and uneducated.... (7) Not all black legislators and administrators were paragons of virtue. (8) In South Carolina, despite their control of the legislature, they broke up into factions repeatedly and failed to press for laws that would improve the lot of poor black farm workers.... (9) One Arkansas black took $9,000 from the state for repairing a bridge that had cost $500 to build....

(10) However, the corruption must be seen in perspective.... (11) [G]raft and callous disregard of the public interest characterized government in every section and at every level during the decade after Appomattox.... (12) The New York City Tweed Rig probably made off with more money than all the southern thieves, black and white, combined. (13) While the evidence does not justify the southern corruption, (14) it suggests that the unique features of Reconstruction politics ... do not explain it....

(15) In fact, the Radical southern governments accomplished a great deal.... (16) Tax rates zoomed, but the money financed the repair and expansion of the South's dilapidated railroad network, rebuilt crumbling levees, and expanded social services....

---

1. F I J	5. F I J	9. F I J	13. F I J
2. F I J	6. F I J	10. F I J	14. F I J
3. F I J	7. F I J	11. F I J	15. F I J
4. F I J	8. F I J	12. F I J	16. F I J

16: Reconstruction and the South

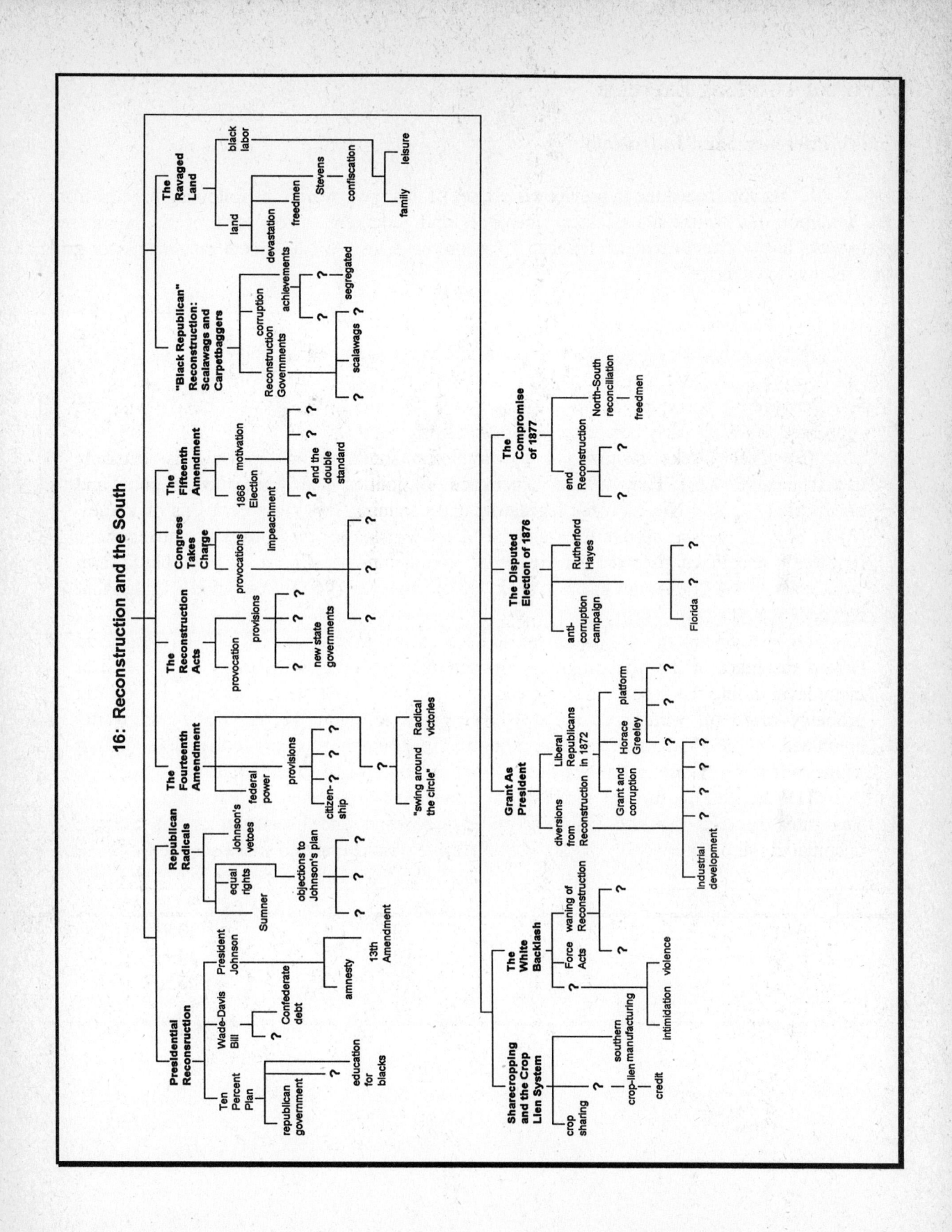

Presidential Reconstruction
- Ten Percent Plan
- republican government
  - ? — education for blacks
- Wade-Davis Bill
  - ? — Confederate debt
- President Johnson
  - amnesty
  - 13th Amendment

Republican Radicals
- equal rights — Sumner
- Johnson's vetoes
- objections to Johnson's plan
  - ? ? ?

The Fourteenth Amendment
- federal power
- provisions
  - citizenship
  - ? ? ?
- "swing around the circle" — Radical victories

The Reconstruction Acts
- provocation
- provisions
  - ? ?
- new state governments — ?

Congress Takes Charge
- provocations — Impeachment
- 1868 Election — motivation
- end the double standard — ? ?

The Fifteenth Amendment

"Black Republican" Reconstruction: Scalawags and Carpetbaggers
- Reconstruction Governments
  - corruption
  - achievements
    - ? ?
    - segregated
  - scalawags — ?
  - ? ?

The Ravaged Land
- land
  - devastation
  - freedmen
    - black labor
    - Stevens — confiscation
      - family
      - leisure

Sharecropping and the Crop Lien System
- crop sharing — ?
- southern manufacturing
- crop-lien
  - credit
  - intimidation
  - violence

The White Backlash
- Force Acts — ?
- waning of Reconstruction — ?

Grant As President
- diversions from Reconstruction
- Liberal Republicans in 1872
- Grant and corruption
- Horace Greeley
  - platform — ?
  - ? ? ?
- Industrial development

The Disputed Election of 1876
- anti-corruption campaign
- Rutherford Hayes — ?
- Florida — ?

The Compromise of 1877
- end Reconstruction
  - ? ?
- North-South reconciliation
- freedmen

CHAPTER 1

Map Locations

1. Labrador (2)
2. Caribbean Islands (12)
3. Newfoundland (3)
4. Jamestown, Virginia (7)
5. Manhattan Island (6)
6. Barbados (13)
7. St. Lawrence River (5)
8. Massachusetts (4), New Hampshire (3), Connecticut (6), Rhode Island (5), New York (7), New Jersey (9), Pennsylvania (8), Delaware (11), Virginia (13), Maryland (12), North Carolina (14), South Carolina (15)

Multiple-Choice Questions

1. **C**   2. **A**   3. **B**   4. **D**   5. **D**   6. **B**   7. **A**   8. **D**   9. **A**   10. **D**
11. **B**   12. **A**   13. **B**   14. **D**   15. **D**   16. **A**   17. **B**   18. **A**   19. **D**   20. **C**

Critical Thinking Exercise

1. De Leon, De Soto, and Coronado were all Spanish explorers of areas eventually included in the United States.

2. Native Americans in what became the United States were generally a deeply religious people who were conscious of their place in the environment, and who practiced communal land ownership.

3. Raleigh, Gilbert, and Hakluyt were all English proponents of colonization in the New World.

4. The first English colonies in the New World were founded in Newfoundland (Gilbert), Roanoke Island (Raleigh), and the first permanent settlement was in the Chesapeake Bay area (Jamestown, Virginia).

5. Quakers, Separatists, and Puritans were all dissenting sects that were critical of the Anglican church (Church of England).

6. Bradford (Plymouth), Winthrop (Massachusetts Bay), and Smith (Jamestown) were all governors of early English colonies.

7. Revelation, Arminianism, and antinomianism were all "heretical" beliefs in the eyes of the Puritan church.

8. Maine, Connecticut, and New Hampshire were all spin-off colonies from the Massachusetts Bay colony.

Answer Section

9. Colonial companies and proprietors came to see the wisdom of offering access to land, political rights, and religious toleration to attract settlers to their colonies.

10. New York, Pennsylvania, and the Carolinas were all proprietary colonies founded after the restoration of the monarchy in England in 1660.

Chapter 2

Multiple-Choice Questions

1. **D** 2. **C** 3. **B** 4. **A** 5. **A** 6. **B** 7. **A** 8. **D** 9. **D** 10. **C**
11. **C** 12. **C** 13. **D** 14. **A** 15. **D** 16. **C** 17. **D** 18. **D** 19. **A** 20. **C**

Critical Thinking Exercise

| \ | *A COMPARISON OF NEW ENGLAND AND SOUTHERN COLONIES* ||
	SOUTH	*NEW ENGLAND*
Economy	*cash crop agriculture*	*fishing, trade, agriculture*
	undiversified	*diversified*
	farms, plantations	*self-sufficient farms*
	slavery was vital to the economy	*slavery was legal, but not vital*
Society	*rural, no cities*	*towns and port cities*
	obedience expected	*strict child discipline*
	female subordination	*female subordination*
	ethnic and religious diversity	*Protestant English settlers*
	low literacy rates	*high literacy*
Demography	*unhealthy environment*	*good water, healthy environment*
	low life expectancy	*grandparents common*
	high infant mortality rate	*low infant mortality*

Demographyy (ctd.)	unstable families	strong families
	scarcity of women	equal sex ratio
	many single, male indentured servants	immigration in family units
Politics	deference to wealthy planters	deference to wealthy merchants
	East-West conflict	East-West conflict
	popularly elected assemblies	popularly elected assemblies
	appointed governors and councils	appointed governors and councils
	local county government	township governments
	white male adult suffrage	white male adult suffrage

Chapter 3

Multiple-Choice Questions

1. **B** 2. **D** 3. **A** 4. **B** 5. **B** 6. **C** 7. **C** 8. **B** 9. **D** 10. **C**
11. **D** 12. **A** 13. **A** 14. **C** 15. **C** 16. **D** 17. **C** 18. **C** 19. **B** 20. **B**

Critical Thinking Exercise

Group 1: 3, 2, 4, 1
Group 2: 2, 4, 1, 3
Group 3: 5, 1, 3, 2, 4
Group 4: 2, 1, 4, 3, 5
Group 5: 4, 2, 5, 3, 1

Chapter 4

Map Locations

1. Lexington and Concord (Massachusetts) (4)
2. Bunker Hill (Boston) (3)
3. Trenton and Princeton, New Jersey (7)
4. Valley Forge, Pennsylvania (8)
5. Charleston, South Carolina (11)
6. Saratoga, New York (2)

7. Yorktown, Virginia (10)
8. Trans-Appalachian West (13)
9. Northwest Territory (14)

Multiple-Choice Questions

1. C 2. A 3. A 4. A 5. C 6. C 7. C 8. D 9. C 10. A
11. C 12. B 13. D 14. C 15. C 16. A 17. C 18. C 19. A 20. B

Critical Thinking Exercise

1. I 2. F 3. F 4. J 5. F 6. F 7. J 8. J
9. F 10. I 11. F 12. J 13. F 14. F 15. J 16. F

Chapter 5

Multiple-Choice Questions

1. D 2. C 3. B 4. C 5. A 6. A 7. D 8. C 9. C 10. D
11. C 12. B 13. D 14. B 15. D 16. B 17. B 18. C 19. A 20. A

Critical Thinking Exercise

PRINCIPLES AND POSITIONS OF REPUBLICANS AND FEDERALISTS		
	FEDERALISTS	**REPUBLICANS**
VIEWS ON...		
human nature	*selfish*	*selfish, but improvable*
common people	*disparaged*	*trusted*
blacks	*Hamilton thought them equal*	*Jefferson feared them inferior*
constitutional interpretation	*loose, implied powers*	*strict*
government power	*strong, energetic*	*limited*
states' rights	*opposed*	*demanded*
majority rule	*feared*	*respected*
judicial review	*Supreme Court authority*	*state nullification*
military preparedness	*vital*	*too expensive, unnecessary*

POSITIONS ON...		
funding the national debt	*favored*	*retire the debt*
assumption of state debts	*favored*	*opposed, compromised*
National Bank	*insisted on*	*opposed*
Proclamation of Neutrality	*endorsed*	*endorsed*
French Revolution	*abhorred*	*enthusiasm, excused excesses*
Whiskey Rebellion	*vigorously suppress*	*insignificant*
Jay's Treaty	*supported*	*opposed*
XYZ Affair	*outraged*	*upset*
Kentucky and Virginia Resolves	*opposed*	*endorsed*
Louisiana Purchase	*some opposition, concern for New England*	*constitutionally troublesome, but good for the future*
Embargo Act	*vehemently opposed*	*supported, but repealed*

Chapter 6

Multiple-Choice Questions

1. **C** 2. **A** 3. **C** 4. **C** 5. **C** 6. **A** 7. **B** 8. **C** 9. **B** 10. **D**
11. **C** 12. **B** 13. **C** 14. **C** 15. **C** 16. **C** 17. **B** 18. **D** 19. **D** 20. **A**

Critical Thinking Exercise: Complete the compare-and-contrast matrix in Chapter 5.

Chapter 7

Map Locations

1. Plattsburg (15); Washington D.C. (16); New Orleans (17)
2. Lake Erie (13)
3. Oregon Country (1)
4. eastern: Lake of the Woods (8); western: Rocky Mountains (6)
5. Adams-Onís Treaty or Transcontinental Treaty (18)
6. Florida (4)
7. Tippecanoe (12)

Multiple Choice Questions

1. C   2. C   3. A   4. D   5. B   6. D   7. C   8. B   9. C   10. D
11. B   12. C   13. B   14. D   15. C   16. C   17. C   18. A   19. D   20. B

Critical Thinking Exercise

1. Effect: The War of 1812
   Contributory causes: land hunger, sense of national honor, agricultural depression, violations of neutral rights

2. Effect: Federalists oppose the War of 1812
   Contributory causes: partisan advantage, concern for the health of New England's economy

3. Effect: American military failures in the War of 1812
   Contributory causes: an effective British blockade, disappointing military leadership

4. Effect: Pronouncement of the Monroe Doctrine
   Contributory causes: Russian colonization of the Pacific coast, the threat of European recolonization in Latin America

5. Effect: Dawning of an Era of Good Feelings
   Contributory causes: "victory" in the War of 1812, economic prosperity, Republican adoption of Federalist programs, Monroe's presidential style

6. Effect: Hostile congressional debate over the admission of Missouri to the Union
   Contributory causes: Tallmadge amendment, Three-Fifths Compromise, the North controlled the House of Representatives, Missouri was located north of the Ohio River

Chapter 8

Multiple-Choice Questions

1. C   2. A   3. D   4. C   5. B   6. C   7. A   8. D   9. B   10. A
11. C   12. B   13. C   14. C   15. A   16. C   17. B   18. C   19. D   20. B

Critical Thinking Exercise

1. J   2. I   3. J   4. J   5. I   6. F   7. I   8. J   9. F
10. F   11. I   12. I   13. F   14. F   15. J   16. F   17. I

Chapter 9

Multiple-Choice Questions

1. **D** 2. **C** 3. **C** 4. **A** 5. **C** 6. **C** 7. **D** 8. **B** 9. **C** 10. **A**
11. **D** 12. **D** 13. **B** 14. **D** 15. **B** 16. **C** 17. **D** 18. **D** 19. **C** 20. **D**

Critical Thinking Exercise

PRINCIPLES AND POLICY VIEWS OF DEMOCRATS AND WHIGS		
	WHIGS	**DEMOCRATS**
Views on . . .		
states' rights	*favored*	*nationalists*
equal opportunity	*favored*	
common man	*faith in*	
strong presidency	*favored*	*opposed*
* democracy	*embraced*	*reserved*
* social equality	*endorsed*	
Positions on . . .		
distribution of federal surplus	*opposed*	*favored*
Indian removal	*favored*	
protective tariffs	*opposed*	
Specie Circular	*favored*	
federal internal improvements	*opposed*	*favored*
Independent Treasury	*favored*	*opposed*
* Second National Bank	*opposed*	*favored*
* nullification	*Jackson opposed*	*opposed*

242

Chapter 10

Map Locations

1. New York (5), Philadelphia (6), Boston (4)
2. St. Louis (18), Lexington (15), Louisville (17), Cincinnati (16), Pittsburgh (3)
3. New Orleans (13), Charleston (9), Baltimore (7), Mobile (12), Savannah (10)
4. Upstate New York (19)
5. Great Salt Lake, Utah (21)

Multiple-Choice Questions

1. **C**   2. **B**   3. **B**   4. **C**   5. **D** 6. **B** 7. **D**   8. **C**   9. **B**   10. **A**
11. **C**   12. **D**   13. **C**   14. **B**   15. **B**   16. **A**   17. **C**   18. **A**   19. **C**   20. **C**

Critical Thinking Exercise

1. Cause: Population mobility
   Effects: increase in the number of towns, population growth in the West, growth in size of large cities

2. Cause: Emergence of the factory system
   Effects: division of cities into residential and occupational areas, adoption of a wage payment system, rapid decline of household industry

3. Cause: Growth of industry
   Effects: increased family income, improved living standards, new economic opportunities for women,

4. Cause: Growth of the factory system and cities
   Effects: increased family intimacy, reduced economic importance of the family, increased prestige and authority for wives/mothers.

5. Cause: Second Great Awakening
   Effects: mobilization of women to social action, increasing church membership, decline of Calvinist theology, heightened hopes for personal salvation

6. Cause: Abolitionist movement
   Effect: caused some to question the morality of slavery, provoked controversy among antislavery northerners, spawned a women's rights movement

Chapter 11

Multiple-Choice Questions

1. B 2. B 3. C 4. C 5. D 6. C 7. D 8. A 9. B 10. C
11. A 12. D 13. B 14. B 15. A 16. C 17. D 18. C 19. D 20. B

Critical Thinking Exercise

Additional categories for comparison might include attitudes toward change, social reform, government regulation, political activism, idealism, self-confidence, industrialism, reason, and so on.

Chapter 12

Map Locations

1. Maine (5)
2. The Alamo (8)
3. San Diego (10), San Francisco (11), Puget Sound (1)
4. Rio Grande (9)
5. Texas (17)
6. 49th Parallel from the Rocky Mountains to the Pacific Ocean (2)
7. California (14)
8. New Mexico (16) and Utah (15) Territories

Multiple-Choice Questions

1. B 2. C 3. D 4. D 5. D 6. C 7. B 8. C 9. D 10. D
11. A 12. C 13. A 14. D 15. A 16. C 17. B 18. A 19. D 20. D

Critical Thinking Exercise

Effect: Texas Annexation 3, 1, 4, 2, 5
Effect: Mexican War 4, 1, 5, 2, 3
Effect: Compromise of 1850 2, 3, 1, 4, 5

Chapter 13

Multiple-Choice Questions

1. D 2. C 3. B 4. A 5. D 6. A 7. C 8. B 9. D 10. D
11. C 12. C 13. D 14. A 15. B 16. B 17. C 18. B 19. A 20. C

Critical Thinking Exercise

1. J   2. I   3. I   4. I   5. F   6. F   7. I   8. I
9. I   10. J   11. F   12. F   13. J   14. J   15. I   16. F

Chapter 14

Multiple-Choice Questions

1. A   2. B   3. C   4. A   5. C   6. D   7. C   8. B   9. B   10. B
11. D   12. D   13. A   14. D   15. C   16. B   17. D   18. B   19. B   20. C

Critical Thinking Exercise

1. b   2. b   3. f   4. l   5. i   6. a   7. h
8. d   9. j   10. k   11. c   12. e   13. g

Chapter 15

Map Locations

1. Fort Sumter, Charleston, South Carolina (23)
2. Tennessee (15), North Carolina (5), Arkansas (13), Virginia (2)
3. Bull Run (Manassas Junction, Virginia) (20)
4. Antietam (Sharpsburg, Maryland) (19) and Gettysburg, Pennsylvania (17)
5. Vicksburg, Mississippi (27)
6. Richmond, Virginia (21)
7. Atlanta, Georgia (24)
8. Georgia (7)

Multiple-Choice Questions

1. A   2. B   3. D   4. D   5. B   6. B   7. D   8. B   9. A   10. C
11. A   12. A   13. D   14. D   15. B   16. B   17. A   18. D   19. D   20. A

Critical Thinking Exercise

1. N   2. N   3. S   4. S   5. X   6. S   7. X   8. S   9. S   10. N   11. N   12. X   13. B
14. N   15. B   16. B   17. S   18. B   19. B   20. N   21. B   22. N   23. B   24. N   25. X

Chapter 16

Multiple-Choice Question

1. **D**   2. **D**   3. **C**   4. **C**   5. **C**   6. **C**   7. **A**   8. **A**   9. **C**   10. **C**
11. **C**   12. **B**   13. **C**   14. **A**   15. **A**   16. **D**   17. **C**   18. **B**   19. **C**   20. **B**

Critical Thinking Exercise

1. **F**   2. **F**   3. **F**   4. **F**   5. **I**   6. **F**   7. **J**   8. **F**   9. **F**
10. **J**   11. **F**   12. **I**   13. **I**   14. **I**   15. **J**   16. **F**